Human Being

Human Being

Reclaim 12 Vital Skills We're Losing to Technology

GRAHAM LEE

Michael O'Mara Books Limited

For Hannah, Marnie and Enzo

First published in Great Britain in 2023 by
Michael O'Mara Books Limited
9 Lion Yard
Tremadoc Road
London SW4 7NQ

A CIP catalogue record for this book is available from the British Library.

This product is made of material from well-managed, FSC®-certified forests
and other controlled sources. The manufacturing processes conform to the
environmental regulations of the country of origin.

ISBN: 978-1-78929-525-2 in hardback print format
ISBN: 978-1-78929-613-6 in trade paperback format
ISBN: 978-1-78929-527-6 in ebook format

1 2 3 4 5 6 7 8 9 10

Designed and typeset by Claire Cater

Printed and bound by CPI Group (UK) Ltd, Croydon, CR0 4YY

www.mombooks.com

MIX
Paper | Supporting
responsible forestry
FSC
www.fsc.org
FSC® C171272

Contents

Introduction

What does it mean to be human? Our genetics distinguish us from other species, of course, and the evolution of our bodies and brain has been key to our survival. But I would argue that it is our activities, attributes and skills, rather than our mere physical apparatus, that characterize our humanness. An active life, a fully human life, involves engaging deeply with the world and making sense of it and our place within it. Together, the twelve skills discussed in this book have underpinned the bulk of our daily human existence in the past and continue to do so today. These fundamental capabilities and ways of interacting with our environment are at the heart of what makes us human.

American philosopher Ralph Waldo Emerson's seminal 1841 essay *Self-Reliance* succinctly captured a moment in time as the modern age began to gather pace. Railway travel, the telegraph and a slew of other inventions were beginning to dramatically impact people's lives. In an age of growing comfort, his appeal for self-sufficiency and to trust one's own abilities struck a chord.

Since then, there have been a number of pivotal moments that have dramatically changed how we live. The mass take-up of television in the 1950s was one: we were soon spending several hours a day in front of a flickering screen, and by the end of the next decade, 530 million people simultaneously watched the Moon landing live from the privacy of their own living rooms.

The advent of VHS, cable and satellite television, video game consoles and the PC in the 1980s changed things further. We spent yet more time at screens, this time less passively as we clicked, rewound, recorded, worked and played. The widespread adoption of the internet in the 1990s started to bring all of these technologies into one place, while ever more versatile mobile devices and faster processing speeds set them on the move in the 2000s. And here we are today, when the continual progress of computing and technology sees artificial intelligence taking on ever more complex tasks and encroaching on human capabilities. The technological change facing Emerson almost two centuries ago seems quaint in comparison.

Yet his ideas about freedom from technology are just as relevant. We are surrounded by digital technologies that can do almost anything for us; as a result, we have gained great new possibilities and an ease of living never seen before. At the same time, Emerson's notion of self-reliance – that is, making use of our own innate or learned abilities – is more important than ever.

Much of my daily work focuses on digital skills education. Over time I have noticed detrimental effects on our wider skills from technology use, and the extensive research I have carried out supports this. As we offload chores to our computers, we begin to do less on our own. Technology can of course be helpful – after all, there are lots of tasks we would rather not have to do. But when we rely on our devices to support our core abilities – essential skills we have acquired such as reading or writing, or fundamental capabilities such as memory, navigation or social skills – these can quickly begin to degrade over time. As a result, the benefits we gain from digital technology come at a substantial cost.

In this book, I range across historical periods and continents to uncover and celebrate human capabilities which we may today find extraordinary but were far more commonplace in the past. In comparing these stories with how so many of us live now, I aim to show that technology use is degrading not only our core competencies but also the very essence of what makes us human.

When technologies begin superseding our active moments and lessen the calls we make on our natural abilities, we risk diminishing the scope of that being. Our muscles and minds, once stretched, begin to slacken as we outsource our vital skills to devices and algorithms. Yet we seem all too readily to accept the negative repercussions technology has on the quality of our lives. Worse still, our increasing reliance on our devices can come to seem inevitable, and transhumanist projections of a future in which our bodies are fused with or superseded by hardware direct public debate to focus on technological advance while giving little space for the contemplation of human being.

To be fully human is something worth fighting for, and fortunately, unlike most of the other pressing issues of our time, we as individuals have the agency to do this in our everyday lives, starting from today. The very first step? Not reaching immediately for our devices. Beyond that, each of us, by the very virtue of being human, has the natural potential to excel at the innate or learned skills covered in this book, and the countless examples of achievements in our past illustrate how we might use that potential to the fullest. Human beings are hardwired to master and hone new skills; to learn what we are truly capable of, we just have to get started.

Chapter I

Navigation

POLYNESIAN SEAFARING

Each time the celebrated European explorers of the early modern age set foot on the vast, hitherto uncharted territories of our world, they were met by human faces. Almost all tracts of land, including the most remote oceanic islands, were already inhabited by groups of people who had made their own far earlier journeys of discovery, unaided by navigation technology. The peopling of the Pacific Basin, which occupies one third of the Earth's surface, began millennia before Europeans first made landfall there. Pacific Islanders lived across the entirety of the Pacific Ocean, from the Americas to Australasia, many on improbably small, outlying islets. Throughout this expanse, spanning 165 million square kilometres, an extraordinary uniformity of language and custom was found by explorers such as Captain James Cook. When he and his contemporaries arrived in the region, they were dumbfounded. Where had these people come from? And how exactly did they travel to these far-flung islands?

The Tahitian islands at which Captain Cook's ship HMS *Endeavour* arrived in 1769 were paradisiacal, with luminous green shoots growing from basalt outcrops and huts scattered between coconut trees along sandy shores. All around, the cerulean sea glimmered, with unbroken views to neighbouring isles. The inhabitants looked outwards to the water, their home islands just small rocks in a network of interlinking land masses.

They and neighbouring Polynesians were able to read the sea in ways no one has matched since.

Cook had set sail in pursuit of *Terra Australis Incognita*, a hypothetical continent first posited in Roman times on the presumption that continental land in the Northern Hemisphere would be balanced by an antipodean counterpart. He needed help in his quest, and in Tahiti he was introduced to Tupaia, a high priest and custodian of local astronomical and navigational knowledge. On 15 August 1769, Tupaia set to work drawing a chart of the Pacific Ocean for Cook and his crew, a copy of which is in the British Library today. The map exhibits a staggering mental vista extending from Tahiti to Easter Island and Fiji, encompassing the majority of the Polynesian Triangle, and falling just short of New Zealand. The largest distance between two islands on the map covers over 4,000 kilometres. Tupaia had presented a glimpse of the monumental wayfinding abilities and body of navigation knowledge amassed by his culture over generations. Recruited on board the *Endeavour*, he proceeded to pilot the expedition for six months around the network of islands in Polynesia.

Despite the *Endeavour*'s circuitous route, covering thousands of kilometres, Tupaia was always able to indicate the direction of his home. The crew never thought to enquire deeply into how he did it. Blinded by their own technological prowess, the thought that their native hosts were also in possession of elaborate, advanced methods of navigation never crossed their minds. The *Endeavour* relied on the very latest instruments to chart its way and gauge longitude and latitude at sea, and the notion that native islanders could find their way perfectly well without any of these supports was baffling. Struggling to explain the skills underlying Tupaia's clear aptitude, the European explorers mythologized Polynesian navigation, viewing it as a mysterious sixth sense. But the silence and contemplative serenity Tupaia exhibited on board the *Endeavour* was no form of devotional prayer; rather, he was paying close attention to the world changing around him. The crew was simply oblivious to the highly developed powers of observation Tupaia was using to spot subtle, evolving signs to point him onwards in the right direction.

It's easy to see how Cook and his crew failed to grasp the ways in which Tupaia navigated. Out at sea, waves roll on to a vanishing horizon; explicit signposts are entirely absent on open water. Whereas a shopfront, building or memorable tree might spark a recollection of a route on land, we have to work a lot harder at sea to make the most of elements we can detect with our unaided senses: the movement of water and waves, winds and clouds; underwater life below and birds on high; the Sun, Moon and stars overhead. A Japanese word, *fuubutsushi*, refers to the intuitive first stirrings of recognition we have as the seasons begin to change: after an extended time of seeming monotony, there's a moment when we start to spot differences in the world around us. Polynesian navigators attentively searched for these kinds of small signs as they sailed, keeping open to all change. Their minds were buzzing with activity, constantly gathering data from a multitude of sources, many of which we barely know of today. On board the *Endeavour*, Tupaia was on the lookout for the unexpected, for new information on factors such as wind direction or temperature. Patience was key: signs were elusive and certainly not available all of the time. Studying cloud change or sea swells could take hours. There was a trained art to extracting reliable conclusions from the shifting circumstances at sea: no one set of phenomena was sufficient to guide a sailing vessel in all conditions. Instead, navigators like Tupaia would assimilate diverse observations, much like a detective accumulating circumstantial clues at the scene of a crime, some perhaps seemingly tenuous. They could finely judge the shape of waves in open sea to ascertain the presence or direction of current and would carefully watch how crests broke on the surface or gauge the size of the waves proportional to the strength of the wind behind them. Layers appearing within waves or sub-surface currents were followed, together with the serpentine lines of flotsam gathering at confluences of opposing drifts. An eye was kept out for flying fish, with the knowledge that they always face into the current on re-entering the water.

Swells were one of the most elusive characteristics to distinguish, and notoriously hard to ascertain. Patterns of ocean waves and swells interlace in complex ways, moving across each other from different directions, at various shapes, heights, lengths and speeds. Swells from far away are longer in wavelength and move under a sailing vessel with slow, expanding undulations. An experienced sailor could find his way across the Pacific based on signs from the slightest of swells, most often originating thousands of kilometres away. He would rely on feel rather than sight. It was common practice to retire to a hut on an outrigger platform and lie down to assess the roll and pitch of the ship as it coiled over the waves, and even to more sensitively gauge the feel of the waves through the testicles.

Polynesian sailors would also scout for phosphorescence, the flickers and streaks of light emitted deep beneath the water's surface. These momentary glowing shards of luminescence, or 'underwater lightning', as the Polynesians called them, are best seen by night, at least 50 kilometres from land, darting out from nearby islands. On dark, drizzly evenings it was typical to steer by them.

By day, tall, shimmering columns of light rising above an island, reflecting from the tropical glare of white sands and still lagoons below, could be spotted at great distances. Clouds stalling slowly, as if held in place by a kite line, indicated dry land beyond the horizon. On closer approach, sailors would begin to distinguish colours and different pitches of brightness in clouds overhead, wooded islands yielding a dark green hue, or the slightest of pink tinges signalling a reef below. The protracted movement of clouds was examined at length and watched more closely than any initial formation. On a calm day, pairings of clouds were found to rise over an island like a set of eyebrows.

Getting lost at sea presented serious dangers. Heavy gales in the Marshall Islands in 1830 led to only one canoe out of a flotilla of over 100 surviving. Tales and folklore of failed journeys focused minds to retain bearings wherever possible, but such events were surprisingly rare. The array of signs sailors were trained to keep at their disposal was most often sufficient guidance to get back on track. An important rough indicator of direction was the Sun, with its bearings at the start and end of the day carefully noted, and automatic mental calculations relied upon between dawn and dusk. Sailors would compensate for changes through the year in the Sun's trajectory, but there was room for error. Sailing by night, on the other hand, was far more accurate.

Polynesians conceived of the heavens above them as a dome and traced the courses stars swept across it. Navigators had to become familiar with significant portions of the night sky, memorizing sufficient stars and constellations to be able to orientate themselves when only a few were visible. The Tahitians Cook encountered were found to be able to predict where stars could be seen in any month, at what times they would rise above the horizon, and the seasons of their appearance and disappearance. Sailors observed the sky carefully, noticing how stars rise earlier each day: a star that rises in the evening will appear in the morning six months later, and for half of the year will disappear entirely from the night sky. Stars low in the sky were the easiest to navigate by, and whenever one set below the horizon another was selected to take its place. Navigators incorporated a multitude of stars into a mental 'sidereal' compass, visualized in their minds to help indicate direction at any stage of the year. Stars were chosen that conveniently matched on an axis and were positioned twice – on rising and setting – to designate opposite points, just like our North and South poles. The sidereal compass used in the Caroline Islands has thirty-two of these cardinal points.

The Polynesians combined all of their navigational knowledge into a hugely impressive, dynamic map held in their heads, called 'Etak', a world away from the maps we use today. A voyage would be mentally divided into a series of stages, with each one located by a star position or a well-known island. When a journey was underway, the canoe was set to another fixed coordinate, typically another faraway island, while the rest of the world was seen to drift by. It's akin to sitting in the passenger seat of a car gazing out of a window, with scenery close by slipping past, yet cliff tops in the distance remaining static. Instead of focusing on the movement of the canoe, a sailor would track the bearings of the starting location and destination in relation to the fixed coordinate. By setting to a stable position, difficulties in tacking the boat in different directions could be managed, and risks of storm drift allayed. Islands passing by confirmed the route was on track; swells, currents and wind were used to stay on course and gauge distance travelled or time remaining. Etak created a moving frame of reference, a mental repository into which any observation could be added and answers found.

The Etak system evolved from the personal perspective of an individual standing on deck and watching the relative movements of islands passing. It also stemmed naturally from the way we humans have navigated for most of our history. When early people ventured out in search of food, they needed to be able to get back home. By looking back and keeping a check on the location of their starting point, it was possible to progressively travel further afield while maintaining a connection to a village or encampment for easy retreat upon facing bad weather or other dangers. It's the only way populations of early *Homo sapiens* from eastern and southern Africa could have steadily spread out to inhabit most corners of the globe.

We navigate entirely differently today. Western forms of navigation have for centuries fixed ourselves at the centre, with calculations based on our personal location, wherever that may be. Modern-day GPS is the clearest manifestation of this yet, with directions delivered from a 3D 'egocentric' viewpoint that moves along with us. This has obvious advantages, with it being easier than ever to find our way in a new location, but it also severs our personal connection with the places we travel through. The power of Polynesian navigation was that it combined both egocentric and allocentric, or outward-looking, methods to establish a current location at any time. The sidereal compass, together with navigation by currents, swells or clouds, operated from a personal perspective. The Etak system, on the other hand, was allocentric, with navigators locating islands in relation to other places rather than to themselves. They trained their attention outwards, fixing their position to prominent environmental features as they went.

Finding our way back home to a hotel in an unknown city, we might do the same, counting streets crossed, or looking out for a colourful building we recall. But more often these days, we rely on our phones to tell us where we are. GPS is the latest in a long line of technological advances in navigation aids that have placed us dead centre in our world. Combining egocentric and allocentric perspectives gave the Polynesians a far wider vista, and Tupaia's map is the last fully formed evidence we have of it.

Recent academic research on some of the earliest Palaeolithic paintings found in caves using the open-source software tool Stellarium confidently asserts that humans have been charting the sky for over 40,000 years, and all ancient cultures have had navigation methods similar to those the Polynesians honed to such a fine art, many just as astute. Long-distance seafaring has been dated back to at least the Mesolithic age by historians, with intricate networks of seaways connecting northwest Europe three millennia before the Romans expanded overland. The Vikings successfully navigated 150 to 250 kilometres per day and could journey from the Shetlands to Iceland in a week, across temperate seas with at times very few cloudless, starlit nights. Early settlers discovered that Native Americans were able to point in the direction of places up to 150 kilometres away and, when pressed for detail, could minutely describe landmarks en route. Australian Aborigines developed mental maps in much the same way as the Polynesians, always maintaining an exact bearing to their destination and home, although the land mapping and depiction of star charts in Aboriginal artwork wasn't fully understood by Westerners until relatively recently.

Cook had lost sight of our natural talents of navigation and never managed to find an answer as to how the Polynesians had inhabited the Pacific islands in the first place. It is in fact possible to sail to almost all of the inhabited islands of Oceania from Southeast Asia without making a sea crossing longer than 300 or so kilometres; these were distances short enough for Polynesian sailors to make advancing reconnaissance trips over time. Yet this doesn't explain far longer journeys made to Easter Island, Hawaii and New Zealand. Polynesian migration to New Zealand is believed to have taken place close to a millennium ago. At a distance of 3,600 kilometres from Tahiti, it's a seemingly impossible stretch into the unknown for a twin-hulled Polynesian voyaging canoe.

What wasn't understood by Cook at the time was that, for over 3,000 years, Polynesians had been landfinding by observing and interpreting bird migration. The consensus today is that the first Polynesians set out across the Pacific in pursuit of the long-tailed cuckoo, following its annual flight southwest from Tahiti to New Zealand. Recent scientific findings have discovered that birds also rely on cognitive abilities to recognize habitats and form mental maps, navigating using their senses and celestial cues from the Sun and stars.

The longest recorded bird migration on Earth is 14,000 kilometres. Much like natural human navigation, Western appreciation and understanding of bird migration is only a recent phenomenon, dating from the early twentieth century, when birds were systematically tagged and discovered in far-distant locations. Vast numbers of animal species, including mammals and insects, have since been found to possess highly developed navigation abilities: the wood mouse, for example, picks up and distributes conspicuous objects such as leaves and twigs, using them as landmarks during exploration, before moving the markers when ready to move on. A 2008 study investigating how harbour seals forage for food at night made use of a specially constructed floating planetarium to prove they steered their way just like Polynesian sailors, by tracking the stars overhead.

Why have we remained so blind to the powerful, natural abilities of both humans and animals to find our way around the world? It was not until the German ethnologist Ernst Sarfert began studying Polynesian migration in 1911, followed more comprehensively by David Lewis and Thomas Gladwin in the 1970s, that we began to gain a fuller picture of the remarkable techniques that Cook overlooked. By this time, Polynesian navigation skills were markedly on the wane and nowhere close to the sophisticated techniques exhibited by Tupaia. Western navigation instruments had increasingly infiltrated Polynesia since Cook's arrival, reducing the need for sailors to rely on their own abilities. Today, there are barely any people surviving in the world who retain the natural wayfinding skills of old. Thankfully, studies were conducted prior to the advent of everyday GPS navigation. The repository of research undertaken on Polynesian navigation just a few decades ago is the only substantial and coherent record we have of any ancient wayfinding culture.

The reason Cook began his Pacific journey in Tahiti was to construct an astronomical observatory on the island and attempt to track Venus gliding across the face of the Sun, a rare event taking place every 120 years. Close observation of the transit of Venus was deemed an important step to refine astronomical calculations and surmount the continued troubles European shipping encountered establishing position on the high seas. For years, sailors had been able to use a sextant to observe heights and angles of stars to determine latitude; fixing a ship's longitude, however, had proven frustratingly elusive. Cook had the very latest longitudinal measurement devices on board *Endeavour*, but they were far from perfect. No matter how detailed his charts, he could never know his exact position at sea. The innovations in navigation aids over the centuries, from the map to the magnetic compass to the sextant, had cumulatively adapted Europeans to an increasingly egocentric worldview as they utilized Cartesian coordinates – a numerical system invented by French mathematician and philosopher René Descartes – to mathematically fix their position on a map. The speed and ease of instrumental navigation, particularly as accuracy improved, progressively superseded any reliance on natural abilities. The cultural knowledge and traditions facilitating Celtic or Viking voyages had been long lost to posterity.

There is no evidence in Cook's journals that Tupaia's map made any impact on him: he simply could not read it. There have been a number of recent academic studies seeking to decipher the perspective behind the map. The consensus is that Tupaia was attempting to represent his conception of navigating the Pacific in a format his visitors would understand. He impressively translated his Etak worldview into a European, two-dimensional chart. His efforts were sufficient for Cook to recognize the result, but not enough for him to be able to fully comprehend its contents.

The navigation methods we adopt alter our worldview in subtle but powerful ways. The fundamental difference between the natural Polynesian navigators and the European explorers arriving on their islands was the maps they relied upon. Cartography creates an abstract, fixed view of the world – one that's actually very different to reality. The familiar two-dimensional world maps we use today, for instance, are based on the

Mercator projection, a method first conceived in 1569, and they flatten out the Earth's sphere in a way that distorts the size and shape of larger geographic areas. The Polynesians Cook encountered didn't use charts, but they possessed rich cognitive maps, varied tapestries of terrains woven from evolving memories of their personal journeys. Cook and his crew had impressive charts and the latest navigation instruments; they just couldn't see past them.

CARTOON BUILDINGS AND SWABS OF GREEN

Cook made a second Pacific voyage in 1772, this time aided by a newly invented marine chronometer to accurately measure longitude. Conceived by John Harrison, a self-taught clockmaker, the H4 chronometer revolutionized sea travel and set a path for England's command of the oceans and the growth of the British Empire. Cook was able to make highly accurate shipping charts of the Pacific, allowing others to follow in his wake. The sea watch compared Greenwich Mean Time with the time at a current location, ascertained by observing celestial bodies above. It was a seminal invention and allowed anyone to determine their precise location on the globe. Chronometers were used well into the twentieth century and became the eventual precursor to the Global Positioning System (GPS) that supports our digital navigation apps today.

GPS relies on a constellation of satellites orbiting the Earth, the first of which was launched by the US military in 1967. Each satellite transmits a signal from 20,000 kilometres away in space, detailing a current position and the time the message was sent. GPS chips in our phones collect faint signals from at least four satellites to determine a highly precise location to within 30 centimetres. It's precisely the same principle Harrison cracked for his chronometer and is very similar to the Etak system. Whereas a Polynesian sailor would observe star courses to pinpoint location, GPS relies on artificial celestial bodies to do just the same.

The accuracy of GPS and the ease with which it allows us to travel around is staggeringly impressive; the short time it's taken to arrive in our pockets is equally remarkable. We have tended to view digital navigation apps as interactive versions of the maps we have been using for centuries. In actual fact, they are much more. A traditional map requires us to work out our own route by determining our current location and visualizing how it connects to our destination. We create our own cognitive maps in the process. Properly reading a map sharpens our thinking about space and increases our wayfinding skills: there is a confidence to be gained by adapting and inventing our own itinerary. Few beginners examine maps in anything close to sufficient detail; the ability to grasp everything a map shows and then act on the information is a skill that takes time to develop. But academic studies have found that the more we use traditional maps, the easier we find it to get around without them. Proficient map-users are also far more able to sketch precise diagrams of routes and form visual memories of their surroundings.

Satnav does all of this cognitive work for us, swiftly calculating a best route and delivering a simple set of step-by-step directions to follow. The first commercially available computer navigation system for cars, released in 1985, was called Etak, an appropriate name, as satnavs work in very much the same way as the Polynesian Etak method, pinpointing start and end locations and splitting journeys into stages. The crucial difference of course is that the route planning is all automated for us. Although we have often relied on tools to navigate in the past, we have always played an active role in the decision-making, taking stock of our location and relying on our senses. The manner in which route-planning apps dispatch us on our way with next to no involvement in the process is an entirely new phenomenon. The automated, trusted accuracy of satnav separates us from the very environmental cues we need to shape our own cognitive maps. Our ancestors, by contrast, investigated their environment with zeal, paying close attention to their surroundings and where they were going. Polynesian navigation drew on concepts relating to physics, biology, meteorology, astronomy and more, the very working mechanics and principles of our world.

Although we may not be aware of it, our overall sensory and cognitive experiences when we travel today are substantially subdued. Route-finding apps deliberately display simple information to avoid any distraction or confusion: we swap the infinite detail of the world around us for cartoon buildings and generic swabs of green, the terrain condensed to shapes and lines. Happenstance or the chance to learn from failed routes is wholly removed as we smoothly glide through the route. Using GPS, we can find our way without comprehending where we are, where we have been, or the direction in which we are heading. It's a phenomenal transformation, and it has a profound effect on us. For one, we are far less attuned to our environs: the question of location that once required a close interaction with our surroundings now no longer applies. And as we neglect to take in our environment, spatial memories are prevented from being formed, so our ability to find our way back home later or to recall a route taken before is inhibited. Even more concerning is the fact that we are at risk of losing innate and fundamental cognitive abilities beyond navigation itself.

The early development of GPS navigation technologies in the 1970s happened to coincide with important neurological breakthroughs in the study of how we process spatial information. Experiments conducted by Professor John O'Keefe at University College London (UCL) discovered 'place cells' – individual neurons in an area of the brain called the hippocampus – that fire every time a rat visits the same location, over time forming a map of a room. In 2005, May-Britt and Edvard Moser, a husband-and-wife team from the Norwegian University of Science and Technology, identified complementary 'grid cells' that enable rats to generate a coordinate system and determine their precise location. Further studies at UCL in 2010 uncovered the same place and grid cells in humans. Exact parts of the brain were later identified as predicting distance to a destination, together with head-direction cells that work as an internal compass. At the very same time that smartphones were making GPS navigation available to all (the first iPhone was released in 2007), science was only just discovering the physical nature of the comprehensive positioning system we hold in our brains. In 2011, a major UCL study captured headlines by revealing that the hippocampus of London taxi drivers increased in size as a result of having to learn 25,000 streets in the course of acquiring 'The Knowledge' – the renowned test they must pass in order to secure a licence. The volume of grey matter of the brain was discovered to decrease when this capability was no longer required.

These illuminating findings began to trigger concern about the possible effects of GPS navigation. With growing understanding of neuroplasticity – our brain's natural ability to change as a result of experience – studies were conducted on people undertaking intensive exercises to improve their navigation skills. The same physical growth in the hippocampus was found. What would happen when the opposite takes place? Could GPS detrimentally affect our cognitive capabilities? The UCL team behind the London taxi-driver study cautioned that conducting a rigorous human study into these issues would be extremely difficult and most likely prohibitively expensive. Numerous attempts have been made to surmount this challenge, and a growing body of results now confirms that GPS negatively impacts our spatial memory and disables parts of the brain that would otherwise be used.

A study published in 2020 by McGill University in Montreal offers the clearest view yet, with results compiled over a number of years concluding that the more we rely on GPS, the steeper the decline in our cognitive abilities. This impairment remains with us when we navigate on our own. GPS reduces the ability to register and recall information relating to our surroundings and damages our propensity to form accurate cognitive maps. Research has also been completed recently on the likely impending effects of GPS navigation in augmented reality glasses, and again measurable neurobiological consequences have been found, mirroring the physical hippocampal changes reported in taxi drivers. A growing dependency on GPS technology has been discovered, even after a short period of ten to twelve weeks. The next instalment of GPS devices looks set to infiltrate our day-to-day lives in increasingly intimate ways, yet wider studies on the likely physiological and psychological consequences of wearable devices are non-existent.

In 2014, the Nobel Prize in Physiology or Medicine was awarded to John O'Keefe, May-Britt Moser and Edvard Moser for their work since the 1970s on place and grid cells. By offering the first demonstrable proof of how we navigate complex environments, their work was seen to have prompted a paradigm shift in our understanding of how specialized cells work together in service of higher cognitive functions. These discoveries were billed by the Nobel Committee as having 'opened new avenues for understanding other cognitive processes, such as memory, thinking and planning'. This is exactly what has happened since. Research more recently by Princeton University has found that the parts of the brain that create mental maps of our environment also play a much broader role in memory and learning. Common mechanisms in the hippocampal region of the brain were found to perform a diverse range of tasks. We now understand that when we visit a new location, we don't just make a mental map: we also form memories in situ. Our brain does not just register our location, it also takes in and stores other fuller features of our day-to-day experience at the same time: neurologists refer to this as 'episodic memory'. The way our brain makes sense of space creates the repositories in our mind to hold on to events that happen to us. It's why ancient recollection aids hinged on visualizing imaginary locations to store information. By thinking of a place where something happened, it's far easier to recall it later.

The growing awareness today of the close interaction between navigation and memory is a prescient concern, as we fundamentally rely on our memories to make sense of the world around us. And spatial thinking has been connected with a collection of other vital cognitive functions, including abstract thinking, imagination and even language. There are apprehensions raised today by many scientists that reducing the amount we actively navigate could lead to earlier onset of Alzheimer's disease or dementia. So to what extent does GPS affect our memory and cognitive abilities?

Unfortunately, there's a point where the science runs out. Whereas formalized procedures are regulated in clinical pharmacological research and testing, there are no standards to ensure the safety of technology devices intended to supplant or enhance our cognitive abilities. GPS devices designed to spare the cognitive efforts inherent in navigation have been released to market with no scientific investigation into the psychological or medical risks their use may cause. As such, investigation into the real effects on our minds is lacking and only at a nascent stage.

Polynesian sailors trained their minds. Formal instruction began on land, sitting together in a canoe house making diagrams with pebbles to commit star positions to memory. Gilbertese islanders sat in a quadrilateral, thatched-roofed hall, with the high beams and rafters used to represent the night sky, arranging sticks to mark star courses and swells between islands. The Etak system required a formidable body of knowledge, but the vast majority of learning took place at sea. Senior navigators demonstrated the movement of waves and clouds, pointing out any fluctuations in sunlight or temperature – details that had to be seen or felt. Apprentices were taught to watch for the unexpected, for any signs of strangeness. Researchers working with the last well-versed Polynesian navigators struggled with what seemed at times impenetrable obscurity. Some concepts were easily shared, but many proved too elusive to describe in words, particularly with a language barrier. Polynesian navigation was hard-won from personal experience and trial and error over innumerable canoe voyages – only by overcoming one problem at a time could a sailor become an accomplished navigator.

Rather than our 'How are you doing?', Pacific Islanders were found to greet each other with 'Where are you going?'. Their worldly know-how bred an outlook of spontaneity and adventure. Knowing our way in the world and understanding our surroundings grounds us. We forget that who we are as humans is so closely connected with *where* we are, with the spaces in which our lives literally 'take place'. The remote Pacific islands found in the 1970s to be the last vestige of these ancient ways of life were vibrant places bustling with a sense of purpose and fulfilment, but today, modern navigation has played a part in decimating local seafaring cultures.

In 1976, a Polynesian double-hulled voyaging canoe named *Hōkūleʻa* set sail from Hawaii on the 2,500-mile journey to Tahiti, with no modern navigation instruments on board. The purpose of the trip was to demonstrate the potential of Polynesian navigation techniques to locate land over such extensive distances, and it was a success. *Hōkūleʻa* proceeded to complete numerous other voyages over the next few decades, stemming out from Hawaii across Polynesia and Micronesia, and to Japan, Canada and the mainland United States. The crews on board benefitted from the tutorship of Mau Piailug, a master navigator from the Caroline Islands who still retained remnants of the Polynesian wayfinding practices of old; but mostly, they had to master these methods for themselves. Navigation is a fundamental human skill we can all cultivate, but we need the chance to practice, develop and hone our connections with a world that technology too easily obscures.

TRAIN YOUR NATURAL NAVIGATION SKILLS

In a number of Scandinavian countries, orienteering is taught in schools as part of the general curriculum. This focused time learning wayfinding spans an array of connected disciplines and promotes an invaluable lifelong skill: being able to determine where you are and where you're going, at any point in time. Navigation is fundamental to daily life, from retracing your steps in a familiar place to exploring a city for the first time. Skilful navigation relies on a number of core abilities that are inherent in how you live moment to moment: the ways in which you perceive your environment, how you direct your attention to useful parts of it, and your ability to remember those features in the future. How you navigate is inseparable from the impressions and memories that connect you with reality – the more able a navigator you become, the more vibrant and refined your perceptions are in turn. Proper navigation is not a simple matter of practicalities or well-being, it's an essential basis of how you fundamentally exist in the world. Sadly, the extended rites of passage in ancient civilizations that saw navigational knowledge passed down generations have altogether halted today: the vast majority of us receive no foundational navigation training, and it's almost entirely missing from most school curriculums. Whereas Polynesians would steadily learn intricate details about how to navigate their world from their elders over many years and journeys, the knowledge we hold today is held within maps and devices that we start using early in life with next to no precautionary guidance or education.

How you tackle today's endemic reliance on GPS and the resulting decline of your navigation skills brings an individual challenge; natural navigation is a discipline that's long been forgotten in our culture, and there are few supports at your disposal. Yet the opportunity to reclaim your navigation skills is in plain sight: you just need to put down your phone and look outwards. The habit of noticing details around you can be easily developed with practice and, with continued effort, be finessed to levels where remarkable navigational feats are within your grasp.

Pay attention to your route

The crucial first step in developing your natural navigation skills is to begin to rely more on your own senses and cut out the mediation of any navigation aid, in particular your phone and other GPS devices. Satnav apps are habit-forming, so it takes specific efforts to break your reliance on them. A useful habit to start is the 'one-leg rule', using GPS to get you somewhere new, but switching it off for your return journey. By doing so, you create a more urgent need to pay attention on the outbound leg of your trip, making a mental note of landmarks and street signs so you can find your way back. Your level of focus naturally increases on your return, as there's no option but to look out for landmarks to guide you home. Even better is to follow this with the 'one-trip pony rule', forbidding yourself to rely on GPS on any route you have used it on previously. These techniques can encourage you to view your satnav app as a useful tool to teach you new routes rather than as an ongoing crutch.

Another useful method is the 'home rule', switching off GPS whenever you are in your local area. Making unaided trips from home is a natural starting point, mirroring the way our forebears struck further out by keeping a connecting link back. On foot is best, as you're more physically attuned to your environment. In city locations in particular, we retain pockets of knowledge about our surroundings – small radii around our home, office and other places we frequently visit – but we rarely connect these places together. Set out in new directions along unfamiliar routes, again to create the necessity to pay more attention to the details – including good old street signs – that will help you find your way.

The pioneering French aviator Antoine de Saint-Exupéry flew during the nascent years of air travel in the early 1900s, making his own way from southern Europe down the west coast of Africa. Rather than just rely on conventional maps and charts, he searched for memorable peculiarities in the landscape stretching below, imagining faces on mountainsides, monstrous eyes and bulging noses. You can do just the same, and urban environments in particular can be remarkable places. Keep a playful eye out for incongruous symmetry or juxtaposition and look for the unexpected, such as strangely named roads, lop-sided buildings, undulations in the road or oddly shaped trees.

There's a world of difference between absent-mindedly walking down a street and paying close attention to what you find. Absent-mindedness is exactly that: you're not mentally present. Relying on GPS either keeps you staring at the screen to find your way or gives you a level of assurance so you breeze along with your mind on other matters. Reducing your use of satnav with the 'one-leg', 'one-trip pony' and 'home' rules means you only become absent-minded when you truly know a location: the rest of the time you pay attention, because you have to.

TAKE ACTION

- **Reduce your use of satnav:** Give the 'one-leg', 'one-trip pony' and 'home' rules a try.
- **Start with some trips close to home:** Seek out new routes, and visit neighbourhoods you've never been to before, then try to make your way home unaided.

Find your own way

Competent navigation is a combination of observation and deduction: taking stock of the information you can find around you and, with some logical reasoning, thinking through a problem to get to an answer. Adept navigators maintain an idea of their direction, place and position at all times, and understanding the places they visit in relation to each other. The most impressive facet of Polynesian navigation was combinatorial, with sailors assimilating disparate details from a wide variety of natural phenomena to deduce where they were and decide where to go next. They read the world much as we read text on a page, a series of signs from which they could decipher logical conclusions. You can also do the same. Try to deliberately make journeys on your own at first, so you're not distracted by conversation or inadvertently guided by someone else. Give yourself the mental space to focus and interpret the combined evidence from a number of different indicators.

Reading the streets, buildings and land itself offers you clues no map can capture. It's helpful to know, for instance, that churches are aligned west–east, with the main entrance at the west end, while any tennis courts you spot will typically have a north–south orientation. And it often doesn't take long to learn the general layout of main roads, particularly in the US or other newer metropolitan areas, where grid planning is easy to decipher: cities such as Chicago, Denver and Kansas City are even aligned to compass points. All urban spaces have some form of natural arrangement, whether that be at the foot of a mountain, aligned either side of a river, or clustered around a port.

Rely as much as possible on *all* of your senses, not just what you can see in front of you. Hearing in particular is tremendous for orientation, so be wary of cutting out a lot of navigational cues when you wear headphones. We constantly hear sounds – at bewildering volumes in cities – and when you take the time to register and localize their source it's possible to navigate by them. Busy streets hum for a large radius, and music and the murmur of crowds can carry just as far, particularly with a good wind. Noise can be used in the same way as visual landmarks for finding your bearings, or can be set as useful targets for your destination. Your sense of smell too can easily place local eateries or breweries, while fresh sea air is distinguishable even hundreds of metres from the coast. Learn to trust your own impressions.

There's no such thing as an innate sense of direction. Working out where you are going always requires observation and deduction. By stopping and scanning a 360-degree view, you can quickly place the profile of mountain ranges or skyscrapers on the horizon, setting landmarks to easily use for bearings and noting the position of the Sun overhead. In rural spaces, signs such as the configuration of hills, the orientation of valleys and the way windblown trees lean can be related to each other to help orient you. With a good view, you can build a picture of the shape and patterns of the land itself and read its characteristics. Hills and rivers in particular have a close relationship, betraying the direction of movements of glaciers and ice sheets millennia ago. Streams flowing downwards tend to run in a fairly straight line; it's only on flat plains that they meander. By looking more attentively at what can at first seem random or chaotic, you will begin to see patterns and signs in the landscape, enabling you to better understand it and navigate your way through it. As you form far more detailed and personal views of your surroundings, you become ever more capable of making your own way in the future.

TAKE ACTION

- **Deliberately switch off your phone:** Get into the habit of only using satnav when you absolutely need to.
- **Get to know local landmarks:** Take in details of your local areas as you walk or drive; aim to find new geographical markers with which to orient yourself.
- **Allow yourself to get lost:** Challenge yourself by setting out on a more complicated route; rely solely on the clues you find in your surroundings to get to your destination.

Build your own cognitive maps

The spatial nature of your memory means it responds readily to use: the more you pay attention on your travels and work out a route for yourself, the more detailed the personal cognitive maps you grow in response. All the same, there are a number of deliberate map-reading and map-making techniques that offer powerful ways to speed up the learning process and grow your mental vista.

A simple change, but one that can quickly help develop your own geography, is to swap from digital to printed maps. An Ordnance Survey or other high-quality map spread wide over a table offers a number of advantages, with comprehensive amounts of information at your disposal, but with a rich variety of signs and symbols that you have to interpret to understand the topography you plan to travel through. In contrast, when route-finding apps deliver directions to you in easy steps, you are prevented from doing the cognitive work yourself and forming your own memories in the process. Reading a map properly enables you to compare and contrast further details with the physical clues you encounter, while a map's grid system forces you to take a wider view before you zoom into a specific location; this is a fantastic way to gain a wider perspective of your area and connect different locales together.

Another straightforward adjustment, but one that again helps you grow your own cognitive maps, is to change how you read digital maps. GPS route-finding apps have an egocentric view as standard, automatically orienting the map view to your perspective. This innovation has been central to removing much of the intellectual work traditionally needed when map-reading. But the setting can typically be removed in most apps at the touch of a button, and once you do so, a GPS map becomes more allocentric, adopting the mode of a printed map more closely. It's highly recommended. Suddenly, you are forced to translate the map to the direction your body is facing and as a result more properly understand its contents in relation to your own positioning. It's useful to maintain an allocentric view on any map you use on your phone when walking. By car, standard egocentric satnav directions can be invaluable in a new town with a complicated one-way road system, or when you're trying to get somewhere quickly. But again, where possible, try to use an allocentric view, which will help strengthen your own cognitive maps.

The more you use maps properly, the better able you are to memorize what's coming ahead and reduce potential wayfinding errors. Try studying a map carefully before navigating a specific section of your journey, remembering important features to look out for on your way, then put away the map, whether it's digital or physical, and on a piece of paper, sketch the route you plan to follow. Try to keep this sketch out of sight in your pocket. Get into the habit of checking your progress as you travel by taking stock of your bearings (or referring to a map or your sketch if you really must). Slowly you will begin to develop a more natural sense of where you are at all times.

For journeys you are keen to remember, go over a trip in your mind afterwards and test yourself on how much you can recall: street names, thoroughfares, directions taken and any other points of interest. Try to get used to fixing an idea of north in your mind as you go and bear it in mind as you sketch a quick map afterwards. Most smartphones include a compass as a standard, and it's useful to practise using it to keep a more continued awareness of your bearings. Progressively, mental map-making becomes a natural habit that doesn't rely on pen and paper, though writing things down initially can be extremely helpful.

Planning more complex or longer routes, and remembering them, is one of the most complicated navigation challenges you are likely to face, and this takes time and practice. For a simple route, you can simply fix a line between two landmarks; but for anything more complicated, it's necessary to determine the different legs of a journey. Similar challenges led the Polynesians to the Etak system, and as you become an increasingly adept navigator, you will begin to naturally develop the very same methods for yourself, fixing your position to prominent landmarks and closely monitoring your progress as you go. Test yourself by planning a new, more complex route across town and see how you fare. Refer to a printed map, then sketch your own maps and memorize them before setting out. Try to spot early on if you are straying from your course, and attempt to remedy this before looking back at your maps or asking for help. Over time, you will be able to head further and further afield.

The kind of rich cognitive maps the Polynesians held in their minds are within your grasp. Furthermore, the digital navigation technologies at your disposal today give you unrivalled information to plan your journeys, and, if things go wrong, to find a way back. Used sparingly and properly, digital navigation devices such as smartphone compasses and online maps can reconnect us with our environments.

TAKE ACTION

- **Purchase a high-quality printed map of your local area:** Pin it to the wall or spread it out over a table and put time aside to study it closely.
- **Disable the 'egocentric' view settings on your GPS devices:** Ensure the digital maps you use are always oriented to north.
- **Try sketching your own maps to plan a journey:** Refer to a printed or online map at home to plan a journey then draw a simplified version on a piece of paper to help you recall it later.
- **Test yourself with more complex routes:** Plan and memorize a more extended route for yourself in a new area, then set out with the aim of not referring to notes or a map, unless you really need to.

Chapter 2

Motion

OUR LIGHT-FOOTED ANCESTRY

In April 2017, a twenty-two-year-old woman arrived in the state of Puebla, in Mexico, to compete in a 50-kilometre ultramarathon. María Lorena Ramírez had not formally trained for the event and wore no professional running equipment: she ran in her handmade skirt and huarache sandals; nor did she carry any energy sweets or gels. Ramírez set off strongly at a steady pace, and as the hours unfolded, the 500 other runners from twelve countries across the globe began to slow or fall away. Running with a low gait and fluid grace, she soon gained an insurmountable lead. The UltraTrail Cerro Rojo is an internationally renowned race, and when Ramírez crossed the finishing line in first place, it created a stir in the running community. She had held her stride for seven hours and twenty minutes and had outcompeted the other Lycra-clad runners dotted along the course. After her victory, she went on to compete in longer races of up to 100 kilometres in distance and raced internationally. Ramírez continues to run today and ranks highly in major ultramarathon events worldwide.

Yet for some, Ramírez's natural talent is no surprise. She was born in the Copper Canyon system in the Sierra Madre Occidental mountain range in Chihuahua, Mexico, and lives there to this day, looking after her family's stock of goats. Home to 3,000-metre-high conifer-forested mountaintops, the area is inhabited by the Rarámuri, a group of some 60,000 indigenous people who are proud to be known as 'those with light feet' – *rara* meaning feet, and *muri*, to run. From childhood into old age, the Rarámuri walk and run across difficult terrain, scaling the steep-walled ravines wearing sandals made from plant fibres, or, more often today, rubber from car tyres. As there are few roads, farming is conducted almost entirely without any motorized vehicles, and children begin climbing mountainsides to herd goats, sheep and cattle when they are just five or six years old. A 2019 study of a group of Rarámuri men aged over thirty-five found they daily travelled 15 kilometres with an average of 18,800 steps, almost double the 10,000 recommended by health practitioners today. Many of these steps were up steep inclines, and older members of the community were found to hike ascents of 1,000 metres on a regular basis. Although influences from distant towns are beginning to increase obesity and other indicators of chronic disease, the Rarámuri have excellent cardiovascular health across their society.

Long-distance running is in the Ramírez family's blood. Three of the seven siblings – as well as their father, Santiago – ran with María Lorena in a recent Chihuahua ultramarathon, and her elder brother, Mario, was also among the competitors in Puebla, coming tenth in the 30-kilometre category. Santiago has run since he was a child, just like his father and grandfather before him. Running is less an activity than a way of life for the Rarámuri: it is their prime means of transport and allows different groups to come together and celebrate festivities. *Rarajípare* foot races requiring high stamina are an integral part of their culture, with villages competing against one another at events often arranged spontaneously. Distances of 65 kilometres or more are run while kicking a hard wooden ball, with teams of all ages relaying through the night and weaker runners progressively dropping out of the race.

Recently, the surge of interest in ultramarathons has seen runners from elsewhere visit the region in an attempt to discover the training techniques behind the Rarámuri's phenomenal range. Yet there are no secrets: running a 100-kilometre distance is the same challenge for Ramírez as it is for any other ultramarathoner, and the strongest runners attain a high level of fitness quite simply by exerting themselves in training. Rarámuri runners have essentially the same genetic make-up as all of us, and a similar natural ability too: they just make more active use of it in their daily lives. The survival of their culture gives a glimpse of how much further we used to travel on our own feet. Humankind has always been capable of covering phenomenal distances, and for much of our past it was our primary way of being; indeed, walking and running are natural capabilities that are fundamental to our biological evolution.

The running abilities that Ramírez and her family exhibit today used to be commonplace not only throughout their region, but also across the entire American continent. Trails and thoroughfares, travelled along exclusively by foot, have criss-crossed the expanse of North and South America since humans arrived some 14,000 years ago. Networks of routes have been found that ultimately connected Hudson Bay in Canada to the Gulf of Mexico and beyond. The forms these routes took varied vastly, from simple clearings and pathways to the 200 kilometres of curbed roadways and staircases over cliff edges found in the Chaco Canyon in New Mexico. Whatever ground these tracks covered, whether that be the white limestone roads laid by the Mayans on the Yucatan Peninsula, brushland trails across much of the central US or mountainous passes in the Sierra Nevada or Andes, they were all undertaken on foot.

In surviving accounts from the first Spanish and Portuguese landings from the 1490s onwards, the running abilities of Native Americans feature regularly: even on foot they could escape their colonizers on horseback. Upon arriving in Mexico in 1519, the Spanish conquistador Hernán Cortés reported on the rapidity at which runners communicated messages about his ships, men, guns and horses to Montezuma, the emperor of the Aztec Empire, based at Tenochtitlán (the location of Mexico City today), 400 kilometres away. Indeed, runners supplied Montezuma's kitchen with fresh fish from the Gulf of Mexico, 150 kilometres from Tenochtitlán. Admiration of the native population's physical fitness, stamina and endurance features in many of the logs and reports from Europeans at this time. During the conflicts after the Spanish conquest, native runners were routinely found to outspeed battalions of horses over long distances, and whereas Spanish mail between Lima and Cuzco took twelve days to arrive in the sixteenth century, native runners were reported to have covered the distance in just three.

In North America too, European settlers were consistently surprised by the speed and range of indigenous populations on foot, and there are many illuminating examples documented by anthropologists, historians, travellers and Native Americans themselves. These accounts serve as a reminder that, in our relatively recent past, we humans possessed far greater physical abilities that enabled us to traverse distances difficult for most of us to comprehend today.

Running made swift communication and trade possible: in Native American tribes, individuals held posts as courier runners and were responsible for transporting goods or dispatching urgent news. They were also revered as indispensable bearers of the latest developments and wider culture. People ran across intricate networks of pathways and shortcuts – often in relays – carrying raw hides marked with hieroglyphs, or knotted and coloured strings to communicate events. Their messages allowed administration across large areas; as today, speed of delivery of any correspondence was critical, particularly if it related to threats of attack, and runners trained accordingly, ready for any emergency. A runner in his mid-fifties from the Mesquakie tribe is documented as having raced over 600 kilometres from Green Bay in Wisconsin to warn Sauk Indians on the Missouri River of an impending enemy attack: missions such as these could determine the survival of a community.

In an extensive programme of field research on Native North American culture in the early 1900s, the anthropologist Truman Michelson found similar levels of training among a large number of tribes. From childhood, runners were trained to manage their stride and energy reserves. Running strategy was paramount, and extended time was dedicated to guiding young members of a tribe on how to plan and pace a journey. Fables akin to Aesop's 'The Tortoise and the Hare' have been preserved in various Native American communities, and these instructed learners on how to maintain stamina over extended distances and harness proper breathing techniques, as well as when to sprint when necessary. Differentiation was made between different running styles, with names for each to help better describe variations such as dodging movements or the quality of a tight and controlled speed.

Strength training was common, and exercises progressed from running with small rocks to carrying boulders uphill. Runners also trained carrying logs of various weights, some as heavy as 60 kilograms or more. Couriers vigilantly switched any item that they were carrying between their right and left hands to balance strain on their bodies as they ran, and many trained with ankle weights. Sprint training was often saved for the morning, with marathon distances covered in the afternoon. A common tactic was to take a mouthful of water and hold it during the run, breathing only through the nose to build stamina; some also ran with icicles in their mouths. More extreme training regimes were saved for ceremonial runners or soldiers – Mesquakie runners, for instance, adopted a vow of celibacy and observed very strict diets. They would start walking barefoot once springtime came and train until the skin on the soles of their feet was almost a centimetre thick. In winter, members of the Navajo tribe would roll in snow or take ice baths before setting off on a training run, and it was common, even on the chilliest mornings, to run in the dark wearing only moccasins and a loincloth.

Although reports on Native American running tend to focus on the most impressive feats of endurance, speed or distances, running was also everyday in nature, and pervasive across all ages. Elders encouraged everyone to run where possible, and a large number of exercise practices were adopted throughout a tribe. A lightness of foot was much admired, and running prowess was an important source of pride.

The roots of Native American running – and indeed running in any culture – lie in persistence hunting, an ancient method of pursuing animals that has existed in most societies and environments from the earliest records of humanity. Hunters would target suitable quarry and proceed to chase it on foot over long distances, persevering until an animal slowed, collapsed or was driven into an ambush or trap. Abundant evidence indicates that persistence hunting was a major part of life for native populations living across the Americas, and a 2020 study of the Rarámuri presents one of the last glimpses into this vanishing way of life – rifles, mining and logging are now common in the region, and the last recorded persistence hunt was in 2011. Surviving hunters give accounts of chasing deer, wild pigs and smaller prey such as rabbits or squirrels, heading out in all conditions through summer and winter. The duration of a hunt would vary from the more typical four to six hours to as long as two or three days, with hunters setting off early in the morning and continuing until it was too dark to follow an animal's tracks. They ran at a steady, moderate pace throughout, interspersed with purposeful sprints or periods of walking when needed, covering on average 10 kilometres or so in an hour. The same pace and combination of walking and running is seen in ultramarathon runners today. Persistence hunts were carried out in groups of as few as three to as many as fifteen participants, all working together to strategically track and chase. Only the strongest and fittest in the community would attempt a hunt, and it was common to drop out because of fatigue; chases could be long, tough and required the highest levels of endurance.

The Rarámuri originally inhabited much of the surrounding area in Chihuahua but, in order to evade Spanish colonizers in the sixteenth century, retreated to the Sierra Madre Occidental. The tropical canyons, carpeted with orange groves below the high peaks, offered sufficient respite from the cold in the winter, so they were able to live in the region all year round. Over the years, the region has remained sufficiently remote to avoid full integration with Mexico's market economy, but inevitably, life has changed. As remote as the Ramírez family are from wider life in Mexico, their native culture is progressively influenced by modern lifestyles, and while they are still far more active than the majority of us today, the Rarámuri are not as exertive as they once were when persistence hunting was a way of life. Centuries ago, their average number of daily steps is certain to have far exceeded today's 18,800.

To explore what everyday human running would have looked like in its original form, it helps to look at fossil records and the workings of the human body. Palaeontological and ethnographic studies suggest that persistence hunting extends back through the majority of our past, originating in Africa. According to human evolutionary biologists, the successful hunter-gatherer way of life in the Great Rift Valley and surrounding areas of East Africa helps explain the form of the human body today. Around 6 million years ago, our ancestors began to diverge from other primates, venturing out of forests into open or semi-open plains. With plants far sparser, longer distances had to be travelled to find food, and diets were increasingly supplemented with meat. Persistence hunting became essential for survival, and over time we humans evolved a wide range of anatomical and physiological adaptations to run long distances safely.

It's easy to take for granted that we stand upright, yet it is highly rare for most other animals (aside from birds or kangaroos), and biologists agree it is likely to have been the first major transformation in human evolution. Becoming bipedal afforded us new opportunities, freeing our hands to use tools and allowing us to develop running endurance. Walking or running upright is far more efficient over longer ranges, allowing for better thermoregulation and reduced direct radiation from the Sun. So we swapped the fast pace and power of running on all fours for a short span – a cheetah, for instance, can run at 100 kilometres per hour, but only for thirty seconds, and could never cover the distances we do – for endurance. In chasing the weakest prey in groups, we began to adapt further, gaining other advantages so we could cover more ground.

For instance, becoming progressively less hairy across most of our bodies and developing the high numbers of well-developed sweat glands that we have today eventually made it possible for us to run continuously for more than 100 kilometres on a moderately cool day. An ultramarathoner might lose 10 kilograms of weight from sweat alone as the body naturally cools itself, carefully balancing salt and water levels in the process and routing blood to skin level to dissipate heat. This propensity to sweat is exceptionally rare, as most animals on arid lands evolved instead to conserve water, and it gave us another advantage to outrun prey over long distances.

Our feet also evolved mechanisms to reduce the heavy impact when we hit the ground to further save energy: our Achilles tendon stretches on landing, and the foot rebounds with a sprightly lift from the toes. The short stumps of toes we are left with today evolved from five digits we would have used, just like our hands, for climbing. Now, our toes allow us to hit top speed when we run, and they only momentarily touch the ground when we shift our weight onto them. When we sprint at full flight, we in fact barely touch the ground. A special mix of fast and slow twitch fibres in our leg muscles allow us both power and endurance, and the longitudinal arches of our feet and expanded gluteus maximus muscles on our hips keep us going for longer.

When we run, our body synchronizes the delicate movement of hundreds of muscles into a powerful reflex that we can control at will: each part of our body unifies as one with enormous efficiency. Our arms swing in tandem with the strides of our legs, and our breathing and heart rate steady in rhythm. The length of our stride at pace could create tremendous instability, yet we balance perfectly by holding our head and fixing our gaze ahead, relying on loop-shaped canals and hairlike sensors in our inner ears to make fine adjustments.

The ease with which we walk or run hides the sheer number of complexities involved, and we move with an intelligence that is buried deep within our flesh and bones. Comparative examinations of fossil records of extinct hominids over the years have cumulatively shown the genus *Homo* (which includes *Homo sapiens* and extinct species such as *Homo neanderthalensis* and *Homo erectus*) to possess a multitude of adaptations across the body that allow us to walk, run and make carefully orchestrated movements as we move through the world. In other words, running is the chief reason why our bodies are the way we find them: it is not simply something we might choose to do; rather, it's at the heart of who we are as a species.

María Lorena Ramírez's running prowess surprises crowds at ultramarathon events because they equate prolonged training schedules and high-tech sportswear with success. In much the same way, the speed and endurance of Native Americans surprised early settlers because it contrasted so starkly with their own abilities. Societal developments in the Western world by that time, primarily as a result of agriculture and technological advance, had so thoroughly disrupted day-to-day life that the need to walk, run or generally exert oneself physically had already been substantially reduced. The trend has continued since: the distances that we travel on foot and the amount we exercise have substantially declined over the years. Yet the most abrupt change has only been in the past few decades: the advent of screens – first TVs, then PCs and consoles and now the multitude of devices we use today – has had a profound effect on our mobility.

The extensiveness of these changes and the significant negative repercussions they have on our health and well-being are only now becoming clear. Yet the Ramírez family shows us what is still possible today: most of us have the capacity to walk and run and exert ourselves in exactly the same ways as humans have always done. We have a natural-born ability to stand, and move, on our own two feet, but it takes a little more proactivity today to make sure that we do.

THE MOST SEDENTARY HUMAN BEINGS OF ALL TIME

In 1980, the technologist and futurologist Stewart Brand encouraged the anthropologists Peter Nabokov and Margaret MacLean to write a cover story for his *CoEvolution Quarterly* magazine. 'Ways of Native American Running' assembled the fragments of existing historical records and presented for the first time the little remaining knowledge we have today of humankind's natural running cultures. Nabokov, who lived and worked on the Sioux, Navajo, Crow, Penobscot and Alabama–Coushatta reservations for several decades, proceeded to widen the research with keyword searches across a whole mass of surviving ethnographic documentation held at the Human Relations Area Files in New Haven, Connecticut. His resulting book, *Indian Running* (1987), remains the only comprehensive overview we have today of Native American running, and indeed of any traditional running civilization worldwide. The written and pictorial accounts it documents give a sense of how regularly we used to walk and run over long distances, but it also poignantly shows that the vast majority of our running record over the preceding millennia has been entirely lost.

Brand is most renowned today for his conception of the *Whole Earth Catalog*, an American counterculture magazine (of which the *CoEvolution Quarterly* was an offshoot) that sought to act as a compendium of useful technological tools. The covers of his early publications featured never-before-seen satellite images of planet Earth hovering delicately in space to evoke a sense of shared destiny and adaptive strategies for the world's people. Brand's ability to grasp the potential of modern-day technologies while at the same time adopting a deeper view of time that allowed for the full span of humankind's past and its potential future have more recently manifested in his San Francisco-based Long Now Foundation, a cultural institute which promotes perspectives on societal change that extend forward for tens of thousands of years. This longer stretch of human time that Brand has striven to contemplate through much of his work is highly prescient today: whereas the technical tools that populated the pages of the *Whole Earth Catalog* – and the innovations in digital technology that have burgeoned since – have only existed for the past few decades, human societies and cultures have more typically spanned centuries and millennia.

If our evolutionary past is conceived of as a sprint track, with our first bipedal ancestors standing upright at the starting line, then the course of time over which their progeny has competed to arrive at our present-day finishing line totals some 5.6 million years. Our most direct ancestor, *Homo erectus*, arrived 1.9 million years ago – 66 metres into a 100-metre sprint – and we *Homo sapiens* emerged 200,000 years ago, with just 4 metres and a few final strides to the finishing line. Yet, the advent of farming, the first major development to have disrupted the physicality of our day-to-day lives, was only 12,000 years ago: on the 100-metre track of our evolutionary past, it falls just 20 centimetres from the finish line. Much of civilization today rests on this change, as increasing portions of society were freed from the daily labours of finding sustenance.

In evolutionary terms, 12,000 years is a very short period of time – only some 500 generations – and one that is markedly insufficient for our bodies to have adapted to our societal change. If the earliest bipedal ape that we have found to exist 5.6 million years ago is indeed our first upright ancestor, it stands 225,000 generations away from us today – 450 times longer in timespan than the period between the advent of agriculture and the present day. Biological evolutionary change requires tens, if not hundreds, of thousands of generations to advance. It is clear, therefore, that while some aspects of our physical anatomy such as height or jaw size have changed, our bodies are designed in much the same way as our hunter-gatherer forebears, even if they are mismatched with the lifestyles we follow today.

The industrial and technological revolutions have also played their part in making us increasingly immobile. In the eighteenth and nineteenth centuries in Europe, North America and beyond, people progressively migrated from the countryside, where they had primarily spent their days working in the fields, and took to more sedentary work, controlling new machines in factories. Changes in technology in the nineteenth and twentieth centuries also stimulated the advent of the modern-day office: Morse's telegraph, Bell's telephone and Edison's dictating machine allowed administrative work to be undertaken separately from factories and warehouses, and people began to spend increasing proportions of their working lives at desks. The invention of different modes of transport, from the railway to the car to the aeroplane, have all further reduced the amount that we travel by foot. Yet for all the societal and technological change over the past few centuries, the greatest factor in increasing our sedentariness – and we are the most sedentary generation of humans of all time – is the advent of screens, which, on the 100-metre sprint track of humankind's 5.6-million-year bipedal history, arrive at just 0.1 millimetres from the finishing line. Even today's photo-finish technology couldn't capture that; there has certainly been no time for adaptive physical change.

A landmark study of more than 300,000 people conducted by the University of Cambridge in 2015 showed that inactivity was found to be the single greatest risk of early death and a cause of 676,000 deaths in Europe each year – more than double that attributed to obesity. The study is the clearest affirmation yet of a 'mismatch theory' long promoted by evolutionary biologists to explain how the physical traits evolved by humans to survive in earlier times have since become maladaptive in today's world. The seasonal vagaries and haphazardness of hunting success left our ancestors switching regularly from times of plenty to periods of hardship and want. Our bodies have adapted historically to slow down in times of abundance and conserve any excess food as fat deposits. This reduced mobility and activity is a natural protection to save energy for scarcer times ahead, leaving us ready to burn off our own stored calories to survive. Yet, whereas some other animals have evolved to cope better with periods of sustained inactivity, we humans have not entirely: historically, it was rare for us to stop hunting and gathering food for extended periods of time. A bear's bones, for example, do not grow brittle after six months of prolonged hibernation, whereas ours become much weaker if we cease daily exercise. And although food abundance has become the norm for people in most societies today, our bodies are not aware of this profound change: when we are sedentary we build fat stores, just as we have always done, and what was once an evolutionary advantage has become a major health concern.

Although medical advances have lowered mortality rates dramatically in the past century and more, morbidity rates have gone in the opposite direction: we live far longer lives, but there is a far higher propensity for us to suffer from chronic conditions that impact our quality of life, from excess weight gain and type 2 diabetes to heart disease or strokes. Exercise is so often the missing element in our lives that causes us to fall ill and then not improve. Our sedentary lives are the root cause of so many of the physical – and mental – ailments we suffer from today.

The mass adoption of television sets in the 1950s was a pivotal point for our sedentariness: within barely fifteen years, society saw a mass relocation of hundreds of millions of individuals into extended states of total inactivity. The integration of television schedules into everyday life had a fundamental effect on the nomadic instincts of humankind, although we did not realize it at the time: moving images captivate us and command our attention, and the sudden arrival of cultural moments broadcast to our screens felt so novel and otherworldly that we welcomed them with fascination. We were unaware then that the images we encountered on our new televisions – first in black and white and then in colour – stimulated an unprecedented mix of scattered attentiveness and immobilization as our bodies were rendered practically motionless for remarkably long periods of time. Today, the average adult in the UK spends approximately one third of their waking hours watching TV and video content, across all devices – the regulator Ofcom found the daily average to be four hours and fifty-three minutes in 2019, with this increasing as a result of the COVID-19 pandemic to five hours and nineteen minutes in 2021.

Humans have evolved to be watchful of our surroundings and to look for any change, so we are able to sustain our attention on objects of interest for long durations of time; the prefrontal cortex in our brains suppresses other sensory inputs to help us reduce distraction. One of the primary activities that shuts down when we focus on something is our major bodily movement; this is most obvious when we are out and about – if we hear a loud siren for example, we are likely to stop in our tracks in order to pay proper attention. The same happens when we are at a screen: the images sustain our focus to the extent that they reduce most of our bodily awareness. It is possible, of course, to iron a shirt when we are watching television, or to follow an exercise programme, but it is relatively rare overall, and for the majority of the time that we find ourselves at a screen, we sit quite perfectly still. Even when we eat a meal in front of the television, we often pause to take in the action with a spoon, cup or glass hovering mid-air on the way to our mouth.

Since the advent of television, the number of screens in our homes has proliferated, and each of them fixes our attention and holds our bodies motionless. Televisions have become steadily more participative since their first incarnation, and the slew of options on modern smart TVs are set out in much the same way as any mobile app; yet for all the interactive options on display, we remain primarily passive when we watch box sets or streaming services. When we complete digital tasks, whether answering emails, checking our bank balance or browsing the internet, we pay far more direct attention to the screen; yet this is bad news for our physical well-being: whereas a film or soap episode can wash over us languorously, other digital experiences today expect far more of us and hold us even more stationary. Adults typically spend three to four hours on their mobile devices each day globally, and during this time it is near impossible to perform any complex physical moves; despite our phones being mobile by design, the actual time we spend in physical motion when using these devices is actually very limited. When we do move while holding and using them, our physical capacity is substantially reduced, as is evident, for instance, as we awkwardly halt or weave between people in a crowd while sending a message. Most often we sit or lie down when we use our mobile devices, or stop and stand motionless on street corners. Ironically, therefore, the more portable a device is, the more capable it is of rendering us sedentary in new and quite different places. Whereas television infiltrated our living rooms and pinned us motionless to our sofas, our mobiles, laptops and tablets often make us just as stationary, wherever we are.

Our bodies might take a very long period of time to adapt to societal and lifestyle changes, but human beings are able to quickly adjust psychologically to new circumstances. It has not taken us long to accept our daily digital habits and the extended durations of time that we spend sedentary at screens as normal, and ill-health is often required to make us fully aware of our current lifestyles and the health risks we might be facing. Since the 2015 University of Cambridge study, a large number of other research programmes and academic enquiries have continued to investigate the effects of the increase in sedentary time as a result of screen use, and the results have correlated conclusively: without remedially active time away from devices, lengthy durations of time sat sedentary at screens are deleterious to both our physical and mental health.

Over time, our muscles steadily atrophy, particularly the core muscles of the back that stabilize our torso. Prolonged chair rest has almost the same effects as prolonged bed rest, as we do not use any leg muscles to support our weight; equally, if our chair has a backrest, headrest and armrests, it is likely we do not use as many muscles in our upper body either. Muscles deteriorate by losing tissue, especially the slow-twitch fibres we rely on for endurance, and our torso and abdominal muscles in particular weaken and fatigue rapidly. Endless hours of sitting immobilizes our joints, and when our muscles are no longer stretched sufficiently, they soon shorten.

Screen time can permanently shrink our hip flexors: when they become too tight they tilt the pelvis forward and cause an exaggerated curve in the lower back. To counteract this forward tilt, our hamstring muscles along the backs of the thigh compensate by tilting the pelvis backward. This adjustment in the body's alignment can lead to a flat-back posture that hunches our shoulders forward. The lower back pain that so many people struggle with today is also a result of these postural imbalances caused by too much sedentariness.

As Nabokov's *Indian Running* outlines, and as multiple generations of runners in the Ramírez family are testament to today, in Native American societies people ran from their early years, and, until notably late in life, men and women continued to cover large distances. When it comes to sprinting and other high-intensity sports, our performance drops, along with our aerobic capacity, with age. Yet, when it comes to endurance, recent studies have revealed that our bodies can hold out for far longer. The Institute of Physiology and Anatomy in Germany, for example, has found that for non-elite male and female runners, significant age-related losses in endurance performance do not occur before the age of fifty; and even after this threshold, they tail off quite slowly. Analysis of female runners has found the same points of transition from anaerobic to aerobic metabolism as in men, as well as from carbohydrate to fat metabolism. In other words, although men and women have different muscle mass, muscle-fibre types and maximal oxygen uptake (VO_2 max), we share the same physiological, metabolic processes that enable us to run over long distances.

Across our society today, we all remain uniquely disposed to walk and run as a direct result of our evolutionary heritage. Young or old, and whatever our biological sex, each of us has the same natural capability to cover an exceptional amount of ground, even if doing so is no longer a biological imperative. With the radical shift in our daily lifestyles since the advent of screen-based communication, work and entertainment, if we want to retain the physical abilities of our ancestors, we have to make the conscious decision to use them. Deliberate effort and willpower seem to be needed to maintain regular running and walking today, yet it need not be so. Being aware of the unprecedented position in which we find ourselves and instigating some new, simple changes to our habits and daily lifestyles can be enough to make a significant change that can protect our bodily health and mental well-being from the effects of technology and wider digital trends.

GET ON THE MOVE AGAIN

In the same year that the University of Cambridge released its landmark study, the Academy of Medical Royal Colleges also issued its groundbreaking *Exercise: The Miracle Cure and the Role of the Doctor in Promoting It* report. The academy collated a broad base of evidence to show that exercise is better for you than many pharmaceutical drugs in preventing a large number of life-threatening illnesses. Spending just 150 minutes per week briskly walking – that is, undertaking thirty minutes of moderately intense exercise just five times per week – was found to be sufficient to reduce your risk of strokes, many cancers, depression, heart disease and dementia by at least 30 per cent; and the chances of suffering from osteoarthritis, high blood pressure or type 2 diabetes dropped by 50 per cent. Since then, the World Health Organization (WHO) has also investigated the risks of sedentary behaviour and in late 2020 released its own, more strenuous guidelines. The WHO now recommends at least 150 to 300 minutes per week of moderate-intensity physical activity, in addition to 75 to 150 minutes per week of vigorous-intensity exercise, and also sets out further, higher bands of exercise to look after your health fully.

There is a good chance these changes might present quite a turnaround in your lifestyle given that 25 per cent of the UK population has been found to be 'completely physically inactive'. The Sport and Recreation Alliance recently uncovered that although 40 per cent of men thought they met government targets for physical activity, only 6 per cent of them actually did. If you drive to work or use public transport, or work from home, and, like the majority of adults in the developed world, have a sedentary job, your opportunities for physical exercise are already substantially reduced. If your spare moments outside of work are also spent in front of screens, your daily physical activity may be little more than a medley of sitting positions.

A first conscious step to moving more is to pay more attention to how much time you are indeed sedentary. The causes of your own inactivity might seem innocuous and everyday, but over days, weeks, months and years, inactivity presents one of the largest health risks you are likely to face – just as dangerous as drinking, overeating or smoking, and according to some, even more so.

Fortunately, you are gifted with a latent ability to quite quickly adapt your strength and physique. The changes are often highly enjoyable and need not be too arduous; the most important thing is to listen to your body and not to overreach. The popularity of marathons and other running events – not to mention the rise in wearable technology to track and measure your results – can too often spur abrupt changes in the amount you exert yourself, and these are the cause of most running injuries today. Small, incremental changes are best to make sure you give your body the time it needs to recover and improve.

Running in itself – although it can be hugely liberating and rewarding – is not even necessary to restore you back to full health: so long as you cover enough ground each week, walking alone can keep you perfectly fit and healthy. Not all of us can walk or run, but there are often other ways to stay active and maintain good health. The most important thing is to keep moving when you can, and a number of useful techniques can help with this.

Be sedentary-aware

The amount of time each day that we spend sitting or lying down can often come as a surprise. Getting a better sense of how sedentary you are day to day is important so you can properly gauge the changes you need to make to become more active, and it pays to revisit this again at regular, but infrequent, intervals.

Pedometers are the commonly prescribed means for tracking how much you move in a day, and they are useful at the start to give you a measure of how much you typically move. You will most likely be aware of the general guideline of aiming for 10,000 steps per day, but on average, most of us only cover 4,000–5,000, typically consisting of short bursts of movement around the home or office, and doctors consider a lifestyle with fewer than 5,000 steps a day as sedentary. Rather than relying too much on an app or being forced to carry your phone with you throughout the day, a simple pedometer the size of a small pebble can be bought online for less than £20 ($25) and easily dropped into your pocket. Keep it with you for a few days to get a sense of your current base level, then pop it away in a drawer for safekeeping. You can carry it again later to check how you are progressing, but there is no need to quantitatively monitor your movement on a daily basis – listening to your own body and gauging how you actually feel is just as important.

As pervasive as pedometers are on mobile health apps or as independent devices, there are no reliable tracking tools on the consumer market for monitoring how much time you spend standing versus sitting. Academic researchers typically use activPAL accelerometers for studies on levels of sedentariness today. These can closely monitor the exact time you spend lying down, sitting or standing and can distinguish between commuting, walking or running, but the technology is not widely available to the general public at affordable prices.

Happily, all you really need to track your sedentariness is a small notebook and pen. Choose a standard day of the week – preferably a working day – and carry your notepad with you wherever you go; write down the specific times that you start a new activity and note whether you are lying down, sitting or standing. Be honest and try to capture the details of a typical day; even better, track a few days on the trot and look for variations. You are likely to find that the vast majority of your hours are spent stationary, and that any moments on your feet are generally brief in duration. Look out for what is primarily causing your sedentariness: do you not take any breaks away from your desk at work, or do you watch TV all evening? Do you get outside much? Aim to establish a clear view of the rhythms of your days and consciously pay attention to when you stop moving.

TAKE ACTION

- **Check how much you move:** Buy a simple pedometer and carry it in your pocket for a few days.
- **Investigate how sedentary you are:** Carry a notepad with you for a day or two and note how much time you spend lying down, sitting or standing.
- **Find the primary causes of your sedentariness:** Reflect on your daily routine and the habits that most cause you to be inactive.
- **Stay aware:** Try to pay attention more consciously to when you stop moving and revisit your baseline activity from time to time.

Adapt your daily routines

With a few small tweaks and changes, you can easily create more physically active moments in your day and, over time, form new, healthier routines. An easy first step is to examine your commute, if you have one. If you drive or take public transport to work, would you be able to run or walk some of the route instead? Perhaps you could walk rather than drive to the railway station, or park a little further away from your office. Finding ways to travel on foot to somewhere you have to visit daily, or at least regularly, instantly creates a routine that increases your baseline of physical activity. Start with walking, rather than running, and if the distance is trying, perhaps do it only on your return journey, so you can rest and recover at home at the end of the day. Investing in a good running bag gives you the freedom to carry your laptop and a change of clothes, opening up some or all of your commute as a running course. Begin with only short stretches of the commute, and rest for several days in between. As your fitness and stamina build, you can take on longer distances and explore new routes.

Outside of your commute, or if you work from home, consider regular short journeys you make in the car or on public transport and decide which ones you could walk instead – the school run perhaps, or trips to the shops. Multiple opportunities to get you back on your feet more, even for a short time, can cumulatively make a big difference. It's recommended to take short breaks from your desk every thirty to sixty minutes, so try to keep that in mind; setting a timer for a few days can quickly get you into the habit of leaving your seat regularly. Stretching your muscles every hour or so, particularly those in your neck, shoulders, back and legs, can help hugely to alleviate tension and improve posture. Walk-and-talk meetings can be another great way to get you standing again – if you need to discuss something with a colleague or make a phone call, consider taking a walk around the office or head outside. If you work from home, you can incorporate short, simple exercises into your breaks instead: setting a specific time of day for a few squats, lunges, push-ups or jumping jacks can notably improve your circulation and overall fitness.

TAKE ACTION

- **Create space in your commute to walk or run:** Even if your commute is long, try to find sections you could cover on your own two feet.
- **Avoid short car journeys:** Determine which car journeys that you make regularly could be done instead on foot.
- **Set an hourly reminder for a few days:** Use the timer on your phone to get into the habit of taking regular breaks away from your desk, then switch it off and try to keep the routine going.
- **Try out a standing desk for the day:** Do you feel changes to your comfort, alertness and productivity?

In addition, standing desks are an excellent way to dramatically reduce the amount of time you spend sitting in a day. The idea of a standing desk can seem unappealing at first, yet using one quickly reveals your natural propensity to stand, and it often feels more comfortable over longer stretches of time. If you have a desk job, the time you spend at your workstation will likely represent the largest portion of your screen time: switching to a standing desk instantly releases this time from being sedentary. Your leg muscles, core and upper torso all benefit, and you burn more calories too. Most people feel more alert and productive when they stand; your posture naturally begins to improve, and your risks of compression of the spine and back pain decrease.

Build your strength and stamina

Climbing stairs burns more calories per minute than jogging, and any medical practitioner would count it as vigorous-intensity exercise. Swap lifts and escalators for the stairs to help build and maintain the strength of your bones, joints and muscles: doing so is as close as you can get to a high-intensity training (HIT) workout within the regular routines of daily life.

Building in a few extra activities that train your strength over time can help hugely to improve the range of motion in your muscles, ligaments and tendons. You can also reinforce your knees, hips, ankles and other major joints in ways that give you extra protection from injury. Implementing a few proactive changes to preserve your muscle mass not only makes your daily chores a lot easier – shopping bags certainly begin to feel a lot lighter – but it also gives you extra power and endurance when you walk and run.

There's no need to join a gym: you can find the exercise you need simply by walking and running more in your wider surroundings, but if you were to add one strength-training or high-intensity exercise to your daily drill, a good choice would be the kettlebell swing, which can be done in your back garden or front room and gives you an intensive workout in just a few minutes. Originating in Russia, the kettlebell is a cast-iron or steel ball with a flat base and handle attached to the top. It was originally used as a counterweight in markets to measure grains, but over time, people have begun to recognize the health and fitness benefits of using it for strength training. When swinging the kettlebell, muscles in your upper and lower body as well as your core are targeted, and the strength you gain in your posterior chain – the muscles extending down through your back, glutes, hamstrings and calves – helps to propel you forwards when you are on the move. Quick searches online will reveal rafts of videos and articles on how to do a kettlebell swing safely: carefully work out which weight is best for you to start with and begin with a low number of reps once every few days, then progress onwards from there to feel the benefits.

TAKE ACTION

- **Take the stairs:** Avoid lifts and escalators whenever you can and take the opportunity to add quick HIT workouts to your daily schedule.
- **Buy a kettlebell weight:** Start with low numbers of reps and build them into your weekly routine.
- **Make time for simple sprints:** Try sprinting a short distance a few times, ideally up a hill, and repeat for a few weeks to see the benefits.

The more you walk and run, the stronger you become, but regular sprint reps can also boost your power and stamina, which can help you negotiate longer distances or higher climbs more comfortably. Put aside a bit of time in the day to sprint the same short distance a few times; if possible, choose a hill to run up and then walk back down each time. Start with three repetitions on your first attempt; progress to five and then seven on your follow-up sessions: push yourself close to your aerobic limit and then give yourself a full recovery before you try again – often a couple of minutes is sufficient for your breathing to level off again. After even just a few sessions, you will begin to find your walks and runs easier and far more enjoyable; the power and stamina you build will carry you further and progressively attune your body to natural levels of effort and strain. One sprint session every week or two is more than enough and in itself makes for an invigorating break away from a screen. You might even begin to enjoy the challenge!

Run in nature

When you run for a sufficiently long distance and allow yourself to become immersed in the experience, you find yourself settling deeply into the landscape and becoming part of it. You feel the solid substance of the rock and pebbles reverberate through your body, and the softness of the earth and grass under your weight. Noises and smells ebb and flow. Whereas your digital experiences are largely just visual, when you walk and run outside, you are far more fully connected, with all your senses, to the real world around you. When you run, you see with your body too; and the more you do it, the better your physical interpretations can become. Whereas so much digital content is simply delivered to you, when you walk and run you are in total control and play a wholly active role in the experience you create. So when you next go out on foot, head off-road and try to more attentively make sense of the world as you pass through it: focus on the sensory experience of walking or running, the feel of the Sun or breeze on your skin, and the sound of your footsteps on different surfaces. Notice how your muscles stretch and your breath synchronizes with the rhythm of your movement and beating heart; be aware of the differences in texture of the ground underfoot and try to fully take in your natural surroundings.

Let someone know where you are going, and leave your phone at home, unless you are in a remote area. Avoid listening to music or podcasts, as they sever your connection with your surroundings. Try not to use any wearable devices or overly track your times or distances. Listen instead to your body and know when it feels right to turn back; your capability and range will naturally improve, but be patient. Most running or walking injuries are avoidable: listen to any aches and pains and don't push yourself when your body says you shouldn't.

TAKE ACTION

- **Pay more attention when you run and walk:** Try to focus on your physical sensations rather than getting lost in your own thoughts.
- **Take in your environment with all your senses:** Notice the effects the landscape has on you and enjoy the exhilaration of being in the natural world.
- **Leave your phone at home:** Avoid listening to music or podcasts and leave behind any wearables or tracking devices.
- **Listen carefully to your body:** Be alert to aches and pains and trust your instincts on when it is time to slow down or turn back.

Meditate as you run

When you walk and run over longer distances your thoughts naturally begin to clear. There is serenity to be found in the rhythm of your own movement, and more technical moments in particular demand your total attention, when you cross loose ground or undulations or navigate a busy street for instance. As the initial stiffness of your limbs loosens, running can feel like flying as your surroundings whisk past. Even small amounts of walking and running can do wonders for depression and lift your spirits; you'll sleep better too.

In its purest form, running connects you with your body and breath, and there are a number of techniques to help you focus on these and get out of your own head. Instead of chest breathing when you walk and run, try instead to 'belly breathe' to make the most of your full lung capacity. Belly breathing, also known as diaphragmatic breathing, is the natural and more efficient way to breathe, and it is how infants naturally breathe. Focus on filling your abdomen, rather than your chest, with air – when you are doing it correctly, you will notice your belly button moving outward. Give it some practice on the move and, when you feel comfortable, try exhaling on alternate foot strikes to help spread the force of your impact with the ground across both sides of your body. This can potentially reduce the risk of injury or discomfort later. When your diaphragm relaxes on the exhale, your core becomes less stable and bears more of the brunt force of foot impact; if you land on the same foot with each exhale, you effectively double the force of the impact on that side of the body. But if you breathe with a 3:2 ratio, counting 1-2-3 steps on the inhale and then 1-2 steps on every exhale – you balance the force of impact across both sides of your body. The pattern will quickly become second nature and as you stay focused on your breath, your thoughts and worries melt away into the cadence of your footsteps.

TAKE ACTION

- **Try to 'belly breathe' when you walk or run:** Fill your abdomen instead of your chest – your belly button should move outward with each inhalation.
- **Exhale on alternate foot strikes:** Belly breathe with a 3:2 ratio between in-breaths and out-breaths.
- **Focus on your breath and let your thoughts go:** Keep the rhythm of your breathing in sync with your steps and settle into the flow.

Chapter 3

Conversation

TRANSIENT EXPRESSIONS

In 1872, Charles Darwin published a book that many describe today as his forgotten masterpiece, obscured in popular consciousness by his *On the Origin of Species*, which came out thirteen years earlier. *The Expression of the Emotions in Man and Animals* was the first exploration of the ancestral sources of many of the human characteristics we take for granted: lifting our eyebrows in moments of surprise, for example, or sneering when we are angry. During his work on evolutionary biology, Darwin had filled notebooks with thoughts on the possible interactions between hereditary factors and the social aspects of our daily lives. He noticed that our facial expressions of emotion seem globally consistent – indeed, this is backed up by numerous recent studies of literate and preliterate cultures. He also argued, controversially at the time, that emotions are not unique to humans but can be found in many other species. Darwin saw our facial expressions as being not only the richest source of information about our emotions, but also a present-day link to our evolutionary past. For instance, why *do* we raise our upper lip when we are angry? Because, Darwin argued, millennia ago, our primate ancestors exposed their teeth when they felt under threat, to signal and prepare for attack. When we feel angry – however momentarily – we also glare and reveal the whites of our eyes, pulling our eyebrows down tightly together, enhancing the intensity of our gaze and making us appear more threatening and intimidating to others. The anatomy of our facial expressions and body movement that we rely on to communicate is primal, deeply embedded within our genetic code.

Darwin kept all of his written correspondence and organized his notebooks neatly by letter. In 1948, the majority of his archive was transferred to Cambridge University Library. Notebooks *M* and *N* predominantly cover his ideas about emotional expression, but a wealth of other observations can be found on all aspects of human communication throughout the rest of his notes. Darwin began thinking about human interaction early in his career, long before publishing his famous theories of evolution, and it was a project that he would continue for the rest of his life. He was particularly interested in the origins of language, and he conducted extensive research on the subject, including studying the language development of his own children. Yet he was most interested in understanding the physicality and evolutionary significance of human communication – not only our facial expressions but also our gestures and any other forms of non-verbal cues that we rely on when we speak to one another.

The Cambridge archive also includes a collection of original photographs, drawings, paintings and prints commissioned by Darwin, and it's here that his deepest efforts to understand human conversation are most visible. Darwin recognized that our facial expressions and gestures are transient, most composed of a complex association of muscle contractions or movements, and a non-verbal expression most typically unfolds in a quick succession of phases over a short span of time. Darwin was keen to study natural human expressions more closely, and in realizing that they could not be sampled in a conventional manner, he began to search for alternative sources. First, he studied traditional artworks, looking for consistencies and themes in how people held themselves over different periods and cultural traditions; but soon he started to investigate the potential of photography, only then recently invented, to reveal more detail about each facial expression or gesture he was investigating.

It was very rare at the time for photography, a slow and awkward process, to capture our true expressions of laughter, sadness or anger. Darwin had to arrange a series of photoshoots to overcome limits of the medium, and he also found some other unexpected solutions. He was introduced to the work of the French neurologist Guillaume-Benjamin Duchenne de Boulogne, who, by using electric probes, could artificially induce a variety of recognizable facial expressions for long enough for a photo to be taken. Duchenne would sit a person in a chair and position their head between two rods, which were connected to a battery and a series of wires that led to different parts of the face. By passing an electric current through specific facial muscles, he was able to induce the movements we make for a variety of expressions. (His work has been influential more recently in the development of facial recognition technology, which relies on the ability to detect and analyse subtle changes in our expressions to identify individuals based on their facial features.) When Darwin received final prints from Duchenne, he decided to commission wood-carving reproductions of the photographs, so that he could edit out the wires on display to avoid them being a visual distraction. *Expression* was one of the first scientific books to be published with printed photos of this kind, or indeed any images capturing human emotion, and most readers were unaware of how Darwin had produced his natural, realistic depictions of human emotion. Their compelling quality quickly made the book a mainstream success.

Our faces are capable of making more than 10,000 expressions, giving a phenomenal boost to the average active vocabulary of an adult English speaker, which is around 20,000 words. Facial expressions are part of our evolutionary heritage and share the emotions we are experiencing with others quickly and easily. In everyday life, this is highly effective. We rely on our emotions to automatically appraise any situation and prepare us to deal with whatever we find important; we are not typically aware of our split-second reactions, yet they motivate and mobilize the majority of our activity. The emotional signals we send to others with our facial expressions and body movements happen almost instantaneously: micro-expressions are the most subtle and pass across our faces in less than one fifth of a second. And while it is possible to dampen non-verbal cues, it is practically impossible to inhibit them entirely. Our heritage as *Homo sapiens* is, after all, tribal: we have survived and prospered in the past by living in large groups, and by being able to understand each other's concerns and deepest feelings in an instant, we have been able to act together in unison. What we read on people's faces reveals nothing less than our humanity and can connect us in ways that outmatch any words.

Darwin was an active member of the Royal Society and was elected as a Fellow in 1839 at the age of thirty, remaining a member for the rest of his life. He would join meetings and debates in London, and in 1858 he presented a paper on his theory of evolution by natural selection with Alfred Russel Wallace – a presentation now known as the Darwin–Wallace paper and considered to be one of the most important scientific papers in history. In Darwin's day, the Royal Society was a prominent place for scientific discussion and debate, and it helped to shape the intellectual and cultural climate of the era. The lively, collegiate atmosphere at its meetings and public lectures provided a conducive space for people to exchange ideas, and the founding members of the Royal Society had met regularly in coffeehouses to discuss and debate experiments – there is even a record of the physicist Isaac Newton, eventual president of the Royal Society from 1703 to 1727, dissecting a dolphin for an audience in the Grecian Coffee House at Wapping Old Stairs in London.

The first coffeehouse had opened in Oxford in 1651 and became a popular spot for students and the local scientific community to congregate together to read, learn and debate. Away from the more raucous alehouses and taverns, a serious and open-minded civility was quickly established. When coffeehouses began opening in London the next year, the city was experiencing massive population growth, with the number of residents increasing from 375,000 to 490,000 between 1650 and 1700 alone. Newcomers struggling with a lack of social networks – a situation exacerbated by the displacement of many communities as a result of the Great Fire – quickly began to rely on coffeehouses as a first port of call to find professional work and contacts. In a short period of time, coffeehouses spread fast across the city. The protocols recognizing rank and precedence, common at that time in other social settings such as the salons held at great houses, were abandoned to make people feel quickly at ease; and the easy-going, unforced conversations that naturally developed are well documented by Samuel Pepys, Jonathan Swift and Samuel Johnson.

Visitors would pay a penny to enter for a coffee, social company, newspapers, lectures or intellectual debate. These so-called 'Penny Universities' were regular stopping places, somewhere to visit to catch the latest news or find a friend, and the scientist Robert Hooke records in his diaries visiting at least sixty-four different establishments between 1672 and 1680, frequently as many as three in a day. Hooke himself relied on coffeehouses to draw on the knowledge of a wide variety of individuals, from servants to skilled labourers or aristocrats, and found his conversations an important complement to his work in the laboratory.

The spread of coffeehouses across metropolitan London coincided with Britain's commercial and colonial empire expanding across the globe. Coffeehouses became synonymous with the sharing of information; these were places where the latest business news was heard or new opportunities could be found. The London Stock Exchange itself started life in the late seventeenth century in Jonathan's Coffee House, in Exchange Alley in the City of London, an inception point of a financial revolution that funded most of England's endeavours overseas. Lloyd's Coffee House opened on Tower Street in 1686 and became a popular meeting place for sailors, merchants and ship owners, and exchange of shipping news at the venue eventually led to the Lloyd's of London insurance market, which still exists today. The growing functions of coffeehouses as postal centres, employment agencies and business addresses lodged them at the heart of mercantile activity across the city. Auction rooms proliferated in coffeehouses, selling anything from bulk goods to prize ships or artwork, and they increasingly catered for a taste for the foreign and exotic, selling collections of curiosities – ancient books, fine garments, even an elephant or rhino. These sales brought a mass of people together in the beginning stages of global consumerism.

Yet, for all this commerce and activity, coffeehouses were largely informal spaces dependent on the free actions and patronage of their customers. Often little more than a room, but sometimes spread through several enclosed areas, coffeehouses were bustling, voluble and energetic. No one was responsible for adjudicating the larger debates that took place. The cultivation of an art of conversation became an esteemed quality in coffeehouses, and articles began to appear in periodicals at the time offering advice on how to put someone at ease or better learn self-control during more heated debates: an ability to measure one's political zeal or religious views to accommodate others was a particular aspiration. Although people did read up on how to improve their conversation skills, they mostly learned by joining in. A large central table was typically a focal point, open for new arrivals to jump straight into any debate, and smaller tables were often available, set apart for groups to pursue their own interests. Thoughts and ideas would ripple through a room through vocal remarks, murmurs of encouragement or exclamations of agreement or contestation. Practised speakers became capable of building and sustaining their argument to meet the demands of the situation around them and of handling heckles or interjections with good grace.

Coffeehouses advanced to become the settings through which public opinion collected and communicated itself in a 'fourth estate of the realm', as historian Thomas Babington Macaulay put it. Here, anyone, whatever their background, could gather together to reason and share their views. The energetic, bustling conversations in the individual coffeehouses across London and other urban areas in Britain collectively gathered force to drive social change, and a clear analogy can be drawn with the cultural shifts we are experiencing today as a result of social media. The functionalities on our devices – from social platforms and text messages to email and video calls – have equally changed the way we converse and have had profound effects on how we shop, work, gather together and digest news. Yet, conversation in early modern coffeehouses had an inescapable physicality – the close quarters of the building itself and the personal space shared within it, the immediacy of the body movements, gestures and eye contact to support any words spoken – these are the very aspects of human expression that Darwin closely studied, and what we miss out on most when we speak online.

Darwin found gesture to be just as fundamental to communication as our facial movements. He observed that, in contrast to the universal language of facial expressions across all human populations, our body language is far more idiosyncratic and variable across different cultures or situations. Darwin was a little off the mark as to why we gesture with our hands and other parts of our bodies when we speak: he attributed it correctly again to our evolutionary past, but he also accepted the commonly understood explanation at the time that we gesture for the most part to bring emphasis, energy and ornamentation to our speech. It has only been in recent years that an explosion of research in the field of gesture studies has revealed that we rely on gesture for far more profound reasons. Findings have shown that language and gesture are deeply intertwined – our hand and body movements help us not only to express our thoughts and ideas to others but also to generate those thoughts in the first place: in other words, we produce gestures to help clarify our thinking, as much for our own benefit as for our listeners'.

Physically orchestrating our thoughts and communicating with the full array of our body's fine motor movements enhances the impact of anything that we say. When we talk in person, our perceptual states when we gesture rely on the activation of the same neural pathways involved in any life experience. Moving our hands can trigger recall of past events in our minds, and we can inhabit an idea more fully. We almost physically handle our thoughts as we speak, stretching and exploring them with our hand movements to add perceptual detail, and our body movements too can quicken our creativity and help us develop our thoughts in new directions.

Physical gestures can also help us listen. We have a natural ability to mentally simulate each other's body language – mirror neurons fire in our brains when we see someone else performing a gesture, as if we were making it ourselves. When a friend hunches their shoulders sorrowfully and their face becomes crestfallen before us, we can genuinely empathize with them as we experience an intuitive stirring of the same feelings, triggered by their body language.

✧ ✧ ✧

Darwin published *The Descent of Man* just a year before *Expression*, more fully exploring the evolutionary history of human beings within it, and concluded that 'gesture-language was, no doubt, the universal means of communication between the members of the human family, before the invention of articulate speech'. He came to firmly believe that non-verbal forms of communication were crucial for our ancestors' survival, and that their deep-rooted versatility and intuitive use were inevitably incorporated into human language – a theory that continues to be supported by the latest research in linguistics, cognitive psychology and neuroscience. The brain regions responsible for language processing and gesture recognition are closely interconnected, and if we are prevented from viewing each other's body language, we miss out on a lot of contextual information and find it much harder to understand one another.

Physical conversation is a live performance, much more like a stage show or concert than we might first realize, with complex patterns and regulations of behaviour in each person being influenced by, and influencing, that of the other interlocutors. Academic research in gestural studies has taken Darwin's lead in recording different types of human expressions to try to explain them, but researchers are able to use video today to more closely analyse conversations. In observing slowed-down footage of everyday interactions and monitoring the fine correspondence of body movement, scientists have found that people mirror and react to each other's gestures in the most subtle of ways. A listener's body motion coordinates in rhythm with the speaker, syncing with the syllables and words of their speech. Cups are raised and coffee sipped in unison, and the start and end points of the major components of action, such as adjusting one's seat or standing up to stretch one's legs, often coincide with others'. Even our eye shifts, blinks and mouth movements have been found to sync to the same tempo as those of our conversation partners.

Darwin himself struggled with shyness and social anxiety in public settings, but he found his own ways to overcome them, developing a wide extended network of close friends and other scientists, intellectuals and notable figures from his time. He was a thoughtful and engaging conversationalist and, as the German botanist Anton Kerner von Marilaun described, 'when one talked with Darwin, he had such a way of listening, that one was encouraged to express oneself freely, and without restraint'.

Recent academic research has uncovered the important role of 'joint attention' – the ability to closely follow one another – in any conversation. This allows us to arrive at our deepest levels of mutual understanding. We use our own mental and emotional experiences whenever we try to understand the motivations that might be driving another person, and we expand their range with the help of our imagination so that we can estimate what might be playing out in their mind. When we meet face to face, we have the best chance of getting right this so-called 'social cognition', the natural ability we can all develop to process and use the information we gain in conversation to explain and predict each other's behaviour. We are more empathetic when we speak offline, more perceptive, nuanced and balanced.

When a physical conversation is in full flow, when we are engrossed, responding intuitively or being moved emotionally, we are able to share perspectives and assimilate another person's worldview with our own outlook. One of the most important differences when we meet in person is that the ways in which we attend to one another become direct experience and something palpable that we can learn from. The simplicity of some of these actions can too easily obscure their power and importance – a brief glance is one of the easiest ways for us to share our thoughts, however complex or multi-layered they might be, or to fix and align our views on something. Gaze-following, the tendency to look where we see someone else is looking, is another crucial aspect of physical conversation that we too easily take for granted. Without it, we cannot widen our shared focus to take in the three dimensions around us and establish literal – and often metaphorical – common ground.

Darwin strongly believed that we can improve how we communicate, particularly when it comes to our facial expressions and body language. He tried not to limit his research on physical communication to the English language, and in 1867 he created a questionnaire 'Queries about

Expression', which he sent to correspondents at outposts throughout the British Empire. He found great similarities in physical communication across populations of human beings across the globe, but he also uncovered that wherever there were differences, people were perfectly able to learn and adapt to them. Darwin's ideas about evolution and natural selection were highly controversial at the time, and he faced significant opposition in wider society. It took him twenty years to decide to publish his thoughts, and it was only through his extended conversations and debates with his colleagues and friends that he was able to gather the feedback he needed to identify weaknesses in his arguments and refine his reasoning.

It has since been unequivocally proven that conversation is a skill that each of us can improve at – we just need the opportunity to practise. When we meet as a group, reading posture shifts and body movements can help us measure whether or not everyone is closely coordinated in their thoughts, and practised speakers can discern when someone is showing the first signs of disliking the direction a conversation is taking solely from their body language. At its highest levels, social cognition allows a true meeting of minds: when we fully pay attention to one another, a shared understanding takes shape, and steadily a new consensus can be reached.

When we meet online, however, we lose recourse to the majority of our evolutionary heritage of facial expression and communicative gesture. Fortunately, physical conversation is always there whenever we need it. How might we reclaim some of the assuredness, perceptiveness and restraint so evident in seventeenth- and eighteenth- century coffeehouses? And can we too make use of some of these conversational abilities when we are online?

AN EVOLUTION OF EMOJIS AND GIFS

At the height of the Cold War, in the early 1960s, Paul Baran, an engineer working at the RAND Corporation – a think-tank founded by the US armed forces after Second World War – was tasked with developing a new type of communication system that could keep operating, even if part of it was shut down by a nuclear blast. Baran invented a distributed network to divide communications into tiny pieces and spread them around: in this way, if any part of the network was knocked out, the remaining sections could carry on regardless. He published a paper on his new system in 1964, and its findings emerged a few years later in the form of the United States Department of Defense's ARPAnet, an innovation that would eventually evolve to become today's internet.

Digital technology has given us an astounding ability to communicate, irrespective of our location, and the ease with which we can send emails or connect via video calls across the globe is an enormous privilege and luxury. Our decentralized communication networks are phenomenally powerful, dividing our messages into tiny packets of information and delivering them far and wide. But increasingly we rely on these systems not just for speedy communication across long distances or when, for health reasons, say, it is impossible to meet, but also to replace perfectly feasible in-person conversations.

The social and digital media tools we use today are simulations of how human beings actually interact in the real world: expertly designed, they try to approximate the intricacies of our natural face-to-face encounters as much as possible. They do a commendable job, with most communication apps offering a spectrum of options from basic text messaging to high-definition video calls. Yet even a video stream captures only a small, two-dimensional slice of the actual events in each physical location. There is simply no way to replicate the complete reality of human connection online; even the most sophisticated current virtual reality technology constricts body movement, and a digital environment could never be as sensorily rich and complex as our own physical world.

Today's cafes are very different to the coffeehouses of the late 1600s. A branch of Starbucks might fill the same four walls as an early modern coffeehouse and be furnished similarly. But despite the potential for possible community, today we are more likely to find there are large numbers of people sitting alone looking at screens. The decentralized nature of our digital technology can have the unfortunate effect of dispersing our collective social potential – instead, we increasingly gather together as an aggregation of discrete individuals. Much like when standing in a queue or being stuck in traffic, we might all share a physical location, but our attention and thoughts are scattered elsewhere. Digital communication has become so habitual, compulsive even, that we often use it by default, emailing a colleague at the next desk, for example, even when a face-to-face conversation would be more efficient and enjoyable. The more we rely on digital technology to communicate, the more we risk swapping intimacy for distance and progressively detaching from a present sense of shared place.

On the morning of 19 September 1982, Professor Scott Fahlman, a computer scientist at Carnegie Mellon University, used the first smiley face :) emoticon. He typed it on an internal computer bulletin board and added a note recommending that students use it to indicate if any of their posts were intended as jokes. The immateriality of digital networks had always been part of their explicit promise: the efficiencies gained by virtual communications or a paperless office were always a sales pitch of early internet companies, but the negative repercussions on our interpersonal relations were not anticipated. Fahlman was early to spot the difficulties posed by the paucity of facial expressions in most digital communications, and he was one of the first people to try to find a sensible way around them.

It was not until 1999 that the first set of 176 emojis ('*e*', meaning 'picture', and '*moji*', 'character' in Japanese) was invented by Shigetaka Kurita, an artist and designer working for the Japanese telecommunications company NTT Docomo. Kurita had been tasked with creating a set of simple icons that could be used to convey information or emotions in a limited amount of space, and he drew inspiration from not only emoticons but also Japanese kanji characters, street signs, and manga comics. The use of emojis spread beyond Japan in the early 2000s with the advent of smartphones and social media, and they are a ubiquitous part of online communication today. As Darwin might have predicted, emojis with faces are understood globally.

The growing banks of colourful emojis we find on our apps have evolved over time to try to bridge the gap between our written messages and the emotions we feel when we type them. They can seem novel, playful and fun; but their cartoonish simplicity can't encompass the subtle range of emotions in real human faces. The Unicode Consortium releases new emojis at regular intervals, and its most recent version 15.0 includes 3,664: a far cry from the 10,000 facial expressions each of us can make. Naturally, emojis help make our written exchanges more fluid and less misconstrued, but the very need for them and the crudeness of what they offer in comparison to the real thing only goes to emphasize what is missing when we communicate by text online.

In an effort to overcome the limitations of emojis, a variety of other digital symbols that attempt to replicate our facial expressions and gestures have become increasingly popular. Pre-designed images or animations are now often added as 'stickers' to a message to convey a particular emotion or add personality. Bitmoji avatars were invented by a Canadian company called Bitstrips in 2014 and can be customized to look like the user expressing a wide range of feelings and emotions; and in 2017, Apple released its own 'Memojis', which use the TrueDepth camera system on newer iPhones and iPads to track our movements and create more accurate renditions of our facial expressions.

Each of these new evolutions make the expressions we can communicate online that little more nuanced, but it's simply impossible to fully emulate our facial features or body movement without a live, fully accurate three-dimensional rendering of our whole body being made available to the person with whom we are speaking. Our facial movements – such as nods, smiles, frowns or raised eyebrows – support and supplement our speech in all sorts of complex ways. Our faces naturally give one another feedback live in the moment and help us to regulate our behaviour while conversing. When our faces disappear online, it becomes far more difficult for us to coordinate our conversations responsibly, particularly if things get heated.

In both speech and the written word humans have always been constrained by the essential linearity of language – one word follows another in a consecutive sequence. Gesture is not restricted at all in this way, and it's a flexible, visual mode of communication that we carry with us wherever we go to enhance our speech. When we communicate online, of course, most physical gesture is removed entirely, but social media has matured over time to become increasingly visual: thumbs-up and other gestural icons have become commonplace, and many posts today incorporate an image or video. Developed by a team at CompuServe in 1987, the Graphics Interchange Format (GIF) has only recently exploded in popularity. GIFs today most commonly consist of short video loops excerpted from film or vintage TV footage, and often feature a celebrity gesturing or exhibiting an exaggerated facial expression. Available via readymade selections on most messaging apps, we primarily use them to wittily communicate a thought or when we struggle to find the right words. Today, GIFs are often complemented by use of 'cinemagraphs', still photos that have a small area of motion repeated in a loop and are often designed to evoke a certain mood or atmosphere, from rage, humour or whimsy to feelings of awe.

GIFs, cinemagraphs or looped videos use repetition and movement to convey actions that static images cannot capture: they're often used to show a person nodding, waving or breaking into a smile, and they can give an indication of agreement, just as a physical gesture might. This requires only a few swipes, but the lack of physical movement needed to generate this imagery reflects its lesser impact.

In the midst of a physical conversation when we snatch a quick peek at our phone, it might feel inconsequential, yet cumulatively, the harm can be significant. The dance of glances and gestures we rely on is broken, and the rapport we can so easily build when we meet face-to-face risks rupture, however momentary. It is by no means seen as bad etiquette these days for us to take our spots around a table and place our phones down in front of us, but when we speak, we often find ourselves addressing heads peering down, focused on worlds away from the table.

Over weeks, months and years, the interruptions and stalling that our in-person encounters suffer as a result of technology use – not to mention the times when we opt to avoid meeting entirely and send messages instead – impoverish and diminish our opportunity to fully connect with one another and fuel a growing sense of disunity. We generally know that we should be focusing on those around us, but the worry about what we might be missing elsewhere is often too much to endure. We can become very adept, therefore, at maintaining the illusion we are present in a conversation while we check a notification. When we instead deliberately ignore the ping of a message and give someone our full attention, we let them know that we really are listening and that the conversation can flourish in its own natural direction.

Eye contact is our most simple and intuitive way of connecting as humans. Each look we share is confirmation that we are receiving one another's focus. It is also the principal means by which we can fully inhabit a thought or experience with someone else. We share all sorts of fleeting glances: brief 'initiation looks' to start a conversation, 'knowing looks' when we strike accord, and 'reference looks' whenever we call each other's attention somewhere else. The ways in which we share eye contact stem back to some of the earliest stages of our evolution as a species. The cerebellum, one of our most ancient brain regions, has developed over millennia to automatically coordinate our head and eye movements when we shift the direction of our gaze. Our vestibulo-ocular reflex system is a crucial mechanism that enables us to maintain stable vision during rapid head movements, and it makes us enormously proficient at sharing and maintaining eye contact, even when we are in the midst of complex body manoeuvres or running at a fast pace. We share our gaze so intuitively and are often entirely unaware of this, yet eye contact is essential not only to share our psychological states, but also for most stages of human development and our everyday well-being. Even in the heat of a startling, dramatic moment – such as a bank robbery unfolding – our motivation to share an experience can be so strong that we risk missing what might happen next in order to turn around and share the experience with the person next to us.

The effect that losing eye contact can have on us is most obvious on a video call: being filmed in different locations makes it impossible to exchange glances in the way we do in person. We cannot follow where the other is looking, and in response to our overriding instinct to share our attention when we speak, inevitably our eyes fix straight at the screen, creating a semblance of eye contact, enough to trick our minds that it is real, but with some damaging consequences.

This standard mode of a video call, with everyone looking at everyone else all of the time, would make for an exceptionally intense encounter in the real world. When we meet in person, we intersperse our eye contact with large portions of time taking in other events around us, and prolonged eye contact is saved for only the most emotional of encounters. In addition, the positioning of cameras on our devices fills most of the screen with our head and shoulders, creating an impression of proximity that we would normally only grant to someone we know intimately. The simulated closeness and eye contact during video calls conflict with how our minds have evolved to decipher our physical encounters: if someone were to move as close to us in real life, our most intuitive reaction would be to interpret it as a sexual advance or a threat of violence. Peering so closely at one another for such prolonged periods of time moves us instinctively into an unsustainable, hyper-vigilant state, and this is one of the prime reasons we find video calls so tiring.

The interconnected computer networks that facilitate our digital conversations work in ways that our bodies and minds are not primed to handle. For the full evolutionary span of our past, we have adapted as a cooperative species. We need the company of others to thrive. The power our technology has to dislocate us from our surroundings enables us to socialize everywhere at once, and our natural sociability makes it enormously tempting to spread ourselves as far and wide as we can, but when we disconnect too much from the people that physically surround us, we ultimately forgo any proper social contact. True conversation skills take time and effort to nurture, and amid the proliferation of texts, online chat and social apps, we may need to take active steps to recover and then strengthen our ability to fully connect in person.

HONE YOUR CONVERSATION SKILLS

Conversation is a skill that you can get better at. Each of us is gifted with an intuitive ability to attend to others, and we learn how to read one another's eyes and major body movements from a young age, but as with any natural capability, there are far more nuanced levels of competence that we can come to master. A proper conversation, when we actively listen, share news and ideas, and respond thoughtfully to one another, requires generous amounts of time, patience and attention.

It is illuminating to contemplate how many hours of the day your ancestors, even just a few generations ago before the widespread adoption of telephones and then the internet, would have spoken in person. Before the invention of writing, which is to say, for the vast majority of human existence, the only way we were able to converse was in the company of others. While our methods of communication have become increasingly digital and society has changed accordingly, the evolutionary heritage that primes you to connect and cooperate with others face-to-face certainly hasn't.

Conversationalists in London coffeehouses had a distinct advantage over you today: they lived at a time when the ramifications of the invention of the printing press and other new forms of written communication were only just beginning to alter society; a naturally human oral culture was still primarily intact. The practical inability to properly connect outside of one another's presence, save for a delayed receipt of letters, gave a different quality to the times that were shared together. People in coffeehouses had to pay attention to one another when they met, as there were no other quick conversational means to fall back on once apart. The far greater amounts of time spent in each other's company gave them ample opportunity to practise the art of conversation. They were alive to every tiny drama in an exchange, from the smallest eyebrow raise to the change in tenor of someone's voice, and they could deftly control their entire bodily communicative range in skilled response.

Some of the insights that were gained from the care and attention so diligently invested in physical conversation in coffeehouses in the seventeenth and eighteenth centuries survive today in essays that were written at the time and circulated across London in printed periodicals and pamphlets. You have the good fortune to be able to connect with people wherever you might be, and with some simple changes to how you communicate both on- and offline, you can make the most of the time you *do* spend with others.

Physical conversation

When to meet face-to-face

There are occasions when you really should meet in person. Major life events such as weddings and funerals can only get the focus they deserve when you share proper time with those close to you; complex, sensitive topics equally benefit from the increased understanding and cooperation that you can only arrive at through face-to-face conversations. The ease of catching others online, and the always-on spirit of availability most people try to sustain on social apps make it very tempting to share developments as soon as they arise. But it pays to consider the gaps of time people in our extended past would have waited to share important news: when they finally had the occasion to meet, topics that they had saved ready to share would propel a conversation forward. Being constantly available online today can mean that when you do meet in person you're forced to run over it all again or switch to less meaningful topics: either way, the vigour of finally meeting can be lost.

The Anglo-Irish writer and satirist Jonathan Swift, most remembered for *Gulliver's Travels*, was a regular visitor to coffeehouses. In his 1713 essay 'Hints Toward an Essay on Conversation', Swift elaborates on the ways that you can more thoroughly learn about another person's perspectives, experiences and opinions in physical conversation, and he emphasizes how important this can be in building meaningful relationships and understanding. In particular, Swift suggests being willing to listen to others' perspectives with an open mind, even if they differ from your own; equally, he advises not talking too much about yourself, so that a conversation gets the space it needs to develop in its own way.

It can be useful to keep in mind that digital conversations are always less consequential and memorable. A tendency to rely on texts, messaging or video calls risks degrading your physical conversations when they do happen. A key change you can make to revive your social life is to reserve digital messages, as much as is possible, for arranging only logistical details and other essentials. Stop sharing your news online or checking in by message to see how someone is doing, and save it instead for when you meet in person. Of course, you will still want to respond to inbound messages, but by being less proactive in your conversations online, you will be more disposed to arrange a meeting sooner, and the difference in energy levels and overall attentiveness when you do meet can be quite noticeable. Naturally, circumstances can make it harder to meet in person, particularly geographical distance: save your news for phone or video calls when this is the case, rather than relying on message exchanges – you'll get much more from your conversations.

It's common to feel an inclination to move some of your most difficult or emotional encounters online, yet these are precisely the exchanges that most benefit from you meeting in the flesh. Speaking in person is often the best way to defuse a situation, however difficult it might feel. Try viewing a fraught or complex conversation as an opportunity to learn both more about yourself and the other person. Whenever you notice an urge to text or email, keep in mind that you can far better control the eventual outcome of an exchange when you meet in person.

TAKE ACTION

- **Cut back on your digital messages:** Save news to share in person and observe the effect this has on energy levels and attentiveness when you do meet.
- **Make time for conversation:** Carve out a full morning or afternoon to meet up with a friend purely for a catch-up.

Become a good listener

Swift stresses that one of the most important conversation skills is being a good listener. He finds that when you are quieter and listen more in conversation, happily ceding the floor and control over a conversation's direction to others, you can more thoughtfully respond to those around you and, over time, become a better speaker. He suggests listening more actively by clarifying questions and paraphrasing what others have said to ensure that you have understood their meaning correctly.

When you are in the flow of a physical conversation, see if you can begin to more consciously take in the full combination of body motion, gestures and facial expressions of the people you are talking to. Are they leaning back languorously, or are they pitched forwards, with wide eyes? How fidgety or quiet are they in their movements; are there any repeating 'tells' you can spot? We give away so much more of our thoughts and feelings with our gesticulations than you might realize, and more actively paying attention to these in others can be very revealing.

Give deep listening a go and see what other differences you can find: intentionally focus as much as possible on what your friend is saying and attempt to quieten your inner voice. Often in conversation, you're poised to speak, quip or comment and spend as much time thinking of what to say next as following what your friend is saying. The rapid-fire stimulus of digital communications can only quicken this instinct, so try to notice it when it happens and then deliberately calm it. Spend more time instead absorbing the words and ideas the other person is communicating and if you find yourself struggling a little in conversation, take Swift's advice to paraphrase back what you've heard the other say to help you stay on common ground.

It also helps to watch your own body language. Do you keep your arms open in front of you or regularly cross them? Look out for when you most actively gesture: are there any types of hand movements that you often repeat? Consider what motions you can make to help people feel more at ease. Touch is one of our most intimate and emotionally resonant forms of communication, and totally impossible of course online. Try tapping a friend on the arm or the shoulder when you feel it might strike a chord and see what its effect is.

TAKE ACTION

- **Listen deeply during an in-person conversation:** Intentionally focus as much as possible on what your friend is saying and attempt to quieten your inner voice.
- **Try paraphrasing:** Ask questions to clarify things and paraphrase back what someone is saying to help you arrive at a mutual understanding.
- **Attend to body motion, gestures and facial expressions:** Pay close attention to the way someone's physical actions punctuate and complement their speech.
- **Watch your own body language:** Notice when you most actively gesture and consider which physical actions you can make to help people feel more at ease.

Tackle social anxiety head-on

The lexicographer and literary critic Samuel Johnson, who was responsible for the first comprehensive English-language dictionary, also frequented coffeehouses in the 1700s and in a collection of essays in his periodical *The Rambler* wrote extensively about the importance of regularly engaging in conversation to develop your skills. For Johnson, meaningful interactions with others are essential for personal growth and happiness, and the ability to engage in stimulating and insightful conversation is a key part of building strong relationships and developing a sense of community. By improving your conversation skills, he argues, you can enjoy more rewarding encounters with others and lead a more fulfilling life overall.

In Johnson's view, conversation is not something that comes naturally to everyone, and even those who are innately gifted conversationalists still need to practise and refine their skills in order to truly excel at the art. Over time, he argues, you can become more comfortable with the open-ended nature of conversation, learn to express yourself more clearly and effectively, and hone your capacity to listen attentively and respond thoughtfully. But there are often hurdles to overcome. Johnson struggled with several physical and emotional challenges throughout his life, including symptoms of Tourette's syndrome and a number of mental-health struggles, and he likely had to persist with conversation even at times when he felt anxious or self-conscious. He was successful in doing so, becoming renowned for his witty and engaging conversation, and he grew a wide network of contacts in his lifetime, including many prominent writers, intellectuals and politicians.

Today, technology use is one of the common hurdles preventing you from developing your conversation skills. The more you communicate online, the more likely it is that you will experience social anxiety and discomfort offline. Each time you mull over a written reply or social-media post, you are crafting a persona, one which can quickly dissolve when you meet in person and take part in real-time, physical conversations, which unfold rapidly, with levels of complexity and nuance unparalleled online. Johnson thought that open-ended and spontaneous conversations are an important way to learn and grow as a person, yet sadly an over-reliance on digital communication can make us anxious about meeting in person, leading us to spend increasingly more time online.

TAKE ACTION

- **Be curious about your social anxiety:** View moments of shyness or awkwardness in conversation as indicators of the types of face-to-face exchanges that you might benefit from practising more.
- **Don't fight the silences:** Resist the urge to fill a gap in a conversation; notice any feelings of discomfort and observe how and when they pass.

When you do experience pangs of shyness or anxiety in the company of others, or find yourself avoiding a social situation, ask yourself why. As uncomfortable as it might be to experience social awkwardness, moments when you stall, blush or stammer can indicate to you the types of face-to-face exchanges that you need to practise more.

Johnson also believed that conversations progress best with a certain level of natural flow and that it is best not to force or overly structure them. Unfortunately, a common tendency when feeling uncomfortable in a social situation is to jump in to fill a gap in a conversation, rather than sitting back a little and letting the silence develop. When you next find yourself doing this, try to hold yourself back: don't ignore or suppress any feelings of discomfort; instead turn your attention inwards and live within them until they pass. Relaxing silently in another person's company can be as powerful a means to connect as any words you might say.

Improve your digital conversations

Video calls

Video calls are the closest digital equivalent today to meeting in person, but by keeping in mind the variety of ways in which they contrast with your real-life encounters, you can make a few small changes to handle them more naturally. Be sure to disable the square video of yourself that appears on the screen: most video platforms include this as standard to flag that you are being filmed, but it creates the unnatural, distracting and sometimes stressful experience of a 'gesture mirror', displaying your own gestures and facial expressions back to you.

Reducing the size of your browser window can help you to more closely emulate the distance you would naturally maintain in a normal conversation; connecting an external keyboard to your laptop can help further by increasing the personal space between you and the faces on your screen.

Creating some extra physical room between you and your computer gives you the space you need to gesture with your hands. There's no need to always remain sitting down. Perhaps you can even pace about your desk while talking. If you feel self-conscious while you try this initially on a video call, turn off your video for a while.

Give yourself breaks at other times too by turning your video off to avoid staring at the screen for too long. When you do, turn away from the call entirely, particularly during group calls or long meetings. You can still follow the thread of the conversation as you scan your eyes around the room, but as you ground yourself again in your physical setting you will get a much-needed break from the intense, simulated eye contact that can feel so draining.

TAKE ACTION

- **Use the 'hide self-view' button on a video call:** Not seeing yourself can help reduce stress and mental taxation.
- **Connect an external keyboard to your laptop:** Create a more natural sense of space between you and the faces on the screen during a video call, and give yourself extra room to gesture and move around.

Step away from your keyboard

Joseph Addison is another influential writer from the coffeehouse era, perhaps best known for his work as an editor of *The Spectator*, a periodical which focused on social etiquette and conversation skills. In his essay 'On Anger', published in *The Spectator* in 1711, Addison gives advice on how best to control anger when in conversation. In particular, he argues that one should avoid speaking or acting impulsively when angry, as this can often lead to regrettable words or actions. This mindset is perhaps even more relevant online. The inability of written messages to fully convey your emotions, together with a lack of facial expressions and body language, makes digital channels highly unsuited for fraught, heated exchanges. Whenever you find anger or negative emotions rising as you type a message, post or email, stop and take a break. Return to your device only once your thoughts have settled; unleashed anger never translates well online, and it often lives on in digital formats well past any fleeting moment of outrage.

TAKE ACTION

- **Don't type in anger:** Take a break and return to your device only once you are ready to respond with a cool head.

Fully commit to an online conversation

One of the most common themes among writers from the coffeehouse era is the importance of dedicating oneself to a conversation. Swift, Johnson and Addison all comment regularly on the need to pay full attention when speaking and listening to others. Online, we rarely do this. Digital tools simplify conversations, as a result demanding far less of you. It's common therefore to read and send text messages and attend to online chats while doing other things. You connect with others, but only at snatched intervals, and most often not with your full attention.

Consider the contrast between your digital interactions and your face-to-face conversations. It's typically considered impolite not to give someone your full attention when talking to them in person: try to apply the same level of engagement and focus to your online conversations. Put aside other activities or thoughts when you write an email or respond to a message; and for more important exchanges, if you can't meet in person, try to emulate some of the conditions in a real-life encounter. Setting aside some dedicated time at the end of the day for an unhurried email, message exchange or, better yet, a phone call, gives you far more of a chance to properly share your news and thoughts and to fully consider what your family and friends have to say.

TAKE ACTION

- **Create quiet time for social messages:** Give yourself the opportunity to properly consider and respond. Might a real-life conversation or phone call be more appropriate?

Chapter 4

Solitude

SHIPWRECKED ON MÁS A TIERRA

In 1713, the cofounder of *The Spectator* Richard Steele sat down in a London coffeehouse with the Scottish privateer and Royal Naval officer Alexander Selkirk to hear his story. Selkirk exuded a rough, hardened charm, but what struck Steele most was his serenity of countenance. Selkirk explained how he had been marooned on the Juan Fernández Islands, 580 kilometres off the west coast of Chile, after inciting mutiny against the captain of his ship. Selkirk had stayed on the island for four solitary years with scant possessions and quickly had to adapt to survive, yielding to the rhythms of island life. When he had the good fortune of being rescued, accounts from his rescuers and fellow crewmen began to reach an audience back home. His future acclaim was sealed, however, once Steele penned an article after their meeting. This found its way into the hands of Daniel Defoe, who adapted the tale into one of the first novels written in the English language. *Robinson Crusoe* was an instant success and resounded with readers of the time. Selkirk's story sparked fascination then, and continues to do so, in part because of the abruptness of his marooning and the great length of his enforced solitude.

Selkirk had been an unruly youth and joined a succession of buccaneering voyages to the South Pacific during the War of Spanish Succession. He set sail on the *Cinque Ports* in 1703, on an expedition to search out and plunder Spanish merchant ships sailing with valuable cargo from Acapulco to Manila, across the Pacific Ocean. The venture was privately funded, but with England at war with Spain, it was also made in service to Queen Anne. In command of the expedition was William Dampier, a renowned explorer and the first person to circumnavigate the world three times. He appointed Thomas Stradling as captain.

The *Cinque Ports*'s journey across the Atlantic and around Cape Horn did not go well. The quarters were cramped, many sailors succumbed to scurvy and Selkirk, who had been placed in charge of the ship's navigation, became increasingly aggravated by Captain Stradling's decisions.

When the *Cinque Ports* docked at Más a Tierra in the Juan Fernández Islands in September 1704, its crew had been decimated in number. The survivors were hungry and sick and dressed in tattered clothes. Selkirk turned on Stradling and began to fuel dissent. Frustrations escalated, and Selkirk lashed out at the captain with his fists. He was formally accused of inciting mutiny, and Stradling ordered his sea chest, clothes and bedding to be put ashore with him.

Selkirk watched from the rocky, horseshoe bay of Más a Tierra as the ship that had been his home for six months set sail. The island, uninhabited at the time, is just 19 kilometres long and 6 kilometres wide. Its eastern cliffs rise precipitously from the sea, and two mountains tower at the centre of the island. A Pacific breeze meets the ridged peaks, then cools, condenses and falls torrentially down as rain; hanging gullies and stony streams carry the surface runoff to the seashore. In the valleys, winds gust through sweet-smelling sandalwood trees, tall ferns and brushwood; and while clouds shroud the highest reaches of the island, sunshine bathes the lower hills and beaches. The symbol of a desert island runs deep in our culture, both as an alluring image of paradise and as a challenging environment for survival: Más a Tierra was both of these things.

Selkirk was left with a pistol, gunpowder and bullets, a hatchet knife and a pot to boil his food. He had a Bible and prayer-book in his possession too, as well as his now useless navigation instruments and sea charts. What scraps of food or drops of liquor he rationed himself were soon gone. A steady, sickening realization that he might never escape the island nor see a human face again would have gradually crept over him. But the spiky pangs of thirst and hunger focused his attention away from dread and despair as he quickly adapted to his newfound situation. He began to wash and drink from the streams, found turnips, watercress and berries, and slowly learned to spear turtles and lobsters with his sharp knife. He kept busy: he collected boulders and stones for a fire pit and built a larder to hold his provisions; he hollowed bowls and casks from wood. To shield himself from the squalls and the wildlife while he slept, Selkirk assembled a hut from pimento wood and thatched a roof with sheared lattices of sandalwood. Once he had fired his last bullet, he began to chase goats on foot and soon gained the stamina to catch them.

But amid all of this activity, Selkirk cannot fail to have been regularly awestruck by the immense and imposing silence of the island at times. He was so far from the mainland that building a raft was not a feasible solution. His greatest chance of rescue was by means of a passing ship – but this too was risky, as any Spanish ship would not take kindly to his presence. Selkirk chose a spot on the highest cliffs of the island to keep watch – to this day, it is still called 'Selkirk's Lookout' – and he spent large portions of his time scanning the horizon for any maritime activity. From the lookout, he could see life on the island unfold, from the morning sun splintering its warm glow across the contours of the mountains, to the stars in the evening as they circled over the sea. He made peace with the rhythms of the slow-wheeling globe, and calmly watched the seasons flow. Selkirk's solitude was pristine, and it would have been difficult to surpass it anywhere else in the world. How did it affect him? Did it alter his worldview?

At the heart of nearly any philosophy or religion – whether in Ancient Greece, in the hermetic and monastic traditions around the globe, or in New Age practices – is the notion that solitude is a necessary precondition for introspection and self-understanding. In peace and silence, away from the vicissitudes of daily existence, humankind has consistently sought out answers to the most trying of questions and reflected on the interconnectedness of our world through internal dialogue. Isolated from our daily distractions, we begin to notice new things, find alternative ways of thinking and wonder how we really want to live. Thinkers as varied as Aristotle, Plato, Boethius, Montaigne, Thoreau or Woolf have consistently found that time alone is crucial for taking stock and preparing for our busy social lives.

The religions and belief systems of the world – across all Western and Eastern traditions – repeatedly propose the elusive idea that an elementary ground exists, a universal connection that binds everything together. Spiritual practices have continually sought to help us grasp the fundamental links between our internal lives and the confounding complexities of the external world. Yet merely following doctrine or subscribing to a religious institution does not typically offer the same clarity of insight as first-hand, direct experience – we need to discover the realities of our lived existence for ourselves to get closest to the 'essence' of being alive.

Ancient scriptures and biographies of saints all attest to the need to transcend the ego and follow a simple life in order to get closer to an understanding of the true meaning and larger realities of our existence. Selkirk inadvertently experienced the level of seclusion that a monk or hermit might strenuously strive to achieve. Mental preoccupations as well as habits of analytical thinking and societal distractions have consistently been found to be major obstacles to arriving at an enlightened understanding of the interconnected, material reality of our world, and without these obstacles, as the months progressed on the island, Selkirk's eyes opened ever more. With no one to speak to, his language capabilities began to degrade, and the ingrained habits he had developed from birth to decipher the world through preconceived words progressively fell away.

He would have begun to feel wonder again – one of the purest forms of joy. It might first have happened at night, when his other senses worked harder to make up for his lack of sight, and he started to experience a heightened sense of overall awareness. From his lookout, he could have noticed the horizon curving ever so slightly upwards and, as he turned his head to the sky, begun to see the stars differently, as pinpricks pointing to a distant heritage, far beyond the geological time on the island. He might have been petrified at the scale of it all, his thinking fluttering and stalling.

Selkirk began to encounter experiences of such complexity and grandeur that at times his reasoning capacities would have entirely collapsed. His eyes would have been increasingly opened during the day too: morning sunshine that illuminated the underside of trees could give him an almost tangible feel for the specific quality of light; and as he noticed the minute movements of the island's wildlife, and the flourish and fall of its flora, he could perceive the perpetual perishment of life and also its inevitable renewal. His thoughts were pushed to a limit and eventually at times his ability to reason and understand would no longer have been able to keep up with the profundity of some of his experiences; Selkirk made peace with the vibrancy of change on Más a Tierra and found room in his new life to wordlessly appreciate the sublime.

He also became more comfortable with looking inwards. With few distractions, Selkirk began to directly experience his own mind more, and he would have increasingly recognized that his inner state affected his own reality. As he paid more attention to the natural world, he would have also started to notice his own responses to it – he saw himself seeing, and slowly gained increasing levels of possession over his thoughts. In his mind he would have replayed the scenes of mutiny he had started, until he was reconciled with the reality that he himself had invited his own abandonment and severance from society. His judgements of the island shifted entirely, and he grew to love the verdant flora and fluidity of daily life. Increasingly, he would have appreciated an unseen order in things, and felt a unity and solidarity with the world around him. Most of all, he learned to confront his bare self and face his fears. The decisions he had toiled with at home suddenly felt clearer, and, steadily, he arrived at a more authentic sense of who he was.

Selkirk was out fishing one day when he caught his breath in surprise: a set of cream sails jauntily poked over the waves in the distance. He swam as quickly as he could back to the shore and started preparations. In the years since Selkirk had been cast away, Dampier had managed to persuade a syndicate of Bristol councillors to finance a new expedition. Troubles had once again hit at sea, and the captain, Woodes Rogers, happened to set his sights on the haven of Más a Tierra as a place to drop anchor and recuperate. Selkirk lit a bonfire to draw the ship's attention, confident that this was a singular opportunity to reconnect with civilization once more. Unfortunately, the men on board mistook the flames as signs of an enemy and prepared their weapons to attack; they circled back away from the bay, before making another, stealthier approach onto dry land. Selkirk evacuated to his lookout, and once he believed the crew to be English, he finally made his approach.

Captain Rogers published a book about his adventures, *A Cruising Voyage Round the World*, on his return home, and considerable space is given to the moment the crew first met Selkirk. Rogers recollects a 'man cloth'd in goat-skins, who look'd wilder than the first owners of them', his speech 'for want of use' failing him, as 'he seemed to speak his words by halves'. Rogers and his men were quickly impressed with Selkirk's strength and self-reliance, and particularly admired his temperance of mind. On recommendation, Selkirk was appointed second mate, in charge of twenty-one men, and he thrived with his new responsibility: he took no part in any intrigues or feuds and completed all of the tasks that were assigned to him. Later in the voyage – and after having made his fortune securing prize ships and plunder – Selkirk was promoted to shipmaster, responsible for all of the crew and precious cargo; he arrived home a rich man.

Rogers' descriptions of Selkirk were the first accounts of the castaway to stir interest at home, and these are what prompted Richard Steele to arrange that coffeehouse meeting. Steele reported afterwards that Selkirk had a 'strong but cheerful seriousness in his look' and 'a certain disregard to the ordinary things about him, as if he had been sunk in thought'. Selkirk spoke of moments of real adversity: on one occasion, running up to a summit, he had fallen violently down a precipice after overstretching to seize a goat, and had proceeded to lie helpless for three days. But overall he looked back very fondly at his time on Más a Tierra. He recalled a constant cheeriness and tranquillity, and explained that he had grown thoroughly reconciled to his new condition.

Steele bumped into Selkirk on the street a few months later, and even though they exchanged words, he failed to recognize the former castaway – life in the city had started to have its effect and, according to Steele, had 'quite altered the air on his face'. As the years passed after his arrival home,

Selkirk's bad habits resurfaced. His violent tendencies worsened, and he was eventually charged with common assault. He did not show up for the hearing, however, and soon scouted for more opportunities at sea. He was serving as an officer on board HMS *Weymouth* when he succumbed to the yellow fever that plagued the voyage and died on 13 December 1721; he was buried at sea.

Selkirk had succeeded in finding an enviable serenity through solitude; but, unable to bring his island life home, he failed to sustain this once back in society. His tale is a familiar one: we humans have continually struggled to preserve in our lives with others the peace and perspective we encounter when alone. One of the clearest articulations of this can be found in the *Bhagavad Gītā*, the ancient Hindu scripture which dates from around the second century BCE. In considering whether one should lead a busy life dedicated to one's duty and profession or renounce a householder existence for a life as an ascetic, the text sets out how we might do both: by becoming less attached to the outcomes of our actions and finding space to contemplate the true nature of self and the universe, we can find enlightenment and liberation while also leading a life of responsibility and action. Yet this path has proved challenging for many over the centuries. Societal pressures often push us towards actions driven by personal gain, and our natural human tendencies towards attachment can cloud our judgement.

We grapple with very similar challenges today, but in the fray of our digital lives we have to fight that much harder for uninterrupted, silent time alone. When we do connect online, among the multitudes of digital distraction, we struggle to retain independent thought and the capacity for self-reflection. How can we learn from the solitude that Selkirk achieved on his island? And equally, what lessons can we take from his failings once he arrived back home?

ROBINSON CRUSOE ISLAND

In a bid to attract tourists, Más a Tierra has since been renamed Robinson Crusoe Island, and it has a resident population today of 997. Despite mobile phone reception and Wi-Fi on the island, life remains very remote: visitors arrive via a small six-seater prop plane and a thirty-minute boat ride, and deliveries come just twice a month on a support boat from the Chilean mainland. The physical realities of the island's geography remain the same, but its inhabitants experience nothing like the level of seclusion that Selkirk encountered over 300 years ago – they share instant messages, stream the latest season finales and are plugged into popular culture in much the same way as if they lived on mainland Chile.

The futurologist Arthur C. Clarke once commented that 'any sufficiently advanced technology is indistinguishable from magic'. While Selkirk's only means of connecting to his peers during his stay on the island would have been via telepathy or a very lucky message in a bottle, today we treat as normal the pervasiveness of computer networks and their 'magic' reach across the globe. Our social inclination as humans has seen us adopt communication technology with little active consideration or deliberation on when it may be natural for us to connect or disconnect from society, and in so doing, we have allowed encroachment of the outside world into the most personal parts of our lives. While Selkirk's total solitude was particularly unusual even in the eighteenth century, people of his era typically experienced far more uninterrupted time alone than we do today. Historically, humankind spent lengthier durations of time in one another's physical presence than we do today, but when individuals were alone in the past, they remained almost entirely disconnected from others. For the majority of our existence, people privileged with free time divided it between energetic moments of meeting in person and spells of more contemplative reflection, away from the company of others.

Much of the early flowering of human civilization took place during individuals' free time. In Ancient Greece, for instance, the contemplative life – *bios theoretikos* – was viewed as the only true way to give deep purpose to human existence. *Scholé*, the Greek word for 'leisure', is where our word 'school' and its derivations originate. The sustained thought we need to properly think through a problem most easily comes to us when we are alone, or when we meet together in small, self-selecting groups. True contemplation alternates between alert passivity and focused time concentrating, and for this we need a certain degree of quietude and calm. Solitude allows a mind to experience itself in the act of thinking, to consider its own thoughts and reflections, examine them from multiple perspectives and, in so doing, progress knowledge and understanding. Scientific studies have shown that we become more self-aware in the moments we are on our own and that spending time alone can improve creativity, increase focus and enhance problem-solving capabilities. Silence and calm have been found to promote the growth of new cells in the hippocampus, the part our brain responsible for memory and learning.

But naturally, solitude is also very closely linked to loneliness. When we are in our own company, loneliness – the feeling of sadness or distress that arises when we feel disconnected from others and lack meaningful social contact or relationships – can feel like failure, because much of our personal time is spent, often unconsciously, organizing our lives to avoid feelings of separateness. The same urge also causes us to remain highly attuned to the reactions of others and to strive to fit in or be popular. Yet as subjective beings, we will always feel to some extent cut off from other people. Loneliness is an essential precursor to any form of cultivated solitude, and there is usually uneasiness or disquiet that we have to pass through before we become comfortable again in our own presence.

Selkirk had years of practice doing this, and grew used to solitude. It is unsurprising that he experienced social discomfort when he arrived back in the city after so long away from human contact. He found escape in alcohol, and as he fell back into his old inebriated ways, he became embroiled in increasingly aggressive altercations. Whereas on the island he had little choice but to live within his loneliness and persevere until he came through on the other side, back in civilization he had temptations close by that allowed him temporary relief from difficult emotions but only served to worsen his situation.

Loneliness has become a significant problem in modern times as a direct result of the decline in face-to-face conversation – a trend intensified by the global COVID-19 pandemic. We as a species are primed to respond to real, human engagement, and although we remain connected in other ways – via instant messages, email or texts, or by keeping astride of the latest news – this cannot match the boost to our psychological well-being that real-time physical conversation can give us. To counteract the pain or discomfort of loneliness, it's common to reach instead for pleasurable sensations – whether that be digital distractions, food, drink or TV – and in so doing we tend to fall into habits that do not cure our basic existential malaise: instead, they often perpetuate or exacerbate the problem. Our digital devices, always on hand to take our minds off our discomfort, are the very cause of our predicament in the first place. Our first point of refuge is often to check our messages, but it is equally common to seek out pleasantly passive time online, viewing, clicking and scrolling according to screen prompts, and with little active input or conscious direction on our part. What we tell ourselves are 'breaks' eventually become a goal in their own right, and we lose out on the more productive or creative time that we might have enjoyed had we allowed our restlessness to lead us elsewhere.

It is difficult, by nature, for humans to simply sit and do nothing: our minds' tendency to search for any change in our environment stands in our way. Most commonly today, the temptation to scan the online environment wins over uncomfortable feelings of boredom. Yet the tension that we encounter in the pauses of each day – when we fight to stay with our thoughts, remain focused and be fully present in whatever we are doing – can inform us on how to win back our solitude. Religions and spiritual practices through the ages have adopted and developed methods or ceremonial rites that allow us to calm our thoughts and focus our attention. What they all have in common is a technique – whatever form it might take – that serves to catch the wandering impulses of our attention and to redirect that attention internally. Meditation practices commonly focus on the breath or an internal mantra to steady our mind; yoga and the traditional Chinese practice *qigong* turn our attention to our physical body movement to cultivate a calm energy; and most forms of prayer or devotion rely on repeating memorized sequences of text to silence our thoughts. In recent years, mindfulness has emerged as a practice that draws on the same methods of stilling the mind, repackaged somewhat to make them more relevant to our contemporary world. Each of these different beneficial techniques involves carving out time away from our busy lives, and this is, at least initially, perhaps their most challenging aspect.

The main question set out in the *Bhagavad Gītā* over two millennia ago is a pressing concern to us today: namely, how can we integrate within our daily lives the grounded perspective found in practised moments of solitary calm? If we are to stand a chance against the sophisticated ways in which digital technology captures and manages our attention, we need techniques and practices that we can rely on, not only when we are away from our devices, but also when we are carrying or using them. It is remarkable how little this modern-day need is recognized. The standard restorative solutions that are offered today, whether in mindfulness literature or packaged in mobile apps, consist typically of twenty-minute daily meditation practices, weekly yoga sessions or weekend detox retreats. As useful as these are to preserve spells of full disconnection from online demands, they cannot offer our solitude the full protection it deserves, both on- and offline, and there is practically no mainstream guidance in existence today that tutors people on how to protect their own thoughts and composure while actually using and engaging with the pervasive digital technologies that steal and trade our attention on a daily basis.

One thinker whose work seems highly applicable to these issues is the little-known Armenian philosopher, George Gurdjieff. As a young adult, he travelled across Iran, Central Asia, India and Tibet, before arriving in Moscow in 1912 with a new, original philosophy of self-development. Gurdjieff described his system of thought as the 'Fourth Way', after recognizing the near impossibility of applying the ascetic spiritual practices of monks, yogis or hermits to ordinary, daily life. After meetings with sages, dervishes and a number of other spiritual guides, he consolidated his teachings into one coherent discipline. Gurdjieff claimed that people – despite what they may think – ordinarily exist with little control of their thinking processes and proceed through life semi-automatically. It is only through the intentional act of separating oneself from external influences and distractions, Gurdjieff thought, that we can focus more on our own thoughts and emotions. Later academic research in attention studies and continual findings in user-experience testing have confirmed this to be the case: so many of the decisions we take in life are directed by external prompts or our own embedded expectations, and when we interact with digital technology, our decisions are commonly dictated entirely by the cues we see on-screen. Indeed, the software we use in everyday life is carefully designed to ensure our attention is controlled for us. Our brains function enormously well in this default autopilot mode, and we become quite used to external motivations determining our next move. The advertising industry is of course especially cognizant of this: slogans and simple compelling statements on billboard adverts, for instance, have far more chance of influencing our opinions than we might realize. The innovative leap Gurdjieff made was to utilize the traditional methods of monks, yogis and hermits to take back control of our own thoughts in everyday life. His instructions survive today as one of the few viable methods we have to protect our self-awareness, autonomy and solitude without renouncing our digital lives.

The vague anxieties that spur us to check our phones most often lie outside of our personal awareness. We feel brief triggers of discomfort or negative emotion and, rather than face them to understand their root cause, we turn away to the next digital task we've created for ourselves. Technology makes it all too easy for us to avoid being present in our lives. Yet, when we unplug from any digital experience, and sit still, quietly, without any goal or anything to look at – when we truly stop – there is a sudden onus on us to manage our own thoughts. They certainly do not immediately quieten – in fact they may grow noisy, and temptations may surface. By taking the time to simply watch how our thoughts unfold naturally, it becomes clear how fully a thought can take command of our whole perceptual experience. The prime tenet of any form of meditation is to focus our attention on something else, so that we can slow or ideally stop our thoughts completely. When we succeed, we begin to experience a deep, reviving sense of tranquillity: a restorative state that can stay with us for a good while afterwards. As we become more practised at meditation, we start to spot more easily when our thoughts are beginning to take over and are increasingly able to take our attention back, so we can keep better control of it.

Gurdjieff's methods offer a way to prevent digital technology stealing our focus: we can get better at spotting the times when we unthinkingly jump online and can more keenly observe when our clicks follow paths not of our making. As we become more aware of the specific ways in which our devices impact our thoughts and actions, we gain more power to instigate the changes needed to protect our private moments and personal motivations.

He offered practical advice on how to ground ourselves more readily in everyday life, and advocated an exercise to break automatic patterns and bring awareness of the present moment: by mentally saying 'stop' and freezing in place every so often, we can take note of our thoughts and emotions and allow ourselves to become more present. He also emphasized the importance of reconnecting with the physical body as a means of anchoring oneself in any experience. He argued that, in seminal moments such as the birth or death of a loved one, or in the fleeting fullness of life experienced in times of joy, we become acutely present to all of our senses at once. He noticed that it was at these times of deep awakening that our concept of separateness shifted, and that we naturally gained a more comprehensive grasp of how connected we are with the world around us. By more consciously observing when we experience what Gurdjieff referred to as 'self-remembering' and by exploring the inner experience of these moments as fully as we can, he argued, we can recreate this awakened state, wherever we might be. Today, Gurdjieff's work can offer techniques to enable us to relish rather than fear solitude, and to maintain context and perspective, both online and in our offline lives. There are steps we can take to protect our solitude today, and with just a few changes we can nurture some of the changes of thought and being that Selkirk enjoyed as a castaway in the South Pacific.

CULTIVATE YOUR OWN SOLITUDE

You have a natural ability to thrive alone, but it takes practice to be comfortable in your own company. With time, you can gain confidence in your capacity for solitude, and become better able to rely on your inner resources. The first step is to create the space you need to fully disconnect at times, and there are some simple, effective changes you can make to control the levels of input from your digital devices. You can also improve the quality of your solitary moments with meditation and breathwork techniques: traditional methods that present an intensive way to recuperate from the strains of digital life when you need to.

Yet, as important as they are, retreat and rejuvenation are not sufficient to fully protect your solitude and individuality. Without care, the digital networks you rely on to connect to others can expose you to groupthink and predispose you to unmediated points of view. Even when your devices are switched off, digital connections can disrupt your most intimate thoughts, because the tethers that connect you to the digital world are largely psychological. Yet they are also motivated by instincts that you *can* begin to control. By tweaking your levels of awareness when you are at a screen, you can begin to notice how technology is affecting your decisions, thoughts and moods. As you learn to pinpoint exactly how your time online tinges your personal outlook, it becomes easier to spot how it also affects you even when you are offline. The impulses to reach for your phone in times of loneliness or boredom become more obvious, and it's simpler to bring them under your control – or even make them disappear entirely.

Take control of digital distractions

Reduce interruptions offline

Notifications from your phone are likely to be the main source of interruption when you are on your own, and these can easily be switched off with a few changes to your notifications settings. Ringtones and vibration alerts to grab your attention whenever you receive a message or call are usually set as standard on devices. Relying on factory settings leaves the onus on you to remember to quieten your phone whenever you want to focus – a simple step that we all know is very easy to forget. To protect your solitude, it's far more conducive to have notifications turned off as standard, and to instead switch them on only when you need them. How often do you really need to read a notification as soon as it is received? Other than in an emergency – and for this you can set favourite contacts to reach you regardless of your notification settings – there might well be the odd pressing message you are awaiting, or work commitments to attend to. But the vast majority of messages that steal your attention throughout the day could just as effectively be dealt with a little later when you actively decide to check your messages.

Reaching for your phone can become so habitual that the best solution is often to remove it entirely from your person. Create a new habit where you place it by the front door when you arrive home, or lay it on a charge pad at your desk. Retrieve it when you want to check your messages, but be sure to put it right back once you are done. In the evening, leave it there overnight until after breakfast.

TAKE ACTION

- **Set notifications on your mobile device to 'off' as standard:** Carefully consider how often you really need to read messages as soon as they are received, and only switch notifications back on as needed.
- **Leave your phone in a fixed location:** Create a new habit of only picking it up when you want to check your messages. In addition, keep your phone out of reach during the evening and until after breakfast.

Protect your focus online

Protecting your solitude is just as important when you are online. When you work, read or play on a device, your flow of thoughts is too valuable to fritter away on unwarranted distractions. An uncluttered computer desktop can create the right environment to contemplate and consider your thoughts as carefully as when you are totally offline. Clear out all files on your desktop and tidy them away into folders; equally, try to minimize the number of software icons you can see on the home screen of other devices. Use full-screen mode whenever you can in apps or when you are browsing the internet, to reduce the proliferation of buttons and options, and block your browser from displaying pop-up notifications aside from calendar invitations.

Are there sites you return to in moments of boredom, and then regret wasting your time on? Consider using a website blocker, which can prevent you from accessing specific sites or social-media services on your devices: Cold Turkey Blocker is currently the most powerful and comprehensive of these.

TAKE ACTION

- **Declutter your desktop:** Minimize the app icons on display and choose full-screen mode when you can.
- **Set up a website blocker on your computer:** Consider permanently blocking distracting websites or social-media platforms.

Don't jump back online

Although you may feel perfectly content or happy socially a lot of the time, be aware of moments when you do feel pangs of loneliness. Whenever you are at a screen – whether at work, checking your phone during the day, or relaxing in front of the TV at night – try to keep in mind that, in our not-too-distant past, each of these moments would most likely have been spent in the company of others. Humankind has always lived in close-knit, tribal communities – up to and including your ancestors only a few generations ago – and it is these long-standing customs and behaviours that prime the ways you have naturally evolved to seek out social contact, or to feel discomfort when you are alone. However much it might feel hidden or disconnected from your daily life, recognize that you likely experience levels of alienation and remoteness that your forebears would never have had to contend with, and this burden can cloud your judgements and actions day-to-day.

Remember that loneliness can manifest itself in a number of different ways: most typically as feelings of boredom or restlessness. When you catch yourself feeling bored, or itching to check your phone, deliberately push back and test your comfort zone. Rather than instantly evading your boredom, stay within it and begin to understand it more: investigate what the root causes might be and be alert to impulses to jump back online. With time, it can become easier to spot the associations that might drive a lot of your digital time, such as thoughts or memories that have you scanning for new messages, or feelings of disquiet that might prompt you to find solace in watching TV. By better understanding these motivations, you will be more equipped to decide when it is best for you to remain offline and find longer-term means of calming your mind instead.

TAKE ACTION

- **Sit with feelings of boredom, rather than evading them:** Watch for impulses to check your phone in quiet moments and practise resisting them.
- **Explore any feelings of discontent:** Try to investigate the root causes of your discomfort rather than turning to your phone or TV for distraction.

Improve the quality of your time alone

Meditation is one of the most effective ways to train your capacity to be alone, so long as it is approached in the right way. When you meditate, you still your thoughts and progressively dismantle any unhelpful thinking patterns. Impulses or temptations are muted, and as your thinking settles and stops, a deep peacefulness arrives and stays with you.

Yet for the uninitiated, meditation can be very difficult: sitting alone with your thoughts can feel exceptionally hard at first and takes some getting used to. To give yourself the best chance of achieving positive results straight away, start with breathing exercises. Breathwork is a more intense form of meditation that uses active breathing techniques to train your focus: the physicality of your deep breathing, and the corresponding effort and exertion you put in, make it far harder for your mind to wander. By splitting your meditation practice into two parts, starting with ten minutes of intensive breathwork to prepare your mind and ground you, and then progressing to ten minutes of restorative meditation, you give yourself the best chance of calming your thoughts and increasing self-awareness.

It's easiest to try this at home first. Find a quiet place where you won't be disturbed and sit cross-legged or lie down. Set a timer for ten minutes, so that you don't watch the clock. The 'three-part breath', also known as Dirga Pranyama, is a fantastic technique to begin with as it is simple but offers results straight away. Close your eyes. Breathe deep into the bottom of your belly using your mouth or nose, or both. After filling your abdomen, continue to inhale and fill your chest, expanding your rib cage and the middle portion of your lungs. Finally, breathe up to where your collarbones meet your shoulders, filling the upper part of your lungs. Then breathe out. Keep on repeating this until your timer runs out – there is no right or wrong way: you can breathe athletically, or more slowly and measuredly if that feels better for you. When your phone buzzes, set it for another ten minutes and close your eyes again for your meditation practice. This time, take your focus away from your breath and start repeating a random word or sound in your head – it's best that it has no meaning, to stop any connotations it might hold being a distraction. It can help to imagine a space in your head, with the sound of your word echoing in it. Keep your mind fixed on this repeating mantra, and whenever it wanders, though you most likely will not notice this straight away, simply bring it back to your reverberating word. When your timer goes off again, spend a few moments noticing any differences in how you feel and enjoy the relaxation and calm that you have achieved.

TAKE ACTION

- **Try the 'three-part breath' technique:** Focus on filling your abdomen, chest and then upper part of your lungs on the in-breaths.
- **Investigate other breathing exercises:** The Wim Hof method, for instance, involves simply breathing deeply through the nose or mouth forty times. On the last exhale, expel your breath fully and hold for as long as you can before taking a breath into the top of your lungs and holding again for one minute. Repeat the cycle as many times as you like.
- **Follow breathwork with a simple meditation:** Sit in a quiet place, set a timer for ten minutes, then close your eyes and concentrate on your breath.
- **Follow a daily breathwork and meditation practice:** Choose a fixed slot in your day – ideally in the morning – to commit ten minutes to breathwork and then ten minutes to meditation.

Meditation and breathwork are skills that you can take with you through life. Meditating is a fantastic way to begin the day, or to unwind before bed, and the benefits naturally spill over to the rest of the time you find yourself alone. The intensity of some experiences online inevitably frazzles your nerves at times – whether that be the mental exhaustion of intensely sifting through screens of information or making sense of the vagaries of social contact that you encounter – and meditation is a ready method to counteract this, a time to refresh and reset. You can meditate at home, on the bus, in the park, or perhaps in a quiet church. As you progress in your practice, you can find serenity within reach when you most need it.

Become more present on digital devices

Meditation and breathwork are enormously potent tools, bringing balance between the bright, harsh exposure of your tasks in daily life and the protected calm of your solitude. You retain a level of composure from the peacefulness you can find in meditative states, and this can protect you in your busy moments, back in the travails of active life, but only to a certain extent. Usually, life takes over and leads your attention in untold numbers of new directions.

To help you become more aware of how your attention controls your thoughts and inner experience, and to give you a means to become more present in your daily life, Gurdjieff devised exercises for dividing your attention. He pointed out that as you undertake any intellectual task, it is also possible to follow the sounds or sensations around you, and to experience deep, intense feelings, however unrelated they might be. You are quite able to naturally split your awareness and attend to a number of different events all at the same time.

This capability can also help you become more present online. When you next sit at your computer, allow yourself to proceed with your digital tasks, keeping active what Gurdjieff termed your intellectual centre, but at the same time, deliberately create a second focus of attention. Pull your 'instinctive centre' away from whatever you are doing and let it follow ambient sounds around you – the ticking of a clock, for example, or the sound of workmen down the road. Once you feel you have arrived at two attentions, try then to get your third attention going: this is Gurdjieff's 'emotional centre'. Allow it to rest deeply in a particular feeling – perhaps find a reason to feel joy or thankfulness, or simply search for whatever emotions you are experiencing at that moment and sink deeper into them.

Successfully splitting your attention three ways and living within each of the different experiences you encounter creates a vividness and corporeality to your experience. You might find that your breath shallows and quickens – and if so, allow this to happen. It is also possible to open a fourth attention by observing the three others you have created and allowing a sense of wonder to develop. Hold your attentions separate as long as you can, for a couple of minutes ideally; and when you are ready, bring them all back together as one and be fully present.

Dividing your attention when you use digital technology allows you to become more watchful of how it affects your inner world. As you separate your emotional centre from the tasks you are doing, you can begin to discern more closely how what you encounter online actually makes you feel. When you scroll social-media feeds, look out for any rises of jealousy, anger or anxiety and settle within them to try to understand why you might be experiencing them. Then pull your instinctive centre away from your focus on the screen – for instance, noticing the hardness of your seat, or the smoothness of the table on your forearms – to ground you in your actual physical location and prevent you from getting swept away in what you find online. Mindfulness techniques also work to bring your awareness to the present moment and, with practice, can be used while you are busy doing things, but they are less applicable to online activity. As Gurdjieff's approach specifically targets the division of attention between various centres of the brain, and encourages you to become more aware of the different aspects of your experience, it's well suited to the complex and multi-faceted nature of most online tasks and helps you become more aware of how your online activity affects your emotions, thoughts and physical sensations.

To deepen the benefits, try to cultivate a daily practice of dividing your attention when you are on a digital device: choosing a fixed moment in the day – perhaps when you first check your email in the morning – makes it easier at the start. Over time, try dividing your attention as you go about different tasks to get a more coherent view on the variety of your digital experiences and a keener awareness of how each of them affects you. With practice, you can learn to protect your own perspective and individuality and retain the benefits of solitude even within the busy online world.

TAKE ACTION

- **Divide your attention three ways at your computer:** As you work, pull the focus of your instinctive centre away from your digital tasks to follow a sound outside, then activate your emotional centre by noticing your current feelings; hold these attentions separate for as long as you can.
- **Pay active attention to how being online makes you feel:** Activate your emotional centre to attentively follow the flow of your emotions; stay with any negative moods and try to determine what might be causing them.
- **Ground yourself in your physical setting:** Pull your instinctive centre away from the screen to focus on tangible aspects such as the solidity of the floor under your feet for as long as you can.

Chapter 5

Reading

MARGINALIA, MANICULES AND COMMONPLACES

The great polymath John Dee was one of Tudor England's most active and informed readers. Thought by many to be the inspiration behind Prospero, the learned protagonist of Shakespeare's *The Tempest*, he pursued encyclopaedic branches of learning and was a respected advisor to Queen Elizabeth and her court. His important contributions to mathematics helped lay the groundwork for the scientific revolution that would take place in Europe in the centuries that followed; the highly detailed maps that he helped create advanced navigation and cartography; and his firm grasp of astrology led to his reform of the British calendar, synchronizing it more closely with the solar year. He also wrote books on language and linguistics, cryptography, philosophy and swathes of human history, from Ancient Greece and Rome to more contemporary events across Europe, as well as a comprehensive chronicle of the British monarchy. Extensive reading underpinned all of this knowledge and dedicated work: by the start of the 1580s he had amassed the largest library in the country, totalling around 3,000 printed books and 1,000 manuscripts. Dee was a reader of the highest calibre and a stellar example of the sophisticated reading practices developed during his lifetime.

The Renaissance was a time synonymous with learning and civil advancement. Forgotten knowledge from the past – Greek and Roman times in particular – was energetically reassimilated into culture and learning and put to practical, active use in an educational revolution fuelled by a great esteem for the values and literary accomplishments of the ancients. The key engine for change was '*studia humanitatis*', a new learning curriculum that swept across Europe, with reading a discipline very much at its core. Latin was taught in depth, allowing students to study the historians, rhetoricians and moral philosophers of classical antiquity with incisive methods that heralded the beginning of modern textual research. Grammar schools popped up throughout England, and Dee attended one of them. School-leavers joined the world armed with highly competent reading abilities that they then utilized in their everyday activities and careers and continued to develop over the course of their lives.

Students were trained to read using an assortment of techniques and tools, most of which are quite unknown to us today. They were taught to read actively and learned to focus their full attention on the text in front of them. Readers sat at a desk, fully involved in the process, pen in hand, and were coached to read with diligence and care, selecting only books that warranted the effort – this was the antithesis of reading to kill time. There was a self-consciousness to the reading experience, a wakeful vigilance applied to critically understanding the text, taking from it as much as possible.

Dee travelled widely throughout Europe, meeting other scholars and experts in varied fields and acquiring new books and manuscripts for his collection. By lending his own titles in exchange for others, he maintained a wide network of contacts across the continent. In 1583, when he was overseas, his home and library at Mortlake near London was burgled, and many of his books were stolen. After his death, many of his remaining books were dispersed and lost, but thankfully, not all of them. The British Library holds a significant collection of Dee's hand-annotated books, as do the Bodleian Library at the University of Oxford, the Royal College of Physicians and the Wellcome Collection; through this assortment of rare texts and manuscripts, and thanks to the countless annotations and markings Dee made across their pages, we can get an intimate insight into his life and work as well as the reading practices of the time.

Surviving books from Dee's library demonstrate some of the most refined examples of the information-processing techniques taught to students in Renaissance times. 'Mark my words' first appeared as a phrase during this period and encapsulates the particular importance given to the annotation of books as they were read. Dee adopted this method wholeheartedly, consistently writing in the margins of his books and manuscripts, and he stands out as an exceptional annotator, unequalled by the majority in his time, and certainly since. At their most basic, his annotations consisted of simple marks, lines, brackets or asterisks that drew attention to words or passages. However, he also included margin notes – later to become known as 'marginalia' – that were often carefully scripted; Dee responded to the text as he went, in a form of lucid, and sometimes heated, conversation with the author. These notes reveal vivid, intimate glimpses of him as a reader.

There are also freer scrawls, with heavy underlining or quickly penned topic headings. Here Dee is following the structure of an argument, emphasizing its key points and organizing it further. He also adds cross-references to text within the volume and to other books or manuscripts, and includes summaries at the start and end of sections. He used blank pages in a book to provide fuller compendiums, often including instructive tables or diagrams. And, in a similar vein to the French philosopher Montaigne, Dee wrote an assessment of the book as a whole on its front or back page, a time-saving ploy to save unnecessary future rereads.

He also developed an elaborate system of words or symbols to demarcate subjects and signal his approval or disagreement. A small triangle in the margins marks a section of particular importance; consecutive numbers order passages. Connecting lines are one of the most striking of his techniques, boldly searing across sections of text to join one passage on the page to another. Dee was not afraid to reshape his books, inserting blank leaves for extra annotations, rearranging or adding sections from other texts. He digested his reading into manageable chunks, preparing it for his own future use and intertextual connections.

Dee may have been one of the most skilled and voracious annotators of his era, but annotating text in books was a highly common phenomenon. The sheer volume of notes left by other readers from this time is astonishing. A copy of Aristotle's *Posterior Analytics* printed in Leipzig in the 1500s, for example, holds 59,600 words of marginalia on its sixty-eight pages. There were some conventions – a symbol of a flower in the margin was a standard depiction of quotability, for instance. Paraphrasing was common too, an excellent method for dissecting a point to understand it clearly. Idiosyncrasies developed; personal systems finessed over time. There's endless variety in surviving manuscripts from this period, with techniques deliberately honed to ensure the reader stayed focused and collected what they wanted from a book.

The most common symbol appearing in the margins of Renaissance texts was that of a small pointing hand, a 'manicule', drawn by readers to mark noteworthy passages. Some were just a sparing outline, others complete with sinews, joints or nails. Dee favoured gently arching fingers and perfectly circular sleeves. They were all pointing, an index finger neatly extending out to draw attention to the text, but there was variety: a finger might stretch across the full width of a page or curve impossibly down to indicate a sentence. A manicule was as distinctive as a signature, a personal inscription left on the page.

It's no accident that a hand was the favoured motif of early modern readers to mark books they read. A manicule intuitively mimics the way we use our hands to get a sense of things, and there was certainly a physicality to reading in the Renaissance. Reading, like writing and drawing, was considered as much a faculty of the hand as it was of the eye or mind, and many of the words associated with reading at the time, such as 'manuscript', 'manual' and 'manicule', are derived from the Latin word for hand, *'manus'*.

Another cornerstone of reading in the Renaissance was the commonplace book. Readers collected choice phrases from their reading and life experience and wrote them down in a notebook under '*locus communis*' headings that each denoted a general or common topic. A commonplace book was an indispensable part of how early modern people lived day to day and a continual pursuit that shaped their mental life. Written extensions of the reading enterprise itself, commonplaces spurred new associative patterns and meaning. Topic headings could be adapted to any field and to any level of detail or complexity. For some, commonplacing encompassed staggering volumes of notebooks, exhaustive indexes, cross-references, marginal notes and elaborate tables of contents. For others, loosely gathered scraps of notes sufficed.

Naturally, Dee kept commonplace books to chart his reading and other endeavours. His summaries, reflections and debates drew on books in his library spanning a complex range of subjects. Like other readers of his time, Dee read both intensively and extensively, with a repertoire of reading modes suited to different occasions and materials. He worked from multiple texts at a time, cross-referencing them, often by page and line number. This was a common practice in the Renaissance and led to the invention of the bookwheel, a rotating five-foot-high bookcase in the shape of a water wheel that allowed a person to read multiple books in one location with ease. Dee's library extended through several rooms of a house, furnished not only with books but also with reading equipment, mathematical instruments and laboratories. A commonplace acted as a catalogue to all of this, assimilating the components of Dee's extensive reference apparatus into a condensed guide. Maxims, themes and data were transposed from printed books, conversations and experiments, and the unique ordering of topics imposed a personalized structure on the contents of his library. His reading efforts were by no means mechanistic or routine; this was imaginative work, providing intellectual foundations for new directions, and his inventory made it easier to develop fresh ideas.

One notable responsibility of Dee as advisor to the Queen was to improve the science of navigation and help England acquire new territories overseas. He provided scholarly service to voyages and, in a series of treatises, maps and conferences, developed an expansionist programme that was one of the first clear articulations of ambition for a British empire.

One of the guiding principles of a humanist education was to prepare students to put their scholarship into practice, with reading very much a means to an end. Christopher Columbus also supported his travels with reading, and his New World discoveries were inspired by a wide range of texts, some of which still survive with his annotations intact. Dee exhaustively scrutinized Columbus's writings and ship logs, searching for ways that England could catch up with its Continental rivals. He canvassed European geographers' opinions on countries or passages and collected reports from English explorers, who provided him with maps, accounts of observations and physical artefacts. All of this information was stored in Dee's library, neatly arranged within his tried-and-tested commonplace retrieval system.

Commonplace books have travelled through the centuries under various names: notebooks, miscellanies, pocket books, table books or *vade mecums* (literally 'go with me's). Ralph Waldo Emerson, born almost 300 years after Dee, was another highly competent commonplace user. Emerson's writing has been profoundly influential, informing the lives of thinkers, writers and poets throughout the years, and he remains one of the most quoted American authors. He's most renowned for his lucidity of thought and the ability of his written words to distil the world for us afresh. Yet the role that his active reading and commonplacing played in shaping his thinking processes, working methods and views is often overlooked today. Emerson filled commonplace books at a rough rate of one a month for over forty years. He read widely but systematically and only in aid of specific projects, transferring phrases, facts, details, metaphors and anecdotes to his notebooks, the total of which eventually reached over 260 volumes.

Emerson viewed these notebooks as a storehouse of ideas for his own original writing, and he enthusiastically emphasized how much his own writing was drawn from reading the works of others. The notebooks constituted a well-organized filing system designed to catalogue the vast accumulation of knowledge from his extensive reading, covering every topic that interested him throughout his life. There were so many notes, he had to index their contents so he could access them readily. This took years of rewriting and alphabetizing. A biographical index he created to organize notes pertaining to individuals he found inspiring reached 839 entries alone. He eventually even made indexes of his indexes to keep his notes organized. Emerson had equipped himself with a relational database of interconnecting links and texts that together formed a comprehensive guide to a subject. It was curation of the highest order, perfectly honed to his individual interests and intentions.

Commonplace books have contributed to our culture in unseen ways, providing the foundations for the early production of standard works of reference nowadays taken for granted: encyclopaedias, anthologies, thesauruses, dictionaries and more. An internet search is our modern-day equivalent of Emerson's system of indexes. Google was founded as a result of two academics realizing the power of citation indexing. Without the links between websites allowing Google to gauge importance and deliver results, the internet would be an indecipherable mass of pages. All the same, while web searches can of course query an incomparably larger pool of data than a reader can cover in their lifetime, the sophisticated practices of active reading, meticulously annotating books and writing out passages in a commonplace can enable us to create our own unique logs of our reading and find self-made connections between the texts we have read.

The methods taught in early modern times to interrogate, assimilate and remember text forced the reader to slow down and stop, to go back and reread. They created an important space between an author and a reader, allowing the reader time to think and articulate independent thoughts in response. Dee and Emerson's reading practices are clear reminders of the ways in which active, careful reading can help us to make the text that we encounter our own. By slowing down and more diligently taking things in, using annotation, mark-up and notes as we read, we can better assimilate information. Active reading is a powerful tool to truly understand a text, then dissect, interrogate or reframe it.

Since Dee and Emerson's time, however, almost every aspect of reading has changed. Today, the intricate filing systems we used to create for ourselves are taken care of by algorithms, and where we once slowly and carefully worked our way through a text, these days scrolling and skimming are the norm as we struggle to keep up with the slew of words delivered to us online. Unfortunately, this has left considerable gaps in our personal knowledge and reading ability. If speed-reading is not complemented sufficiently with more active reading, we simply cannot properly digest the information that we encounter: we become less interrogative and more readily accept whatever we read. We then stand in our own way of forming more nuanced opinions and views.

Yet, as with any of our core human skills, each of us has the natural capability to read more actively. Learning from the practices of our bibliophile forebears like Dee and Emerson, we can reclaim our ability to fully grasp and engage with the written word, and in so doing, improve our critical-thinking and information-processing skills, which are vital in our text-saturated, algorithmically engineered information age.

THE GENERATION EFFECT

Shakespeare's work is an excellent Renaissance example of the power of active, wide-ranging reading to support new, imaginative work. *The Tempest* is one of the few plays he wrote with original plots. For all of his other works, he borrowed stories from other writers, re-ordering events with new sub-plots and characters to create plays that were resoundingly his own and that span the entire spectrum of human experience. References can be found in his work to writers across a full millennium and a half of history, from Romans such as Ovid and Seneca in the first century CE and English poets Chaucer and Gower in the medieval period to contemporary sources dating just a few years before Shakespeare's plays first arrived onstage. *Holinshed's Chronicles*, published in 1577, served as a source for almost all of his history plays, and scholars have been able to distinguish which pages he drew from for particular scenes. Yet his plays are in no way a mere hodgepodge of cribbed ideas; they're elegantly conceived, erudite texts of the highest order.

Surprisingly little is known about Shakespeare as he came from a relatively modest family rather than from a well-documented aristocratic background. The few records that do remain indicate that his father worked as a glove-maker and, upon becoming a prominent figure in the town of Stratford, sent his children to the local grammar school. Shakespeare therefore benefitted from a humanist education, but we have no surviving documents exhibiting his reading practices; in fact, no original manuscripts of any of his plays exist today. The opposite is the case for the playwright Ben Jonson, a renowned rival to Shakespeare whose plays influence poetry and stage comedy to this day. A catalogue of Jonson's library still exists, together with annotated texts and one of his commonplace books. Jonson's thoughts and interpretations – like Dee's – were assimilated from a vast and varied corpus of literature adapted to his own interests and purposes. One of Jonson's works, *English Grammar*, articulates his views on the importance of a grammar education, something he also benefitted from contemporaneously with Shakespeare. In his literary criticism and essays on education, Jonson emphasized that reading relies on engagement and interaction with the text. To avoid simply accepting what is read, Jonson argued that it is necessary to critically examine and evaluate a text, making judgements about its meaning, style and structure – an active process that he found to be essential for developing one's own intellectual abilities and acquiring knowledge. It's evident that the rich complexity of Jonson's work, like Shakespeare's, was closely linked to his Renaissance education and sophisticated reading practices.

Studies over the past few decades have definitively shown that actively generating material oneself – rather than just reading or watching something – plays an important role in the learning process and in forming memories that we can remember in the future. This 'generation effect', first reported by Norman Slamecka and Peter Graf at the University of Toronto in 1979, can apply to learning a simple word – for instance, we would be more likely to remember the word 'manicule' if we were asked to generate it from the fragment 'ma_ic_le'. But it also extends to far longer texts: writing our own article about a subject, for example, as opposed to reading an article about it, will result in far higher levels of understanding. The active reading practices Shakespeare and Jonson learned from a young age made it possible for them to draw on an intricate body of knowledge, enabling illuminating leaps of imagination and the coining of new words and phrases that remain with us today.

The richly generative, active process of interrogating text on a page exhibited by Shakespeare, Jonson, Dee and others in the Renaissance are some of the most sophisticated reading practices that we have on record, yet similar approaches of careful reading and analysis to aid comprehension and retention can be found throughout much of our literate past. The development of the Greek alphabet from the eighth century BCE was a significant milestone in the history of reading. It was the earliest known alphabetic script to have distinct letters for vowels as well as consonants, allowing for a far more precise and efficient representation of spoken language; and with just twenty-four letters, it was also markedly easier to read and write than earlier writing systems. Reading became an essential skill for the educated elite to master, and the number of texts produced in papyrus scrolls and stored in private libraries or state-funded collections steadily grew in number over the centuries of Greek civilization, culminating in the 400,000 scrolls reputedly being held at the Library of Alexandria in Egypt in the third century BCE.

It was common practice among Greek scholars to read aloud when alone, with the express intention of understanding things more deeply, and they would often read together in groups, discussing and debating ideas as they went. By paraphrasing and explaining their thoughts to their fellow readers, they would have triggered more of a generation effect than if they had been reading silently. It was in fact only during the late Roman Empire and the early Middle Ages that silent reading became more widespread – as Christian texts were disseminated in increasing numbers, readers were often encouraged to read and reflect on the text quietly and privately, rather than reading aloud or in groups.

Handwritten notes have been discovered in sufficient quantities within

Ancient Greek scrolls to suggest to academics today that annotating and marking up texts was a widespread practice, not just limited to scholars and philosophers. While evidence is sparser from Roman times, as many texts were written on wax tablets and were more prone to decay and damage over time, the same is expected to have been the case, and these foundational reading practices undoubtedly had an impact on later generations and wider cultures. Throughout the Islamic Golden Age – a period of scientific, economic and cultural flourishing in the Middle East, North Africa and parts of Central Asia from the eighth to the thirteenth century CE – scholars were known to add marginalia to manuscripts. Texts were typically produced on paper and copied by hand before being shared among scholars. Not only were Greek and Roman manuscripts translated into Arabic, but the concepts and theories that they contained were frequently expounded upon with commentaries in the margins; further new, formative ideas were generated in the process.

Annotations and illustrations have been found in texts emanating from across Europe in the Middle Ages, between the fall of the Roman Empire and the Renaissance. The Nowell Codex, which contains the only surviving copy of the Old English epic poem *Beowulf*, is one of the most renowned and important documents from this period, and it, like many others, contains marginal notes and glosses made by scribes or readers to clarify its contents. Yet it was not until Johannes Gutenberg's invention of the printing press in the fifteenth century revolutionized the production of books that such reading abilities became more prevalent across society and stopped being largely restricted to the clergy and the nobility. Before the invention of printing, manuscript books in Europe numbered in the thousands. By 1500, after only half a century, there were millions of books in circulation, and literacy rates increased rapidly during the Renaissance era. The rise of humanism at this time emphasized the importance of individual thought and learning, and this was an important catalyst for the more elevated forms of active reading that were cultivated to facilitate learning and intellectual growth; in addition, increasingly generative reading methods, such as commonplacing, helped readers keep abreast of the sudden surge of knowledge available in books.

The information boom we have experienced in recent years, with staggering amounts of data filling and guiding our contemporary digital lives, is of an altogether different order of magnitude. Whereas it was just about possible for an educated and motivated individual in the Renaissance to grasp the knowledge accessible within books over the course of a lifetime, the amount of information we have access to today is unfathomably vast. Four million new book titles are published each year for a start, while every day over a trillion messages are sent via email and social platforms, and 2.5 quintillion bytes of data are created globally. We have adapted as a result. When we are on our digital devices, we most often speed-read and skim out of necessity. We quickly establish patterns and themes, foraging through the range of possibilities we are faced with; we flit between several tabs at a time, sampling sections of text on a page to get the gist before moving on. We browse up and down articles or feeds on the lookout for what to avoid and disregard: most often in a process of elimination, not generation.

Reading in this way is a skill and allows for enormous flexibility. We can switch between different information streams with ease and apply the minimum time and effort needed to get the essence of something. Dee exhibited just the same capabilities as he read extensively through his library, categorizing content for deeper attention and intensive reading – he too would frequently read very rapidly. Our problem today is that we rarely move on to the next step of active reading, for which we need sustained concentration and time to focus. Our modern-day, fast, choppy reading style is a coping mechanism to deal with the mass of data with which we are bombarded. Bookmarks, feed settings and notifications help us to manage and filter information but not to consider it deeply and generate new thoughts for ourselves. A cursory scan of a headline or glance at a tweet is much the same as reading a road sign – we momentarily register the information to determine whether it is of use or not. We are constantly navigating our way through a glut of digital information as best we can. We are certainly not closely interrogating the material or taking steps to more robustly integrate it into our worldview. What is more, we rarely reach an endpoint; the deluge forever delays us, and we keep on wading through it.

A first visit of the day to a news site might typically involve scanning through all of the headlines on the homepage – perhaps fifty to a hundred, or more – to determine articles or events of note, which we then scan in haste. We often repeat the process at regular intervals throughout the day, and, even when we happen upon a major news event or article of significant personal interest, we are unlikely to pause for long enough to fully digest the contents. Our initial habits are formed by our preferences for certain sites or topics. But online, we almost always fail to read with any clear direction, in part because of the struggle to keep up and the myriad distractions online and equally because a significant amount of text we read online is curated by algorithms, compromising our ability to consciously navigate the information we consume.

Much of the reading we indulge in online is escapism, a numbing activity, like easy TV-viewing. Opportunistic looks to our phones during pauses in the day, the brief opening of a new browser tab to check the news: when we submit control to our devices and the content we find on the screen in this way, we indulge in inactive reading, the very opposite of Dee's active efforts. It is impossible to read a web page in a minute or so and expect to remember its content after a passage of time. For text to become meaningful, it must pass properly through our memory and attention; we have to invest considerable mental focus to fully process information and correlate it with our prior knowledge. It is no help that the tools we use the majority of time when we read online, whether internet browsers or news feeds, are deliberately designed for inactive reading, to keep us scrolling on. A social-media feed is the clearest manifestation of this, with the prioritization of content being driven by unseen algorithms and advertising spend. Our eyes lock to the screen as news and posts scroll by, and there is often a mental haze to shake off after a length of time reading inactively. Yes, we can engage with posts, but clicking 'like' or other gestural buttons is a very minimal mental commitment; and while writing a comment requires more consideration, the thoughts that we leave quickly pass out of sight.

Most of the time when we read on our phones and computers, it is impossible to mark up text as we go, whether that be underlining important points or noting thoughts in the margins. Of course, we can easily preserve digital copies, saving a pdf or copying and pasting elsewhere, but it is rare that we make the effort to do so. Equally, there are digital services available that emulate many of the benefits of keeping a commonplace book, but they are far from widespread in use today. While on the printed page of a book we can leave marks wherever we like, and they are ours to keep afterwards, it is impossible to annotate the vast majority of text that we come across online. Most often, articles are read through a browser or live app; they are hosted on a website or delivered via a news feed and are not ours to take away with us. Unless we are taking conscious steps to methodically save material we read for future use, reading becomes very much an ephemeral experience, with any learning quickly vanishing in plain sight.

And it is not just that we forget what we have read: more worryingly, inactive reading disarms our critical faculties, so we are more likely to take an author's opinion to be correct without much interrogation of it, particularly if it syncs with our own beliefs. Inactive reading encourages a rigidity in our opinions, as we miss out on nuances, ambiguity or flaws in an argument and skip the stages of comprehension and appreciation only a proper reading allows. To begin to form a critical understanding of a text, we really need to read it in full; and we need space and time to form more tangible, lasting thoughts in response. By closely reading something and carefully considering it for ourselves, we can stretch to learn new concepts and adjust our perspectives. Simply no tool or device can do this for us.

The British Museum holds a collection of commonplace books compiled by Narcissus Luttrell, an English MP in the early 1700s. Luttrell's entries in his commonplaces are compiled from everyday sources, such as news pamphlets and instructional manuals – the eighteenth-century equivalent of the news articles and how-to guides we are surrounded by online today. Luttrell would carefully distil the arguments put forward in texts into their most economical form, seeking to master them before he moved on to new reading. He clearly sets out a maxim for himself in one of his notebooks: 'It is the privilege and duty of man to enquire and examine before he believes or judges and never give up his assent to anything but good and rational grounds.' How can we follow these principles when we read online today?

The changes in reading practices driven by digital technologies have not gone unnoticed in academic circles, and a vast number of studies in this field have been conducted over the years. An influential meta-analysis published in 2018 by a team of European researchers presents the clearest view yet, combining the results of findings from over 170,000 subjects and 58 separate studies conducted between 2000 and 2017. People were found to have significantly better comprehension skills when reading text in print rather than on screens. The researchers were able to compare the differences between print- and digital-reading comprehension levels as the years progressed, and it turns out that the advantages of paper-based reading have increased since 2000, while the effectiveness of our online reading has diminished – in other words, it seems that the maturation of the digital environment over the years has had a negative impact on our comprehension abilities when reading on-screen as compared to traditional print materials.

So far, though, academic studies comparing print and digital reading have simply tested readers on their passive reading, with no investigations as yet into the generation effect or the impact active reading techniques such as annotation can have when applied to print or online text.

Reading operates at the sensitive, permeable interface between ourselves and the complex media that surround us. Critical, active-reading skills are enormously versatile and transferrable – they can be applied to any media type, whether it be TV, film, images or multimedia content on digital technology platforms, or indeed, to most situations in life. Yet whereas schooling in the Renaissance adapted to the advent of print and the ramifications this had on everyday lifestyles, with pupils being tutored in more advanced reading methods to cope with the increased volumes of information, the same has in no way happened today with respect to digital content. The traditional curriculum for learning to read, up to graduate level and beyond, has remained more or less unchanged over the past few decades. Since 2018, the average time we spend on our phones has continued to increase to now almost four hours daily, not to mention the time when we are sitting at a computer, and the majority of this time is spent consuming text and various forms of visual media. It is astounding therefore that there is no formal education on how to invest this time more effectively, critically and with clearer intention. Personal-development or professional training for reading on digital devices commonly focuses on speed-reading, with various app services striving to help us scan texts as quickly as possible; this, however, is the one area in which we are managing perfectly well already. At a moment when active-reading techniques are paramount as resistance against algorithmic determination, fake news and divisive political rhetoric, we are reading more inactively than ever. Deep, attentive reading is a precious social accomplishment that has taken millennia to cultivate, and we need to preserve it. With some slight tweaks and changes, we can revive and adapt traditional active-reading techniques for our modern lives and more clearly filter, process and critique the information that passes daily before our eyes.

BECOME AN ACTIVE READER

The techniques Dee employed are as relevant as ever. Technology may have changed the types of media you consume, but the methods for actively interpreting information have not fundamentally altered. Close, interrogative reading has the potential to dramatically change your outlook and is a powerful way to understand and appreciate others' viewpoints. It's also the essential means by which to learn any new subject. Many of Dee or Emerson's methods can be followed directly, or with a few adjustments, adapted for online reading.

You're also tremendously fortunate today to be supported by a wealth of information resources that mean you don't always have to work quite as hard as readers did in Renaissance times. At its highest levels, active reading is serious mental work that demands extended periods of focused attention and effort, and it's essential for when you are tackling new, complicated concepts and learning new topics. But there are also many other forms of reading that simply don't require the same levels of exertion they once did, so it's important to be able to discern when and how to use active-reading methods. Keeping a commonplace book, whether physical or digital, is an excellent way to engage actively with what you read as well as organizing your thoughts and logging material in a way that you can easily find later.

When to read actively

When you read, it is typically for one or more of the following reasons: for pleasure, to work through a simple idea, to access specific information, to understand another perspective or to learn a new subject. The mode of passive reading we fall into using digital devices fits the first three types perfectly well and most often just needs a few refinements to become more effective. Search engines and the sheer wealth of resources online mean that we don't need to record information personally in the same ways we did before – there's rarely any requirement for more intensive reading practices such as marking up text, note-taking or commonplacing when you read for pleasure, check the news or look up a fact. A few changes to how you read on digital devices can be all that's needed. But to understand a new worldview or concept, or to learn a new subject, active reading is required. Writing a book, building a shed, raising a four-year-old or retraining in a new job field are the types of personal projects and life pursuits that will benefit most from more conscious efforts and a full assortment of active-reading practices.

Digital reading

Making some small adjustments to the set-up on your digital devices can create a far more conducive reading environment. Install a good ad blocker on your desktop browser to remove the distraction of adverts appearing on web pages: uBlock Origin is very reliable, free and open-source. Take some time to get to grips with the different viewing modes available on your desktop and mobile. Browsers always have a full-screen option that prioritizes the web page you are viewing on your screen, with other settings available to disable toolbars and other static information fields, and mobile browsers often have a reading mode available that simplifies a website's look and feel, prioritizing the text so you can focus more easily. On a computer, using a separate browser that has been preset with the most decluttered views available for your reading or other focused work can be a great help.

Digital screens are perfectly suited for a quick read, whether scanning for a particular technical piece of information or skimming to get the gist of a longer text. Tabbed browser views make it easy to flick between numerous articles at a time, determining what's worth closer attention. Try to register key features of any article, such as the author and their aim, together with the publication date. Slow down to read an introduction or conclusion, and attempt to discern the general structure of an article so you can jump to the most pertinent sections; be ready to reread more complex sections where necessary. If something is of use for any of your more intensive, active-reading projects, quickly file it away for later deeper reading and move on.

Consider all the hours you spend revisiting your preferred news site versus the time you invest in finding new alternative sources: it's so easy to fall into routines and repetitive clickstreams online. Put aside a few hours to find additional sources that complement what you already read, trying where possible to find a balance of articles across a full subject or political spectrum. Think as broadly as you can and run wide web searches. Well-funded, search-optimized websites usually pop up first in search returns, so be sure to dig a lot deeper by asking the right questions. Integrated AI and natural-language search commands give you far more control than more basic keyword searches. Whereas search engines used to rely on simple keyword searches, you can now use AI such as ChatGPT to type in or speak more conversational search commands to find what you need.

Some of the most rewarding sources you can find online are hosted on blog platforms or DIY sites with small, impassioned readership bases:

it takes work to find them. Take note of links existing between different websites, either as suggested reading lists or hyperlinks appearing within posts, and continue widening your reading list as you go. Bookmarking and organizing sites you would like to visit more frequently makes it far easier to integrate them into your ongoing reading.

Avoid social-media sites with large amounts of advertising or opaque algorithms controlling the content you see. If you choose to continue with some, try to cull the profiles you follow to a very low number and only keep those which consistently surprise you with insightful links and thoughts you would not normally find elsewhere.

TAKE ACTION

- **Install an ad blocker:** Add one to your web and mobile browsers to reduce distractions.
- **Fine-tune your viewing modes:** Declutter your reading experience on desktop and mobile.
- **Widen the sources you read regularly online:** Prudently research new sites and use the latest AI natural-language commands to broaden your searches.
- **Avoid social-media sites:** Reduce time spent on social media, and reduce the number of other users you follow. Better yet, delete your social-media accounts entirely.
- **Plan your digital reading:** Choose a focused slot in your day, and save active reading topics for when you can commit deeper focus.

During the gaps in the day when you read on your phone as an escape, you are most prone to inactive, wasteful reading. It's best not to read at all on a device at these moments, and instead try to explore what sensations of discomfort might be propelling you back online in the first place. Certainly avoid pursuing more active reading topics during these short moments; instead, save that reading for when you can commit deeper focus and time. When it comes to keeping up with the news, rather than returning to sites throughout the day, it's far more constructive to set aside a time, usually in the morning, to deliberately work through your chosen sites, then put the news aside for the rest of the day. The space you create between viewing newsfeeds helps you establish a clearer-eyed, less biased view of events rather than simply taking the side of your typical group or political stance. Where possible, let go of the habit of treating reading as something to fill dead time, and instead, put more value on your reading sessions by planning them into your day as conscious activities.

Print reading

Digital reading is indispensable, offering an unrivalled breadth of content on any topic and powerful search algorithms to filter through it all. Yet, as discussed, it also constricts the opportunity for deeper reading and is replete with distraction. Reading words on a printed page, in contrast, is the easiest and most intuitive way to hold focus on a topic and to mark up text and make notes as you go. Consider your reading efforts as funnel-shaped, with initial reading on a topic being broad and diverse at the top – for which digital reading is perfect – and focused and intense at the bottom, for which print reading is essential. For any concentrated projects, strive to move as much of your active reading as possible to print. Choose physical books over e-books and print over digital magazine subscriptions. Invest in a good printer and print out online articles you intend to read more deeply. Organize your books and magazines so you can refer to them easily and compile your printed articles in ring binders.

Annotations

Marking up and annotating text is a vital component of active reading, and it's easiest done with a pen or pencil in your hand as you read printed text. It's also useful to highlight liberally with fluorescent pens: it really helps important sections jump off the page during rereads. Underline or circle phrases, sentences and paragraphs of note. Don't worry if it's messy. There's a tendency today to view books as sacrosanct, not to be marked or amended while in your possession. Try to quickly get past this notion: adding your own scribbles truly makes a book your own and a far more valuable resource to return to. Over time, like Dee, through your scrawls you will slowly begin to develop your own idiosyncratic style, which you can start to take pride in.

TAKE ACTION

- **Experiment with marking up and annotating a book:** Develop your own range of symbols and marks to signpost key points and findings on later rereads.
- **Mark up a challenging article:** Print off an article and annotate your thoughts as you read, questioning the text's accuracy and significance to your personal projects.
- **Try digital annotation:** Sign up to and experiment with a free digital annotation service.

Give some thought to personal projects you have that require more active reading and experiment with marking up some printed articles or books. Mark liberally, responding to the text as you read and emphasizing key points. You may begin to notice that your marks complement your reading experience, striking a rhythm that synchronizes with what you encounter on the page, and supporting you when you struggle to try to make sense of something. Add annotations as you go, putting down thoughts that arise as you progress through the text. Deliberately assess what you read, questioning the text's accuracy and precision, logic and significance, depth and breadth, and relevance to your projects. Develop your own system of symbols and notes, such as exclamation marks next to important conclusions or sentences that summarize key points, or question marks when you do not understand something. Simple prompts are invaluable time-savers when you revisit a text later. Take the time to look over your marginalia when you've finished and see if it helps you jump to the most pertinent sections and recall your first impressions and learnings.

There are inevitably also times when it's simpler to remain at your computer and mark up something quickly there and then. This is where digital services which enable solo and group annotation can come into their own. There are a number available online that allow you to highlight and annotate directly on a web page you are viewing, as well as to archive the annotated page in perpetuity.

Commonplacing

The most important step in any active read is the stage when you analyse, paraphrase and explicate in your own words what you are reading. It's useful to split your active reading into two stages: marking up and annotating a text on a first read, and then revisiting it again to commonplace it, using your jots and scribbles as a personal guide to navigate the text to pull out the most important points. Write these longform in notebooks, copying down quotes or expanding on thoughts or new ideas you have while you read. This is an enormously useful process that can eventually see your notebooks consolidating all of your learning from your reading into a flexible format, which can then become your primary source for any later projects. This method can easily be applied to any project, whatever its scope or complexity.

To get started, buy a simple A4 notebook and put aside the first few pages to work as a contents section. The commonplace method of arranging notes under different topic headings is enormously handy. Take time to carefully consider the structure of topics related to any projects for which you are actively reading: the list of subjects will organically grow from there, but a starting attempt helps organize your notes more thoroughly from the very beginning. Spread your topics through your notebook as headed sections at the top of a page, leaving room for corresponding notes to fall under each, and for other topics to be added later. Number the pages in your notebook and mark the location of each of the headed sections in your contents.

Working between a book you are reading and a notebook in front of you, write down anything that catches your eye or that you find useful, and where you're not logging facts, figures or quotes, try not to simply record text verbatim. Pause to fully take in more detailed points and boost the generation effect by rephrasing them in your notebook. Always take a note of the original title and author of any text, as it makes citations or any further reading far simpler; also include page numbers from the source to link back to any particularly informative sections. Once you've filled a notebook, if you can, take a digital photo of each page and save these on a cloud drive with a clear, numbered file-naming structure so you can easily locate individual pages later. This way, you can easily load them onto your phone or laptop, and you won't need your notebooks physically in front of you all the time.

Digital annotation services allow a similar technique for digital reading, tagging links to articles so you can easily access them later. As they're the same tools you can use for highlighting and annotating text on a web page when reading actively online, all of your mark-up and notes are captured neatly within your arrangement of topics. Set tags in just the same way as the subject headings in a commonplace book; even better, try to match them across digital and your physical notebooks, so you can easily switch between the two.

It can also help hugely to compile your own commonplace index, particularly if you're more rigorously researching something. Proper indexing allows specific information in your notes to be found quickly and also enables a cross-pollination of ideas. Notes recorded in one section are often very relevant for other topics and can offer unexpected vantage points across a range of personal projects.

When you have filled one commonplace book, assign a new notebook as your index, or, better yet, create a spreadsheet, the contents of which can be more easily searched and filtered later. Work through the notes in your commonplace book and begin to itemize different points covered within each topic section. Use a simple number code for subtopics and write the numbers on the commonplace notebook page next to each point. Log these subtopic number codes in your index, with the notebook title and page number for each point relevant to the subtopic so that you can quickly locate the notes in the future.

TAKE ACTION

- **Start your own commonplace book:** Set topic headings for your personal projects and number pages so they're easily found in a contents section.
- **Give your marked-up text a second read:** With your notebook open beside you, use your marginalia as a guide to locate key points and write them down.
- **Keep organized:** Cite the title, author and page numbers of any source; once you've completed a notebook, store digital photos of each page on a cloud drive so you can easily access them later.
- **Start indexing your notes:** Once you have filled one commonplace book, give each point a code according to which commonplace heading or subtopic they fall under. Use a spreadsheet or separate notebook to help you locate these notes in the future.

Chapter 6

Writing

A UNIVERSAL MEASURE OF A HUMAN BEING

In the late 1480s, Leonardo da Vinci began work on one of the most recognizable drawings in the world today. He started with exhaustive anatomical studies sketched in his commonplace books, which he then supplemented with library reading and free-association note-taking. During his studies of Roman architecture, he had discovered a 1,500-year-old postulation that the well-proportioned human body fitted neatly within the perimeter of both a circle and a square. By painstakingly gathering coordinates and fine measurements of each part of the human anatomy, Leonardo amassed volumes of data never collected before. He then proceeded to deftly encapsulate his complex and varied findings in one simple image. His *Vitruvian Man*, elegantly held in its circle and a square, captured for a Renaissance audience the commonly held ideal of a microcosm – namely humanity – existing within, and aligning with, a macrocosm – the universe as a whole.

Almost everything we know about Leonardo today stems from his personal notebooks. He filled an estimated 30,000 manuscript pages over the course of his lifetime, 7,200 of which survive today, and they range from intricate, fine penmanship in large folios to quick scribblings in small pocketbooks that he hung from his belt. Every page is crammed full of miscellaneous drawings, to-do lists and written notes on a myriad of topics that reveal his mental leaps and broad connections of mind. Initially, he primarily recorded ideas for his art or engineering projects – drawings of exaggerated facial features and body gestures or black-sailed stealth ships and submarines – but as he progressed, he began to pursue his curiosity for its own sake. Leonardo spent hours each day writing and drawing in his notebooks, and his work conveys the astonishing powers of a human mind brimming with thought and observation.

Leonardo's father appreciated his son's early burgeoning artistic talent and, when Leonardo was fifteen, apprenticed him to the noted sculptor and painter Andrea del Verrocchio. It was with him in Florence that Leonardo was first introduced to artist copybooks and engineer sketchbooks, and he learned over time to combine these visual mediums with the practical information-processing capabilities of a commonplace book (a *zibaldone*, as it was known then in the Italian vernacular). As a child, he had received only limited schooling – rudimentary training in reading, writing and maths – and it is likely Leonardo taught himself to write in his early years, quickly arriving at his own shorthand and mirror script: as he was left-handed, he composed words backwards from right to left on the page to avoid smearing his hand over wet ink. He quickly became accustomed to seeking out knowledge for himself, and soon observed no real boundaries between his written thoughts and the visual ideas he toyed with for his paintings, jotting down his impressions or composing letters or essays in his notebooks just as much as he drew landscapes, conceived of mechanical designs or mapped out towns and cities.

Leonardo is best known today as an artist, but the complex lines of thought he conveyed through his masterpieces are not always so readily understood. His drawings and paintings demonstrate not only a profound technical ability but also a deep understanding of the mechanical workings and inner cause of things. When Leonardo drew a raised eyebrow or sought to capture the tensed twist of a muscle, he based his decisions, wherever he could, on his own empirical examinations: he continually set himself challenges to discover how things worked, and why. His masterworks stemmed from any number of preparatory studies and scientific experiments, and he communicated his own comprehension of things visually. The pace of his investigations rapidly accelerated over time, expanding to cover almost every conceivable subject of human enquiry. His notebooks reveal not only his mental life and his extraordinary means of visual thinking but also the ever-widening range of his personal interests and autodidactism.

Leonardo discovered for himself the explanatory power of images and that by drawing lines on a page he could better express and clarify his thoughts and intentions. His sketches perfectly exhibit the generative visual activity – a creative gathering and display of information in free, imaginative mode – that people in Renaissance times so frequently interspersed among their handwritten notes. Students in the Renaissance filled their commonplace books with written excerpts, thoughts and ideas and also sketched visual elaborations to try to connect their learnings – it was typical to make use of lines, arrows and diagrams as well as more complicated sketches to explain concepts.

A typical student was far more practised and competent in drawing than the majority of us are today. The Italian concept of *disegno* – fine-art drawing underpinned by intellect – developed in early Renaissance times and eventually spread across Europe. Writing and drawing were understood as cognitive processes, a way of thinking through a problem to come to a solution, and through images students often articulated ideas too difficult to communicate with the written word. As they naturally wrote by hand, students could easily switch between text and illustrations to support their thoughts. The activity of drawing became a central component of training in many topics in schools, with visual representations used as critical tools to organize and explore ideas and large quantities of information. Sketches can be found throughout surviving school notebooks of the time, some made during lectures and others produced later in an attempt to assimilate learning. These show just how much more prevalent it was in our past to use visual strategies to better manage and order information. Drawing classes and training were indeed often maintained until late in life.

What separates Leonardo, however, is his level of ambition and persistence with his visual explorations. In preparation for the portraits that he was commissioned to undertake as an artist – in addition to his work on sculpture and other representations of the human form – Leonardo began to ever more closely research the working mechanics of the human body. In the prime years of his life – and after having already produced some of the world's most revered paintings and drawings – he committed himself to learning Latin so he could read the writings of the Ancient Greeks and Romans, the science of the Islamic tradition and the scholarly works of medieval authorities. He began too late in life to become perfectly fluent, but he worked hard enough to get by and was soon granted access to one of the largest libraries at that time – the personal holdings of Fazio Cardano in Pavia. As Leonardo studied the majority of the medical and anatomical texts existing up until that day, he spotted mistruths and misperceptions and became increasingly frustrated by the basic illustrations and incorrect depictions of the intricacies of human anatomy. He realized that a comprehensive and empirically researched guide to the human body did not exist, and, in early 1489, he decided to undertake it himself.

Leonardo wrote in his notes that his *On the Human Body* anatomical treatise would be unlike anything ever seen before – it would begin with conception in the womb and then proceed to represent the universal conditions of humankind, and the full spectrum of our physicality and movement in life. In a fast flurry of thoughts and ideas in his notebooks, he arrived at the epiphany that his work would be primarily visual. He had just completed a series of engineering and architectural studies and had grown keenly aware of how efficient a tool a carefully penned image could be. Over the ensuing years, Leonardo proceeded to conduct his own hands-on autopsies of over thirty human cadavers and many more animal corpses. He worked with both a pen and a scalpel in hand, drawing what he uncovered as he dissected layer by layer, even as a body lay untreated and decomposed. Stopping at no detail, Leonardo investigated the body in its entirety and even dismembered the deep nerves and muscles controlling the lips to search for the actual mechanisms that transmit emotions into facial expressions and for the emanation of the human smile.

He presented his findings with intimate precision, and by using a range of new architectural and perspective-drawing techniques, he exhibited the full human form with rotations, cutaways and see-through views, with intricately devised plans and elevations. His surviving anatomical studies are astounding: skull and bones, muscles and tissue are all incisively documented from multiple angles, and strong contrasts between light and dark – his famed *chiaroscuro* technique – bring the compositions thoroughly to life. True to form, his written notes engulf his drawings and take up almost as much space to explain his surgical methods and clearly delineate his measurements. What, perhaps, is most astonishing is that none of these eventual 240 drawings or 13,000 words were ever released to the public during Leonardo's lifetime, nor indeed for centuries afterwards: they remained tucked away within his personal notebooks, and he never found time to complete his full, planned treatise. The records that exist today were visual prompts and notes designed solely for his own use.

Primarily, Leonardo was a visual thinker: every diagram, line or scrawl was an imaginative experiment; and by rendering mechanisms on the page – whether to gauge engineering principles or to distinguish how muscles and tendons might control a limb – he was better able to envision how they might work in reality. He brainstormed with his pen, all the while devising new methods to display information, and he had no particular predilection for words or letters, lines or shapes, or full-blown visual expositions. When he found an image more readily articulated an idea than any verbal language, he quickly started drawing; and when writing was enough, he kept going. One of Leonardo's prime skills was this fluid interchange between images and the written word, which enabled him to better delineate relationships between things and more fluidly break down a question or a problem. Leonardo enriched his knowledge with his visualizations, and by combining words and images on a page, he often arrived at more sophisticated levels of comprehension.

One noted distraction Leonardo encountered when he was conducting his grisly dissections and postmortem examinations – and one that inevitably waylaid his anatomical treatise – was his decision to also make an exhaustive survey of human proportions. He began a comparative study of live models and made a series of startlingly thorough measurements, scrutinizing each part of the human body and recording his results meticulously across forty drawings and diagrams and 6,000 words of notes. His models were asked to move, and as they twisted and turned, stood, sat or kneeled, Leonardo recorded the changing proportions and relationships of their corresponding body parts with a measuring string – one of his entries alone consists of eighty calculations as he strives to fathom his 'universal measure' of a human being.

Leonardo's architectural work on the Milan and Pavia cathedrals had led him to study traditional Roman design, and eventually, the writings of Vitruvius, an engineer dating from the first century BCE. His multi-volume *De architectura* sets out key principles for building, with methodologies for arriving at perfect proportions, and Leonardo read it closely. Vitruvius's uncompromising focus on the adoption of circles and squares to inform a natural simplicity of design has inspired many of the most celebrated buildings, from the Pantheon in Rome to the White House. This elementary geometry resonated with Leonardo – he had for a long time wrestled with the ancient mathematical challenge of 'squaring the circle' – particularly as it possessed venerable layers of symbolic meaning. Philosophers, mathematicians and mystics in the ancient world saw the circle as representing unity and wholeness; its absolute uniformity was deemed interchangeable with the all-encompassing system of everything in nature, the cosmos itself. For Vitruvius and his contemporaries, a circle designated the power of nature as an architect; and a square, in correspondence, denoted the earthly presence of human beings.

Vitruvius makes a leap of thought in his *De architectura* that stole Leonardo's attention immediately and held it for a good while afterwards. He leans on the age-old philosophical notion of the human body as a miniaturized version of the universe – and a physical embodiment of the primary laws of nature – to establish a standard system of architectural measurements, based on the ideal human form. Humankind has always used body parts to measure the world – a foot to ascertain distance, the thumb to calibrate an inch, or outstretched arms to quantify a fathom of nautical depth. Yet all bodies, of course, are different in proportion. Vitruvius gets around this by setting out principles for the design and construction of temples in particular: he gives specific recommendations for the exact measurements of the ideal human being and concludes with suggestions as to how such a perfect specimen of humanity might precisely fit inside a circle and a square. *De architectura* contains no illustrations to encapsulate Vitruvius's words, and in the 1,500 years between his writing and Leonardo's reading of the text, no one had ever attempted to test the logic. Leonardo's interest was sufficiently piqued to attempt his own *Vitruvian Man*.

His delicate drawing is locked away today in a climate-controlled room in the Accademia Gallery in Venice, on a simple sheet of paper measuring 35 by 26 centimetres – just slightly larger than an A4 letter. Leonardo drew the circle and square first, using a compass divider and set square to check his measurements, and with a pen and brown ink, placed his human being carefully inside the two shapes. In working through the problem visually, Leonardo addresses the main problem of how to fit a human body inside both a circle and a square and, recognizing that our navel does not actually lie midway between our head and feet, he lowers the square accordingly. He then superimposes two images of the same human figure, to demonstrate how it fits harmoniously within either form.

Leonardo includes a number of other innovations, including a slight twist of the left foot, so it works as a visual key and highlights the human body's role as a fundamental unit of measurement, and adds a further scale at the bottom of his drawing, divided into units of fingers and palms. He uses a lot more measurements than Vitruvius proposes, taking what he can from *De architectura* and testing it thoroughly for himself before then adding a whole depth of other findings from his own extensive data on human proportions. His *Vitruvian Man* encapsulates his months of work measuring the body's minute coordinates and proportional relationships, but in comparison to his abundant pages of notes, it feels almost effortless; displaying everything at a glance, with clarity and concision.

The head of the human figure, dead centre towards the top of the page, looks out directly, and it's hard to escape the feeling that the drawing might depict Leonardo himself. He was thirty-eight when he completed the drawing, and the facial appearance and flowing hair match descriptions offered by his contemporaries. His face, drawn with more detail and emotional intent than the remainder of his body, casts a distinct image of a man looking at himself searchingly in the mirror. The *Vitruvian Man* hovers nakedly as a vibrant act of personal speculation and self-investigation as Leonardo strives to understand the essence of his own nature. It functions as a universal self-portrait of our human being and distils the deeper efforts we make to comprehend ourselves more fully. The Renaissance was an exhilarating time in our past when art, science and philosophy all merged as one to probe the timeless questions about who we really are and how we fit into the grand order of the universe; the *Vitruvian Man* captures the human potential of that era.

Today, the constricted square the human figure nestles within could easily stand for a computer screen, with the surrounding circle our increasingly forgotten physical world. The capabilities of word processors and web tools makes writing on a keyboard frequently a sensible choice; but there are also innumerable times – when we're grasping for new ideas, or striving to come to a conclusion – that switching to a pen and paper simply feels right. Typing at a keyboard orients our thoughts to the screen, the text flowing from left to right, and always downwards, whereas a blank page frees us to connect our thoughts and notes in a non-linear way. Our fingertips alone have the same number of receptors as our entire torso, so when we write or draw by hand, we intuitively make use of the most adept and sensitive parts of our bodies. We can alternate between words and drawing, jot down related ideas next to one another, or group and connect them with lines. This kind of visual thinking allows us to handle complexity more adeptly and become clearer and more critically competent thinkers, in particular when we're seeking to make meaning for ourselves and avoid passively receiving information.

Leonardo's engineering and computational mind would have revelled in the digital technologies we are gifted with today, but if he had forgone his handwritten notes and associated visual thinking, his ability to make links across disciplines – and his reverence for the whole sphere of nature's phenomena – would not have been as far-reaching. When we write and draw by hand we make use of the simplest of tools, but without the spatial constraints on our thinking imposed by software or a screen, we open ourselves up to new connections and a freer way of thinking.

THE MOST EXQUISITE INSTRUMENT WE POSSESS

In 2012, a unique exhibition opened at Buckingham Palace and Holyroodhouse. Upon his death, all of Leonardo's drawings and manuscripts were bequeathed to one of his pupils, and they were eventually pasted into albums that began to change hands across the globe. It is unknown exactly how one of the most celebrated of these books passed into the possession of the British royal family – it was most likely acquired by Charles II in the late 1600s – but its pages, which include all of Leonardo's surviving anatomical studies, are the most valuable treasures held in the Royal Collection today. The 2012 exhibition showcased all of Leonardo's anatomical drawings for the first time and displayed them alongside modern high-tech medical imaging scans. The comparisons revealed that despite his limited prior knowledge or access to technology, Leonardo's studies are indeed incredibly accurate. Much of his work anticipates twenty-first-century medical practice and uses the same sequences of images now relied upon to train medics. If Leonardo's physiological research had been released during his lifetime, it would have fast-tracked the understanding of human anatomy by several hundred years.

One sheet in particular created by Leonardo demonstrates the layered structure of the hand through four illustrations of different stages of dissection: he begins with the bones, then adds the deep muscles of the palm before applying the first and second layers of the tendons. It is one of his most intricate expositions – approximately a quarter of the bones in our bodies are found in our hands alone – and he laboured over it scrupulously. An animated computer simulation was designed at the Royal Collection Trust exhibition to help visitors get closer to Leonardo's appreciation of the fine subtlety of the structure of our hands and their remarkable mechanics. Our hands are perceptual organs that we rely on just as much as our eyes, and they play a crucial role in gathering information about the world around us – our fingertips in particular are layered with thousands of tactile sensors that give us intimate feelings of touch, while the inclinations of our finger joints and wrists offer us a sensitive alertness of movement. Leonardo recognized the human hand as a precision instrument as he studied it, and, of course, deftly used it.

Yet when Leonardo examined the hand closely, his explorations soon extended to the muscles of the shoulder. One of his largest drawings shows a dissected right arm with the muscles and tendons that act upon the thumb displayed; Leonardo was keenly aware that our hands are an integral part of our entire arm: they function in dynamic coordination with the muscles of our neck, back, and even our legs, and synchronize with the rest of our bodies. His realization that the hand links to everywhere in the human body showed a remarkable prescience: recent neuroscientific studies confirm that the hand is so widely represented in the brain – and that its neurological and biomechanical movements are so prone to spontaneous interaction and reorganization in the rest of our nervous system – that our deep-rooted motivations and efforts to use our hands are indistinguishable from the basic imperative of human life. Anthropological and medical research argue that the hand played a formative role in the evolution of human intelligence: neuroscience today deems the brain to exist not only in our skulls, but to also extend throughout the entirety of our bodies, and that it is within our hands that our thinking most prevails when we reach out to the world around us.

Our hands are the most exquisitely formed instruments we possess to make sense of things, yet we do not use them nearly as much as we used to, particularly when we write. Surprisingly, no comprehensive study has been undertaken to date to properly assess to what extent our handwriting has declined since the widespread use of digital technology, but everyday experience confirms that it is by a significant amount. Though many of us continue to fill out forms by hand or scribble quick notes around the house, these days, the majority of our writing is done on a keyboard or phone and, as a result, many of us have seen a significant deterioration in the legibility of our handwriting. Typing at a computer can make writing feel a lot simpler, and in many ways, it is: word processors allow us to cut and paste and move text around, and most email today incorporates some form of autocomplete. For many of our digital tasks, the ease with which our typed words can be copied, shared and searched for later makes a keyboard an obvious choice. Yet, there are also many situations today where handwriting remains a far better option. By understanding how our cognitive processes change when we type – and by paying attention to our own thoughts more closely when we *do* write and draw by hand – we can work out for ourselves when we are best picking up a piece of paper instead.

When we type, our freedom of movement drops substantially: a standard QWERTY keyboard has 101 fixed buttons, and our motion is practically the same, whatever the letter or number we are producing. Typing is predominantly restricted to our fingers, yet handwriting draws on the balance and movement of most of our body. We rely on our core strength to stabilize our posture and to make delicate adjustments when we write by hand, so much so that mothers often find handwriting more difficult after childbirth, until rest and recuperation allows abdominal muscle tissue to sufficiently recover. All of this physical activity is in stark contrast to what our body is doing while typing.

Our brains do different things too: a study completed by the Norwegian University of Science and Technology in 2017 found notable differences in brainwave patterns when children and young adults typed at a keyboard in comparison to when they wrote and drew by hand. An EEG geodesic sensor net – a pebbly hood of 256 metal sensors that neatly pulls over the head – recorded changes in neural electrical activity as a series of written tasks were completed. When people were writing and drawing by hand, their brainwave patterns were those more typically deemed as optimal for learning. Neuronal activation was noticeably less complex and pronounced when typing on a keyboard – a result ascribed to the less delicate and less precisely controlled hand movements when we type. The key findings that cursive handwriting and drawing are more conducive to learning and memory recall have been confirmed by a number of other academic studies, in particular a high-profile report by Princeton

University and the University of California in 2014, and more recently by Johns Hopkins University in 2021, which again found learning rates to be far higher when writing by hand. The researchers suggest that the perceptual-motor experience of using our hands when writing helps us to consolidate and more readily assimilate what we learn.

No academic institution has yet conclusively assessed how language models such as ChatGPT affect our thinking processes when we write, although the effect is likely to be more significant than simply comparing using a keyboard to handwriting. 'GPT' stands for 'generative pre-trained transformer', and it allows any web tool it is connected with to generate original content in the form of human language. AI language models such as ChatGPT can boost our creativity by introducing fresh ideas or perspectives and can help our productivity by analysing and summarizing a vast corpus of text. However, significant diminishment of the 'generation effect' is evident when we offload our writing to AI in this way rather than finding words and phrases to articulate our own thoughts. There is a well-understood risk of 'cognitive outsourcing' when we rely too much on AI to assist our writing, and we risk reducing our capacity to generate new ideas for ourselves and articulate thoughts independently. Counterbalancing time spent writing with AI tools with time using a pen and paper can help mitigate these risks: no AI generative tool can impinge on our thoughts when we write and draw by hand.

When we write on a page, we give ourselves the liberty to think spatially: a blank piece of paper allows us to place marks wherever we like, to connect ideas across the page or easily denote three-dimensional space with shading. We can create our own visual language with a pen, and it can be as simple or complex as we choose: often arrows and lines between words or phrases are enough to expand our thinking. Quick sketches, diagrams or mind maps help us see how pieces fit together as a whole; spatial positioning presents new perspectives and associations that can quite literally turn our ideas around or upside down. Although we can put more polish on something we work up at a computer, for most of us, graphic design software takes far more time and effort and simply does not feel as intuitive or fluent as putting pen to paper.

In a famous letter to the French mathematician Jacques Hadamard in the late 1930s, Albert Einstein explained that, for him, words or language did not play a leading role in the mechanism of thought; rather, his ideas were typically 'visual and some of muscular type'. Einstein relied significantly on visual thought experiments to arrive at some of the most influential breakthroughs in physics, including imagining riding a beam of light for his development of special relativity, and picturing a man in an elevator falling freely in space as he worked out the theory of general relativity. Einstein was astute to spot how closely our thoughts are related to our bodily movement and their kinaesthetic, polysensory quality. By moving our bodies more – either by gesturing or by making marks on the page – we can expand on the limited linearity of language.

When our words are of high volume, are routine or require little creative input, a keyboard is often the most appropriate tool, allowing us to efficiently set down our thoughts – most of us can type faster today than we handwrite, and the productivity of web tools can be hard to match on paper. Yet when it comes to expanding on our ideas with visual concepts, or to arrive at new combinations of ideas freely, technology quickly becomes constricting. Word processors – or indeed any type of software tool – establish standardized ways of working that become very hard to get past: simple menu options may make it easy to switch fonts or change a page layout but difficult to create anything that is more visually freeform; for the majority of us today, the inputs we make into our devices consist almost entirely of prescribed letters and numbers, mouse clicks and screen taps. Even graphic-design professionals, or architects and engineers who use visual software on a regular basis, experience notable levels of constraint on their flexibility and creativity at a computer.

For well over half our waking hours each day we rely entirely on a keyboard, touchscreen or mouse to record our thoughts and decisions. Yet, for all the time that we spend on our digital devices, the words we write with them are far fewer than one might first imagine. Based on data it has collected for the past twenty years or so, the app Whatpulse, which measures keyboard and mouse usage, reveals that on average people type only 941 keys – equivalent to writing only 200 words – a day at a computer. Naturally, some professions will require very little textual work, while others will involve writing thousands of words a day, but it is worth noting that we spend far greater proportions of our time browsing, selecting and consuming information online than we do actually creating it for ourselves. Whatpulse shows that people typically make 497 clicks per day; the Mousotron app finds that the average office worker's mouse travels over one mile in actual distance per week; and 2022 American and Flemish studies reveal that people using smartphones touch, tap or swipe their devices on an average of 2,617 occasions per day. It is clear that we most typically scan, scroll and select when using screens, and when we do type words or sentences, they frequently consist of short search commands to deliver more information or brief message exchanges.

User experience designers and developers use 'heat' maps to closely track and direct where people scroll and click on a web page and then ensure important buttons and elements on a web page are deliberately placed in the most visible sections; users of a website or app home in on those locations, prompted by cues and directions. We repeat very similar gestures with a mouse or a touchscreen, selecting buttons and controls in the same areas of a screen and the accumulation of our moves over the course of a day forms a mush of repetitive lines – entirely different in form to the premeditated marks and designs we make on a piece of paper. The pattern of mouse scrolls and clicks, screen swipes and taps becomes so commonplace that it begins to alter our own thinking processes: when we operate digital devices, our thoughts and impressions are largely sequential in nature, as much dictated by algorithms or software design as they are by our own personal motivations or findings. In contrast, when Leonardo relied on his physical investigations, hand-drawn images and cursive notes as vehicles to produce his own thoughts, he was very much in control and moved freely between each of his different modes. Handwriting and drawing offer us the most intimate means we have to manipulate our thoughts, and in the Renaissance era we got closer than perhaps we ever have to realizing the personal power that they can hold for us.

WRITE AND DRAW BY HAND

Writing and drawing by hand are core life skills, but if you are anything like the vast majority of us today, you will have become so used to typing at a keyboard instead that you will be unaware of the occasions when using pen and paper might enable a deeper level of thinking, help you to organize your thoughts more clearly or spur fresh ideas.

You don't need any special training or artistic ability to collect your thoughts on paper, and good visual thinking is less about knowing how to arrange marks on a page than actually taking the time to do so. With practice, you can grow your own repertoire of penstrokes and develop personal habits of analysing and questioning. Initially choosing a few, simple exercises can help you to develop your own habits of thought. Once you become comfortable with using pen and paper again, you can then find or develop new written tools that enhance your ideas further. Over time, you'll become more alert to the instances when using pen and paper offers benefits, and you will be increasingly inclined to abandon your keyboard.

When to use pen and paper

At any time when you find your thoughts stalling at a computer or when you need some fresh input or ideas, try switching your monitor off or dropping the lid of your laptop down, and reach for a pen instead. Better yet, if you can, step from away your desk and online distractions entirely to give your creativity the time it needs to fully explore a topic.

Carry a small notebook and pen in your work bag and try to keep them with you wherever you go: ideas can arrive in the gaps of the day, often when you least expect them. It can help to keep a writing notebook separate to any commonplace book that you start, as when you're catching your thoughts on the move, or interrogating them, it's more important to get them down on the page than necessarily organize things by topic. Try not to reach for the notes app on your phone – typed text constricts your thinking process and the raft of other apps will too readily distract and disrupt your creative flow. Jotting down notes by hand allows you to more fluidly maintain the associative qualities of your imagination and remain open to further connections and combinations.

Once you have finished a productive scribble of thoughts in your notebook, take a photo if needs be and save it on your phone for safekeeping, or type out some of the most important points on a digital note so you can easily search for them later, but be sure to do this only after you have finished writing them down. Ideas are fleeting, so catch them as soon as you can: treat them with respect and protect them from interruptions.

When you need to take notes in a meeting, a training session or even when you find yourself reading a particularly insightful article or watching an online video, do not type at your laptop there and then. Use a pen and paper and commit things to your commonplace or writing notebook: the physical action of writing by hand, along with the insights offered by any sketched diagrams or visual notes, will better cement your learnings. You will more easily remember the exact location and timing of your first encounter with this new information, and it will remain with you for a good while longer.

TAKE ACTION

- **Close your laptop and reach for a pen instead:** Next time you find your thoughts stalling at a computer, see what ideas you can collect on the page instead.
- **Carry a notebook and pen in your bag:** Be ready to jot down and expand on new thoughts as they arrive.
- **Record new information by hand:** Try where you can to switch to handwritten notes in meetings or seminars and as you read.

Organize your thoughts on the page

Writing simple lists can be enough to get new ideas flowing, but using all the space on a page can be very beneficial too. Mind maps in particular are a fantastic way to represent connections and associations between different topics. They can be found in school notebooks dating back to Renaissance times, and they offer a natural, intuitive way to prompt the visual-spatial techniques our minds use in problem-solving. Leonardo himself used them to clearly articulate, reiterate and generate new prototypes of his ideas. Begin by writing the main concept you are looking to explore at the centre of a piece of paper and then, a small distance out from the middle, note your first related ideas and draw a circle around each phrase. Connect a line from the centre to each of these now orbiting ideas, and for each of these new, individual concepts, repeat the process again. As you progress, you will find your ideas taking shape across the full span of the page, with a web of connections that enables you to follow your own associative links. Where you spot additional connections, mark them with extra lines and arrows, and if you begin to feel hemmed in by the margins of the page, take a particularly fruitful line and move it onto a new piece of paper.

Working through a step-order of ideas or a linear flow of processes is far more easily done by drawing a flow chart on the page than by using software or any web tools. Start by sketching out a first attempt quickly and then look for any gaps or improvements that might be needed: it's simple to make changes and new iterations with pen and paper until you eventually arrive at an optimal sequence.

The Cornell note-taking method can also be very useful for organizing and expanding on your thoughts. Divide a piece of paper into two columns, leaving space at the bottom of the page. The narrower left-hand column is for key words or questions, the wider right-hand column is for detailed notes, and the space at the bottom of the page is for the summary. This method encourages you to think more critically and deeply, identify key concepts and generate questions for yourself.

TAKE ACTION

- **Tackle a creative challenge with a mind map:** Come up with a broad association of ideas and connect them together with lines on the page.
- **Draw your own flow charts:** Test the ordering of your ideas on the page and try out different sequences to find the best solution.
- **Try the Cornell note-taking method:** Divide a piece of paper into three sections for notes, key words and summary.

Find fresh ideas with sketchnotes

You can use a lot of the visual thinking techniques that Leonardo employed in his writing and drawing, and there's no need to for you to be concerned about the end result being anywhere near as accomplished! The goal is to use writing and drawing to get your ideas down rather than to create a perfect artwork.

The designer Mike Rohde coined the term 'sketchnoting' in 2007 to denote the process of note-taking that integrates visual elements such as drawings, icons or diagrams. It's a quick and easy process to learn that you can use to capture, process and recall information, whether you're in a meeting, researching something new or trying to come up with entirely fresh ideas. An active sketchnoting community has developed since, and being unpractised at drawing is regularly found to be an advantage because, as visual artists learn to shape lines, composition and form, the playfulness of visual thinking can all too easily get lost.

Leonardo was distinctive, matching his artistic sensibilities with far more untrained attempts to get to the core of an idea. His fascination with flight, for example, led him to sketch numerous unconstrained designs for helicopters and ornithopters, aircraft that fly by flapping their wings, but the polish of his final drawings had no bearing on their usefulness to support his thinking. He relied just as much on explanatory text to root and ground his visual ideas, and it was the interplay of some his most simple marks on the page and his elaborated written thoughts that helped him clarify his thoughts.

Choose a problem that you have been battling with for a while and sit down with a notebook and pen to work through it. Start by defining your problem or goal and clearly articulate it at the top of page, then list related keywords or phrases. As you progress, begin sketching some of your thoughts in a non-linear, more freeform manner, using a combination of text, icons, symbols or simple illustrations. Search for deeper connections and new ideas using lines, arrows or other visual elements and try to spot patterns, themes and potential solutions. You can easily group and categorize your thoughts on the page, so you can see the bigger picture and identify areas for closer exploration.

TAKE ACTION

- **Make your first sketchnote:** Select a problem that is front of mind, articulate it at the top of the page and then start listing any related thoughts that you might have.
- **Group your thoughts on the page:** Try using lines and arrows to make connections between ideas and help you find new patterns or unexpected answers.
- **Step back:** Once you have finished your sketchnote, take some time to review it as whole and consider if your perspective on the subject has shifted.

One of the most powerful aspects of sketchnoting is that you can easily go back and iterate and refine your thoughts. When you've finished, review your notes, looking for any gaps or inconsistencies – you can add, remove or modify elements as you like to create a clearer representation of your ideas. Give yourself some time to properly assess what you've noted down, and see if your understanding has evolved.

Write by hand at your computer

The computer mouse was invented in 1964 by Douglas Engelbart, an American engineer and inventor. Working at the Stanford Research Institute, his first prototype was made of wood and had two metal wheels, but it was later refined by Xerox and Apple in the 1970s. Mice were designed from the start to be used with the dominant hand to ensure quick and easy adoption. This design choice has not only influenced the arrangement of our desks but also significantly limited our ability to write and draw by hand while using a computer; yet it doesn't have to be this way.

If you are anything like most of us online, the majority of your time at a computer will be spent clicking and scrolling, with your dominant hand resting on your mouse, and your other hand left dormant. It's only when you type that you need to call upon the use of both hands. Yet, whereas it's enormously difficult to become proficient at writing or drawing with your other hand, as you rely on exquisitely fine control of the small muscles in your fingers, hands and wrists, it's far easier to shift to controlling your mouse with your less dominant hand instead.

There are a number of benefits if you do. Once you've got used to using your mouse with your other hand, your activity online is unaffected; but suddenly, you have free use of your writing hand to take notes, doodle ideas or organize your thoughts – it can help to complement and support a lot of your digital work. It's cumbersome to have a notepad and pen next to your mouse, as you need a wide radius to freely move your cursor around the screen. But as soon as you move your mouse mat to the other side, you can keep a pad of paper at the ready, and quite naturally scribble thoughts, even as you scroll, click and browse.

Most mice today are ambidextrous, with a symmetrical shape and buttons on each side, meaning you can easily swap them to your other hand. The only technical change you need to make is altering the button configuration on your computer: most mice have the left-click button set as the primary button as default, and if you are right-handed and moving to your left hand, you will need to switch this setting to the right-click button.

Your non-dominant hand needs time to learn a new skill, but it does come with patience and practice. It gets progressively easier after only a few days, and within a week or two can feel perfectly natural: once you get there, your dominant hand is freed to help you assimilate and interrogate your thoughts in free, visual ways. With care, you can also reduce the risk of repetitive strain injury (RSI) by distributing repetitive tasks more evenly between two hands. Using your non-dominant hand for mouse control can also be a fantastic form of brain training, challenging yourself to develop new neural pathways and strengthen existing ones, improving your dexterity, hand-eye coordination and creativity in the process.

TAKE ACTION

- **Move your mouse to your other hand for a month:** Give yourself the time you need to properly adapt.
- **Rearrange your desk:** With your mouse moved to the other side of your desk, invest in a good-sized blank-paged notepad, and be ready to use it whenever you're at your computer.

Chapter 7

Art

GET ON THE INSIDE AND PRESS OUT

The nineteenth-century American art teacher Robert Henri lived at a time when the invention of photography was upending the function of painting in people's lives. By distinguishing what makes a photo different from a drawing or a painting, he encouraged his students to use the power of their own sight to bring them closer to the world around them. He was first renowned as the leader of a circle of artists, many of whom were skilled draughtsmen from newspaper work prior to the advent of photo reportage and were able to make rapid, accurate drawings from live scenes or memory. He later taught at a number of revered art institutions before founding his own school. Over the course of his lifetime, he became the most influential single force affecting the development of the arts in America for a generation. His influence is still felt today.

Henri's ancestors came from hardy, pioneering families, who, after emigrating from France and the British Isles, went on to establish homesteads across Virginia, Ohio and Kentucky. Born in 1865, Henri spent several years travelling before his family settled in Nebraska and his father founded a flourishing 50,000-acre community and town that he named Cozad. Henri's formative years were true American frontier life: he rode horses over the prairies, swam and fished in the streams and roamed vast expanses of raw, unspoiled nature. Henri and his family supported his father in his day-to-day struggle to establish a growing agricultural settlement, including the large-scale manufacture of bricks and an ambitious attempt to bridge the Platte River. A hotel quickly appeared in the town, together with a school, several businesses and a local newspaper. Yet his father's leadership of the community was soon challenged by a group of ranchers, and in October 1882 a cattle herder in a drunken rage attacked the town's founder with a knife. Raising his pistol in self-defence, Henri's father shot and mortally wounded his attacker; in anticipation of mob violence and revenge, the family fled for safety.

Henri was born Robert Henry Cozad, but in the aftermath of the killing in Nebraska, and while his father was a fugitive for years before being cleared of murder, his family assumed different surnames. They moved to Atlantic City, New Jersey, establishing a more urbane life, and Robert eventually settled into his new identity, but his early pioneering years never left him. He maintained a strength and inquisitiveness throughout his life, and his practical, inventive turn of mind made him quick to find solutions in any situation. This self-reliance and dogged individualism – together with his firm and free grasp of material things – shone through in his creative work and, eventually, became the roots of his teachings that went on to inspire so many.

Henri discovered a joy in art early in life, and soon after he arrived in Nebraska he was making colourful pencil and crayon drawings of a wide array of subjects, frequently from his imagination but also often stimulated by his new, ever-changing environment. He designed adverts promoting Cozad to new arriving settlers and kept his own visual notebooks and scrapbooks. Henri completed his first painting upon arrival in Atlantic City, and he later secured a place at the Pennsylvania Academy of the Fine Arts in Philadelphia, enrolling in 1886. As he set out on his life as an artist, the world was in the midst of a profound transformation in terms of visual culture and technology. The nineteenth century saw a series of inventions that eventually culminated in photography and a host of related techniques for the industrialization of image-making. Images quickly became commoditized and detached from the bodily experience of a single human observer, and the way we looked at and perceived the world changed forever. The growing number of images humans came to be surrounded by – in magazines, on billboards and soon moving in cinemas – became an integral part of the environment, layered on top of, and increasingly obstructing, our view of reality. Henri became increasingly conscious of these changes as he developed his own practice, and his outlook began to evolve and mature, taking its own direction through his work.

During Henri's second year at the academy, a trend developed among students to visit Paris for additional training. Henri went too, to study at the Académie Julian. It was here that he was most thoroughly introduced to the academic tradition of standard conventions and prescribed methods that artists had used for centuries to reproduce realistic depictions of the world. Quickly, Henri began to feel unsettled and disenchanted. Paris at that time was a global centre of visual innovation, and its effects on mass culture were in plain sight: new pictorial devices and photographic imagery were drawing large crowds across the city, and the laboured manual mechanics Henri was being taught in class began to feel quite antiquated.

His stay in Paris happened to coincide with photography's adoption into mainstream culture: photojournalism had become commonplace, celluloid roll film was increasingly available, and in the year Henri arrived in the city, Kodak released its first easy-to-use camera to the general public. These were seismic changes in everyday visual experience, and the unfolding effects were profound, yet in Paris in particular, the technological developments preceding photography had been on show to the general public for a good number of decades prior. Starting in the 1820s, experimental study of afterimages – visions that continue to appear in the eyes after a period of exposure to the original image – led to the invention of a number of different optical devices and techniques initially intended for scientific study. Rapidly, however, the natural interest and intrigue in these new visual forms spurred on new types of popular entertainment. The diorama, a theatrical experience viewed by an audience in a specialized auditorium, originated in Paris and was one of the first of these new visual forms to reach a mass audience. Viewers moved slowly on a circular, revolving platform as a landscape painting shifted past them – different pictures were hand-painted on linen, which was left transparent in selected areas, so multi-layered panels of images could be illuminated by sunlight and coloured blinds to give the effect of an evolving scene. Another French innovation was the phenakistoscope, the first widespread animation device that created a fluent illusion of motion from static images. It consisted of a disc divided into equal segments, each containing a different figure; viewers watched as the disc turned and displayed a distinct sequence of movement. The people of Paris had seen nothing of its like before.

Diorama theatres, phenakistoscope viewers and a host of other devices – from the thaumatrope, Faraday wheel, zoetrope and kaleidoscope to the immensely popular stereoscope, with left-eye and right-eye views of the same image combined to create a single three-dimensional view – sprang up across Paris and other cities of the world throughout the mid to late 1800s. Crowds gathered and queues formed to view these celebrated sensations. It is very hard for us today to ascertain how fundamental a shift this steady release of new visual technology created in people's everyday lives. Suddenly, the actual presence of a physical object was represented in ways that felt undeniably vivid and real – and increasingly, no human hand or artistic creation was required. Photography replaced the practised painter or draughtsman in capturing scenes for posterity. The camera obscura – a wooden box with a small hole or lens to project an image onto a wall or a table – had been used by artists from as early as 500 BCE to capture reality as accurately as possible, but the photographic camera quickly made reproductive art practices almost entirely redundant. Photography was promoted and elevated by central government institutions in France, to much acclaim and widespread attention, and the repercussions on more traditional image-making methods were felt by the wider arts community. Artists realized that photography threatened the role a human being had played to date in recording moments from a single, set point of view. Vigorous new investigations began, exploring the process of perception itself and personal visual assimilation. The fields of science and art, in unison, studied the role our physical sensations and body movement play in affecting our interpretation of the world, and how this differs from the production of photographic images. Burgeoning explorations of interior experience – psychological research and attention studies, in particular – blossomed to reveal the importance of our own judgement and visual understanding.

As Henri wandered the streets of Paris and joined the queues to watch the latest picture shows, the rupture that had been created in the art world would have been evident to him. He realized that an artist could do much more than simply create mirror images of the outside world, and, as his thoughts turned increasingly to his own internal experiences and how they impacted his perceptions in turn, he was drawn to the artistic movements taking shape around him in the same city.

Rather than being discouraged by the advent of the technological reproduction of images, a growing number of artists in France, and eventually across Europe and beyond, began to feel freed instead: artistic vision was no longer limited to a correct or true rendering of the external world, meaning creative possibilities were far greater. Henri's arrival in Paris at the tail end of the nineteenth century coincided with one of most astonishing bursts of invention and experimentation in the art world, and most of it centred initially in the French art community. The artist Paul Cézanne perhaps best encapsulates many of the changes taking place at this time: his mature period overlapped with Henri's stay in France and saw him striving to capture his pure, unalloyed perceptions on the canvas. Cézanne and his contemporaries realized that quick glances and sweeping views of their field of vision did not yield anything new; much like quickly taking a photo, the rote approach to artistic creation so endemic in the established academic tradition revealed only a world of preconceptions already known through custom and familiarity. By patiently looking in a focused way and really questioning what they found for themselves in a scene, the new waves of Impressionist and Post-Impressionist artists could begin to correlate their own subjective experience with the outside world – and in the process create something entirely fresh and new. As Henri gained increasing opportunities in Paris to study the formative work of many of the early Impressionist painters, he became more aware of the interplay between our observations of the world and the active role we can play to assimilate our own conceptions: our vision is constantly holding things around ourselves, and if we don't play a part in constructing what is present, someone else will do the job for us.

When Henri arrived back in the US, he restarted his own art practice with zeal and established a regular routine of painting in the afternoons and drawing in the evenings. His enthusiasm was infectious, and he was soon offered teaching positions, firstly at the School of Design for Women in Philadelphia, and then, after his move to the art capital, at the New York School of Art. He established a weekly open house in his studio, and it quickly became well attended by a group of artists and students. He encouraged free discussion and criticism of one another's work and increasingly held the floor with his impassioned views on the merits of following the artist's life. He was very much a natural leader, and soon a group of modern American painters – known collectively as The Eight – formed around him in determination to bring art closer in touch with the realities of everyday life. In a rally against a prevalent American academic tradition that was subservient to the conventional academies in Europe, they planned a joint exhibition of their work at the Macbeth Galleries, depicting honest, unidealized views of New York's residents in its saloons, tenements, pool halls and slums, and went on to take the show to several other cities across the US. The show became a major centre of interest, first in the city and then beyond, and garnered continued press coverage celebrating its radicalism. The exhibition continues to be recognized today as having paved the way for a modern, distinctly American line of art.

With his gaining notability, Henri proceeded to found his own school. His classes were immensely popular, and a great number of distinguished pupils passed through, including Edward Hopper, who developed an exacting observation of the detached and disconnected strands of modern life. Henri taught artists to train their attention, to cultivate an ability to register their own personal sensations and to find means through which to express them. He espoused close study to form deep impressions: by keeping their eyes alert, students learned to see the influence of one thing on another and to bring a whole scene into concordance. Henri rejected most traditional methods and techniques of teaching art and asked students to find their own means of expression, championing originality over any rote repetition. Principally, he urged students to shed the feeling of being an outside spectator looking in on art and instead to 'get on the inside and press out'.

Henri watched the mainstream uptake of photography and moving pictures with particular interest while recognizing that although a photo or film is a means of taking possession of a moment, it is never full, embodied experience. With each snapshot, we feel we gain a greater sense of the world than we really do; Henri recognized this paucity of experience and strove to counteract it with attentive art practice. He would have been staggered by the progress of technological visual innovation since and the ubiquity of digital imagery, by the fabricated and interactive worlds of websites, online games and the unfolding metaverse that far eclipse the mimetic qualities of photos, TV or film. Our current evolving digital technologies, rather than stimulating powers of observation, capture, shape and control our focus, creating a patchwork of distractions that diminishes our capacity to actively pay attention to our physical environment.

Henri would task his students with creating minute, focused studies, but he also encouraged fast, free-ranging work to quickly capture a gesture or the essence of an object. He found that the stimulation this could spark was often sufficient to propel a student into enthusiastic periods of practice and develop their own means of expression. An artwork brings together a multitude of lived moments, and developing our own art practice opens a way for us to explore the full intensity of our lived experience. A personal approach of the kind Henri advocated can help train our attention and widen our perspective, but is this enough in today's image-saturated consumer culture? What relevant lessons can we take from Henri to help free our own perceptions and loosen the grip digital distractions have on our worldview?

THE WHOLE MIND ON A SINGLE POINT

Posthumously, Henri's philosophical musings and practical advice from his art classes, letters, articles and notes were collected by a former pupil, Margery Ryerson, and published a century ago as *The Art Spirit*. The book remains in print today. Drawing upon Henri's accumulated output across his lifetime, the text follows no logical sequence and is by no means a systematic handbook; instead, it allies with Henri's distrust of too rigid a code of rules. 'The opinions,' he noted, 'are presented more as paintings are hung on the wall, to be looked at at will and taken as rough sketches for what they are worth.' The book was immediately successful, and it found its way into the hands of a large number of burgeoning artists, one of whom has since progressed to become one of the most celebrated of creative auteurs in America today: David Lynch.

Throughout his career as a filmmaker, painter, visual artist, musician and writer, Lynch has continually described the moment his mentor Bushnell Keeler passed him a copy of *The Art Spirit* as the inception point in his life as an artist. Leafing through the pages in his youth, he was buoyed by the thought that he need not follow any established school, method or creative norms, and indeed Lynch follows his own instincts over anything else, informed as much by his own memories or dreams as he is by any external influences. If there were to be one Western modern-day artist that perhaps best demonstrates the power an individual has to make sense of the world today, it is David Lynch. His films, paintings and assorted other creative outputs across a wide array of physical and digital mediums have a distinctly tangible quality and original vision: nothing else is quite like them, and the notion of something being 'Lynchian' has come to denote anything that coordinates more surreal, subjective imagery with the mundane and everyday.

Just like Henri, Lynch also started his own formal art education as a painter at the Pennsylvania Academy of the Fine Arts in Philadelphia. It was here that an epiphany struck him that would eventually culminate in his production of some of the most innovative films to date, including *Eraserhead* (1977), *Blue Velvet* (1986) and *Mulholland Drive* (2001), and the TV series *Twin Peaks* (1990–1; 2017). Lynch recounts that he had no particular interest in motion pictures as a medium at the time, and one day was making a four-foot-square painting. As he sat back to look at his work, he heard a wind that caused him to picture the paint becoming animated. He decided to make his own film, but not in the conventional sense – he set out from the start to produce a 'moving painting'. His resulting first short film won a competition at the school, together with a prize of $1,000 that allowed Lynch to purchase his own camera. He moved to a large space in the Philadelphia suburbs to create other films and was eventually awarded a place at the American Film Institute in Los Angeles.

This sense of a 'wind' – of a hidden, invisible force propelling events in his films or paintings – has never left Lynch's creative efforts. The lack of a clear, narrative form in *Twin Peaks*, for example, or the rejection of fixed pictorial codes in his artwork focuses attention on other indistinguishable or irrepressible forces. Lynch's work reflects back his own creative process and the raw materials of internal experience that he has worked through to arrive at new thoughts and directions of will. This moving wind, this personal exertion of creative intent, underpins all of Lynch's output and equally runs as a theme throughout Henri's *The Art Spirit*. This kind of unique artistic force is what we are at a serious risk of losing in the increasingly manufactured visual realms of our everyday lives, as well as in our growing immersion in digital experiences.

The first attempts to establish measurable norms of perceptive attention were made in the 1850s by the German experimental psychologist Gustav Fechner, whose early work involved a study of retinal afterimages. Fechner's eyes were so seriously injured after gazing at the Sun through coloured glasses that he had to retire to a room painted entirely black. It was during this enforced visual hiatus that he resolved to find a method to examine the relation between our interior sensory experience and events in the outside world. Fechner established measurable units of sensation and correlated them directly with human sight, taste, touch and smell, setting out a scale of varying intensities of sensory exposure. He published a mathematical equation, Fechner's Law, which for the first time quantified human subjective experience and proved that our personal impressions do not always match with reality; further, there are clear, distinguishable thresholds to human attention.

Wilhelm Wundt, the first person to distinguish psychology as its own, distinct branch of science, carried on Fechner's work by establishing in 1879 the world's first psychological laboratory at the University of Leipzig, complete with a finely calibrated suite of apparatus to study human beings exposed to an assortment of artificially produced stimuli. As his investigations advanced, Wundt identified that we rely on 'selective attention' to produce a unity of consciousness and perception in day-to-day life. To ensure the clarity we need when we give something our attentive focus, many of our sensory, motor and mental processes in other areas are inhibited. This process quite typically happens outside of our personal control. The discovery that our attention increases the force of some sensations while at the same time weakening or eradicating the impression of others was a monumental finding, and it triggered a cascade of further attention studies globally.

When moving pictures arrived in cinemas, they marked a distinct break from the historical forms of popular entertainment. Our gaze is fully arrested by a steady flux of moving images, and we largely lose control of our perceptions when we watch a movie, TV episode or online video. To look away is to interrupt the viewing process, and as we continue to watch, the visual scenes primarily take over our sight and sound, body movement and apprehension or memory of what happens next. Unless we make a concerted effort to critique what we see, our responses are rarely internally motivated and by no means spontaneous – we are instead led by the delivery of images on display. The immersion we experience can of course be highly enjoyable and stimulating, offering heady new visions and unexpected outlooks, but these are not of our own control or making.

Charles Féré and Alfred Binet, French contemporaries of Wundt, also explored the dynamics of paying focused attention and found it to be 'a concentration of the whole mind on a single point, resulting in the intensification of the perception of this point and producing all around it a zone of anaesthesia'. Ongoing tests on human subjects in the late nineteenth century continued to elaborate on new, more systematic ways to manage our attention, and it became clear that the more determined, habitual or repetitive our perceptual responses, the less autonomy and personal freedom we have. When our attention is stolen, it really is taken from us, and we lose out not only on the opportunity to deploy it in another way of our choosing but also on our awareness of other events around us.

Today, moving pictures are delivered to us via our devices along with computer-generated imagery and web-design visuals. Every website or app is made up of a complex interplay of visual prompts – underlying code works through untold numbers of sequential operations to display backgrounds, banners, buttons and tools – and the intricate display of pixels lighting our screens changes imperceptibly in real time. Photos and videos are spliced among the sophisticated visual environments that we encounter on our devices in varieties and volumes that we have never consumed before, and at levels which can cause us to reach saturation point. We see the smooth, polished end result but are most often entirely unaware of the working visual mechanics that make our digital experiences possible in the first place. Digital technology has indoctrinated us in new visual codes and grammars of seeing, altering our notions of what is worth looking at, and has changed our relationship with the world around us. To keep pace with the fast, complex visual worlds created on our screens, digital devices require an almost total state of undivided attention from us.

There is a close parallel between our digital lives today and the immersion we find in the cinema or an episode of TV drama, but there is a distinct, important difference. The steady stream of digital content that we consume online amalgamates to form a whole experience; akin to the way in which the sequence of photos in a moving picture coalesces as a sense of motion for us, the assortment of digital imagery we encounter daily accumulates over time to create an entirely new personal reality. While watching a film or a TV show is often an escape or an opportunity to unwind, the time we spend on digital devices today engaged in other activities is steadily taking over the largest portions of our waking hours, particularly our most potently productive moments, and represents not so much a momentary reprieve from the rest of our lives as the defining activity of modern life itself.

As we increasingly accommodate computer operations within our lives, we face a very real and serious challenge to our personal autonomy and creativity. The quantitative study of human attention begun by Fechner and Wundt continues to this day, but most rigorously now by digital technology and media companies. Analytics is used to track and measure people's behaviour on most websites and apps, and even small changes in design are often placed through rounds of split or multivariate testing. By assimilating large quantities of results across a whole pool of visitors to a site, companies can access statistically significant data sets that they can use to robustly predict how people are most likely to respond on a page. Colours are changed and buttons or menu options moved in ways proven to determine human decision-making. 'Call-to-action' buttons are often the most prominent, with bright contrasting colours used to spur us to 'sign up' or 'buy now'. E-commerce sites often use so-called FOMO (fear of missing out) techniques with countdown timers or limited stock availability displayed to create a sense of urgency. If visitor numbers to a site are insufficient to offer statistically significant results, companies often arrange instead for a panel of users to be monitored while they use a site or app, and design decisions are taken accordingly. Although we may feel we are making our own decisions online, other forces are usually behind what we see on screen. If we allow the flow of digital stimuli to ceaselessly prompt us to act on reflex and we do not give ourselves the space and time we need to assimilate our own perceptions, we risk disintegrating our everyday experience, moving from curiosity and independence of thought to a more conditioned, automatic way of living.

When David Lynch's mystery serial drama *Twin Peaks*, cocreated with writer Mark Frost, premiered in 1990 it soon gained a cult following and critical acclaim, and has since become viewed as a landmark in TV drama. It centres on a fictional town of the same name, in the northeast corner of Washington State, and on the murder of a homecoming queen, Laura Palmer. Most TV shows at the time were filmed in studios according to standard soundstage production conventions; in contrast *Twin Peaks*, set in the Pacific Northwest of Lynch's own childhood, had a refreshingly strong sense of place. Lynch's direction portrays events almost in real time, fixing them within the bristling Douglas firs of the surrounding woods, the rising morning fog from the streams, and other resonant memories from his youth. A number of particular motifs are repeated throughout – wind passes through shots of wild, indistinguishable trees, and often the camera hovers ominously at the same crossroads on the freeway through town, where the traffic lights, supported by overhead cables, sway in the breeze: Lynch's creative presence, as ever, is behind everything that appears on screen.

The French philosopher Henri Bergson published his influential book *Matter and Memory* right at the end of the nineteenth century, once photography and cinema were established, and the conclusions he comes to are striking. Bergson insists that every perception we have, however fleeting, has the potential to be truly made our own through the active assimilation of our response to it. He argues that our attention actually operates in two opposite directions – outwards, in direct response to external sensations and events, but also inwards, in reaction to and in comparison with our past experiences. Bergson describes the meeting point of these two quite different reaches of our personal, mental energies as 'a zone of indetermination', and this seems to be exactly where Lynch and other successful artists reside when they complete their most creative work.

In order to develop and improve our lives, to become more resourceful, for example, or arrive at a deeper understanding of what we wish to do with our time, we are obliged to work through points of resistance and opposition; in active reflection on possible solutions and then our adoption of our chosen courses of action, we gain new insight. It is in this kind of direct interaction with the world – a progression through rhythms of energetic activity and contemplative repose to find different ways forward – that art and any creative work truly flourish. The resulting artefacts – whatever their medium – stand as testimony of the work undertaken, but the true value lies in the process of creation itself. Art, regardless of its form, is for Henri and Lynch, a heightened vitality of experience, a connection between our inner selves and our practical, external realities, a mode of being active and alert in the world.

Life would be several degrees flatter without the top-level creative output that continues to spring from the film and TV industries today, and digital technology too can fill our lives with fascinating new perspectives and provocations. But so much of our digital lives is pre-assembled, and we also need to create our own ways of being to untangle what we find in the world and to reframe it in ways that makes better sense for us personally.

Creatives of the calibre of David Lynch, whether filmmakers, coders or digital entrepreneurs, understand the transportative power of the final form of their productions, but if we get too swept away in their final results, we can lose out on our own creative potency. If we overconsume content and experiences created for us and progressively give up on forming our own worlds, life can become a mere flux of brief excitations that passes us by with no deep or lasting personal meaning: a phenomenon that many would agree perfectly encapsulates many of our digital interactions today.

But the lessons set out by Henri and Lynch, and a catalogue of other creatives from the past and living today, also offer clear and tested techniques that we can use to heighten our own perceptions and ultimately sharpen our consciousness day to day; and these can as readily be applied to our digital lives as to our experiences of nature and the physical world. Each of us has the power to develop our creative skills so that we can more actively shape our personal experiences, and in so doing carve out more enjoyable, fulfilling lives.

CREATE YOUR OWN VISION

In 2021, the Metropolitan Museum of Art in New York held a retrospective of the painter Alice Neel (1900–1984). Neel had studied at the Philadelphia School of Design for Women, where Henri had taught for a time, leaving a strong legacy, and throughout her career as a struggling artist, unknown until late in life, Neel had held Henri's assertion of the primacy of human experience central to her creative efforts. 'For me, people come first,' she declared to a journalist in 1950. 'I have tried to assert the dignity and eternal importance of the human being.' It is in Neel's exquisite pictures of real people, which affirm their subjects' agency and autonomy in the face of technology and consumerism, that Henri's philosophy has perhaps most clearly been articulated. Neel evolved her own distinctive mode of direct painting as drawing; she learned to attend to her sitters ever so intently, and deliberately began to leave more traces of her process on the canvas. That process can offer insight on how to control your attention and begin to create your own distinctly personal vision of experience.

Start drawing again

Alice Neel was a great conversationalist and storyteller, but when she painted, she stopped talking. Neel learned most about her sitters not by what they told her, but by the tiny, almost imperceptible body shifts, checks and glances they made as they sat there trying, unsuccessfully, to be still. She discovered a person progressively, line by line, with each mark on the canvas recording what she had seen, the next one following up to double-check its accuracy. Her ways of working as the hours progressed were intense, and she professed to sometimes feeling a profound weariness once she had completed a sitting, but through the process she arrived at a way to question what she saw far more probingly and revealingly.

A real sense of personality and individuality exudes from Neel's portraits, and there is a distinct reason why. Whereas a photo records a moment in an instant, the brush strokes and dabs of colour on the canvas show Neel's direct experience of close observation over a prolonged period of time and record in simultaneity a high quantity of intently focused moments. Any section of the canvas is the result of Neel's active interrogation to find a certain characteristic that epitomizes a sitter, receiving information and measuring things carefully as she put them down. Neel does not hide her working methods, leaving clear evidence of her overlapping assays in her brush strokes. She pays active attention to someone simply through setting down what she sees.

You too have access to this skill, no matter what your level of art training. Drawing is the most powerful and intuitive means you have to see something properly, and in this most sensitive of negotiations between your hand, eye and mind, you gain an intensity of experience that can make you feel remarkably alive.

The predilection most of us have today for taking photos stems from a natural urge to explore and record our world in more detail. But drawing offers a far deeper experience: whereas photography stops time, the act of drawing flows right on with it and takes you far closer to whatever it is that you find interesting. Most of us give up any personal art practice before we reach adulthood, so when you do pick up a pencil and paper again, there is work to be done to train your eyes to notice and your hand to more capably record what you see. However, the benefits of drawing can develop quickly, and it need not require too much of an investment of time, particularly at first. Five or ten minutes a day is more than enough: so long as you try to put aside that time daily, you will find your abilities soon advance.

Henri's advice was that the best way to learn how to draw is simply by getting started. He encouraged drawing from life to develop observation skills. Everyday objects that have simple, recognizable forms are a great starting point, but it is important that you keep motivated and engaged, so prioritize anything that piques your interest. Henri would choose objects with different textures or patterns, such as fabric, wood or metal, and whenever he could he went outside to observe the diverse assortment of textures, shapes and forms found in nature. He challenged his students with increasingly complex subjects to improve their drawing skills, and you can do the same for yourself as you progress.

There are also a few freeform techniques that can quicken your practice. One of Henri's preferred approaches was to furiously record what you see in a short period of time. By scribbling and meshing your lines on top of one another, you can let a form take its own rough shape and progressively get a clearer sense of a scene as a whole. Alternatively, he would also encourage a student to slow right down and work calmly and methodically over a more extended timespan, zeroing in on close details. He found that when you gradually assimilate the features together into a larger image, the excitement and sense of personal accomplishment this brings is often enough to propel you into a more regular practice.

As you become more proficient, you will begin to spot that every mark you make while your eyes are on the page is produced from memory in the interplay between mind and hand. One of Henri's favoured teaching methods was to introduce a model to a class for a short period of time while students made focused sketch studies. He would then ask students to complete a painting from memory once the model was gone. To improve your ability to form your own impressions and remember them later, you can also give this a go by simply sitting with your back to whatever you are drawing: it becomes more of a strain to take another look, so each time you do, you take far more in and quickly learn to improve your powers of observation.

One artist that Henri most revered was Cézanne, in particular the intense attention that he devoted to the subjects of his paintings – and it is another method you can use to get closer to anything that you study. Cézanne tried to dwell as much as he could within his own attention, in search of an authentic vision to penetrate to the very essence of objects beneath the order imposed by our everyday comprehension and habitual patterns of observing the world. By studying a scene with extended levels of focus and unprecedented intensity, he found that he needed to continue looking until he experienced a perceptual decomposition: when he noticed a distinct loss and breakdown of noticeable form he could better understand how things truly related to one another. He described his work proudly as a 'recording machine' or a 'sensitized plate', but what he found himself increasingly capturing was his own internal experience in direct response to the outside world.

Cézanne was practising mindful observation, and you can do the same. Take time to really slow down when you draw, and take in the subject of your drawing with a new level of curiosity. Observe it from different angles, noticing its unique characteristics, and look for new and interesting ways to represent it in your work. The more you do this when you draw, the more you will realize how much you miss when you normally see. With practice, you will become better at noticing details and getting closer to the workings of things and your surroundings, and this can benefit multiple areas of your life.

Most of all, trust your own internal experience and attempt to convey your own unique vision of an object, person or scene, rather than aiming simply to reproduce what is in front of you.

TAKE ACTION

- **Try a quick-fire sketch:** Set aside five minutes and try to draw everything you can see in front of you.
- **Methodically draw a scene:** Commit one hour to moving your attention slowly from feature to feature of a scene or subject and diligently setting down as much detail as you can.
- **Draw from memory:** Sit with your back to what you are sketching. Try to look only sparingly at your subject and instead rely on your memory.
- **Adopt a daily art practice:** Commit to drawing what you see for five minutes a day for one month and notice any improvement in your technical ability and creativity.

Take control of your digital experiences

Shift your attention

There are other lessons you can take from the drawing process when you find yourself at a screen. To reduce the propensity of deliberately designed elements on the screen to steal your focus, try to keep in mind the step-by-step process an artist such as Alice Neel followed to more comprehensively take in something. Particularly when you visit a new website or test an app for the first time, take the time to stop, and in a process of small-scale shifts of your attention, move your focus progressively across the homepage or homescreen – or, if you plan to spend quite a bit of time there, familiarize yourself with the structure of the site or app. As you do this, try to look analytically: deliberately turn your focus from one thing to another and try to connect all of the key elements that you see. Question why buttons and menu options are placed where you find them and try to pinpoint the role each part of the page is designed to play in order to sustain your attention.

By establishing the habit of critiquing what you find on the screen – and of trying to get to the bottom of how digital experiences control your attention – you can get a better handle on the different modes of automatic experience it can be so easy to fall into online. Doing so will help you fight back against distractions and stay more aware and focused.

TAKE ACTION

- **Slow your attention:** When next using a website or an app move your focus slowly across the whole page to get a sense of how the different buttons, menu options and demands on your attention relate to each other.
- **Be analytical:** Choose a site or app that you regularly use and take the time to ascertain the chief motives behind the main elements of its design layout.
- **Watch for when your attention is stolen online:** Backtrack to find what first distracted you.

Create your own digital life

There is a distinct difference in how your attention performs when you create your own experiences online in comparison to simply consuming what you come across. When you begin inputting creatively into anything you do online, like an artist, you take control of the process, sifting through the content that you find and transforming it into something personal to you. Whether it be writing a blog post, building a playlist or coding the next iteration of a website, the generative series of actions you work through when you create online has an altogether different quality to simply following directions on-screen.

TAKE ACTION

- **Monitor your passivity:** For a week, be alert to any online habits you might have developed or sites and apps that you visit where you only consume and never create. Reflect on whether it is in your interest to continue using these.
- **Be more digitally creative:** Take some time to consider what you most enjoy doing online and consider whether you can make that time more creative.
- **Be ready to stop:** When you become aware of times that digital technology is taking over your thinking for an extended duration, stop using it.

Spending time drifting along online is not unlike browsing between TV channels, and it pays to watch how much you do it. Keep an eye out for when you find yourself simply selecting from options rather than inputting new searches and stop to consider if it is the most productive use of your time. Digital technology can offer as much creative potential as it does wasteful personal distraction, so pay attention to what you enjoy doing most online and try to see if there is room for you to play a more active, creative part in the process – if there isn't, it might not be worth your while. The more you simply consume, the less opportunity you have to better understand your own existence and personal desires. So much that is displayed online in advertising or search and social feeds promises the opportunity to transform yourself, but your real-life experience in the moment is inevitably deferred.

Try to view your mobile, tablet or computer as a tool only, an immensely powerful suite of apps that you have at your disposal to create something new. In other words, what can the apps do for you? Stop technology making decisions for you: create personal gaps and step offline whenever you notice that digital experiences are being delivered to you rather than created by you. This is easier said than done, and the tech giants are well practised in retaining your attention, but being aware of and resisting the effects of digital operations on your thinking can help you regain an active space of mental engagement and perceptual control, both on- and offline.

Reignite creative experience

In a review written by Robert Henri, he recalls an artist painting 'like a man going over the hill singing' and in this one memorable phrase consolidates his thoughts on the fullness of life, which he insists it is possible to experience when you set out on your own path to create. When you apply yourself to a creative project, you forge your own rounded experience and exercise your senses. There is novelty in the actions you take, and in the range and depths of insight that you can muster, and you can open yourself up to new depths of emotion and human feeling. For Henri, the experience of thirty minutes spent at this kind of spirited work was worth more than a whole week lived below par.

Artists typically continue their work until the very end of their life (David Lynch, at the time of writing, is in his late seventies and is as prolific as he always has been), and there is a good reason why. An art practice, more than anything else, provides for a vigorous rhythm of life experience, full of variety and complexity, and with a wide deployment of personal capabilities. In the continuous, non-routine work and positive wranglings with the outside world that creative work demands, your attitudes and outlook progressively develop.

Take yourself back to when you last painted, drew or made art or crafts. It may be decades ago now. Try to remember the texture of the paper, the smell of paint or glue, the feel of a sketching pencil, and dwell within the feelings that you experienced. Where else do you experience those sensations today? Expand your thoughts to your working life or school and university projects, and try to pinpoint the times when you really feel you most came on as a person. Henri saw no distinction between any mode of creativity and neither should you: think of creative digital work as well as physical objects you might have made. What have you been most proud of creating in life? What work has given you the deepest sense of personal satisfaction? And are there any special things you would like to create and pass on to your loved ones after you are gone?

Any real, creative work starts with your own impulse, but the first tinglings of inspiration can often be brief: it is only when your thoughts are refined through deeper exploration that a real purpose or plan truly takes shape. Do not worry if you do not have a creative focus right now. Simply watch out for any new ideas surfacing, and when they do, give them time to breathe by investigating them more fully with notes or sketches. Give any new possible creative project the time it needs to gestate, and get started as soon as you feel ready. A creative project's full form and purpose often only materializes when you begin working on it.

TAKE ACTION

- **Recall heightened life experiences:** Set aside some dedicated quiet time with pen and paper to properly consider the moments in your past that you have found most rewarding.
- **Dwell again in a creative moment:** Reflect on one of your top creative experiences and consider whether it is something you get much opportunity to experience today. If not, think of ways in which you could.
- **Find a new catalyst:** Deliberately search for new, creative projects to pursue.

Chapter 8

Craft

THE SPACE TRAVELLER

George Daniels' Space Traveller pocket-watch is one of the most impressive handmade objects ever crafted. Inspired by the NASA Apollo missions, it shows both our conventional 24-hour solar time and sidereal time, measured by the Earth's rotation relative to the stars. It's held entirely in a slim gold case, with engine-turned displays intricately engraved by hand; a calendar, Moon phase and equation of time are shown on the face. The entire piece is self-mechanized by means of a sophisticated movement, complemented by one of the most important horological innovations in centuries: the coaxial escapement, a mechanism conceived by Daniels after waking from a dream in 1974.

The Space Traveller was one of the first mechanical watches to be made in its entirety by a single person in over 400 years. (Only six others had been completed in this period, all of them by Daniels, who made twenty-three pocket-watches in his lifetime.) Since the seventeenth century, watches had been produced by communities of craftspeople divided into a wide assortment of thirty-four distinct trades – watch cases alone were the work of four specialists, for instance. By the twentieth century, industrialization led to the majority of these crafts becoming redundant, with watchmakers increasingly assigned to routine tasks such as regulating, repairing and servicing. Daniels single-handedly re-established the importance of the individual watchmaker and the handmade watch. From the case, dials and hands to screws, jewels and wheels, he learned to make every part himself.

Mastering thirty-four individual crafts was a complex and daunting task. When he made his first handmade watch, completed in 1969 after 3,000 hours of work, Daniels had no formal training – institutions offering education in these areas and at this level had all closed by the 1960s. Nor did he use any computerized machinery. He relied on his practical knowledge and use of traditional tools to ensure the quality and precise fit of each component, and the simple, natural finish he accomplished is remarkable. Minute, interlocking components move together, each triggering the next in a train of actions. There is a fixed, precise orderliness as the individual functions of wheels, cogs and screws coalesce into a unity. It is spellbinding to see his watches literally spring to life.

It's no coincidence that George Daniels started his career as a watch repairer, responsible for fixing whatever came into the shop: his early days were spent surrounded by piles of worn or damaged watches and parts. Repair work forced him to notice details and work through a chain of causes for any problems he came across, and he learned to read the distinctive properties of a watch's components and the materials he was working with. He progressed to opening his own watch-repair business and took on more challenging work restoring antique pieces. He also started a lifelong habit of keeping a record of his horological work, filling a ledger with drawings and comments and photographing all of the components. Opportunities opened up for him to work on celebrated watches that were hundreds of years old.

A craft works through time. Experience passed from generation to generation allows increasing levels of sophistication as a culture evolves. Craft apprenticeships and fraternities in the past provided opportunities to grasp the accumulation of knowledge in a trade. There was a healthy yet intense spirit of emulation and rivalry – not only between contemporaries, but also with predecessors: craftspeople saw their personal development as part of a chapter in a long, unbroken historical line. Lacking an apprenticeship, Daniels learned by studying the watches he worked on, and bit by bit, he began to understand the progression of innovations made to the mechanical watch over the centuries – an arc of improvement that rested on a number of notable masters, including Abraham-Louis Breguet, the most acclaimed and admired of watchmakers.

Breguet had assembled a team of a hundred workmen in the mid-1700s to interpret and manufacture his watch designs. One of his earliest innovations was the self-winding watch, which reset automatically in a wearer's pocket from the movement of their walking. This eventually led to the design of the most famous watch ever created: the Marie-Antoinette, made for the Queen of France and completed after Breguet's death by his son in 1827. Considered one of the most complicated pocket-watches in the world, it features a perpetual calendar and thermometer, and the self-winding movement comprises 823 parts and components. George Daniels was one of the last people for decades to inspect and hold the watch before it vanished in an infamous heist while on display in Jerusalem in 1983, only to resurface in a box of stolen goods in 2006. It's valued at over $50 million today.

Daniels became obsessively focused on Breguet and, upon discovering no clear study had been undertaken of his work, decided to take on the project. The proprietor of the Breguet brand in Paris allowed Daniels access to the archives, including books from the 1700s containing intricate construction details. Daniels meticulously analysed and catalogued Breguet's watches, gaining an unrivalled insight into a centuries-old manufacturing process.

His study of Breguet took fifteen years and concluded with the publication of his book *The Art of Breguet*. By that time, Breguet's watches were so valuable that collectors withdrew into anonymity, fearing for their security. Daniels was the last to get close and scrutinized each piece, marvelling at the handmade elegance of Breguet's work. There are 109 line drawings by Daniels in his Breguet book, each one investigating and interpreting complicated workings and innovations. He was particularly impressed by Breguet's invention of new mechanical principles in the construction of a watch, many of which are still used today. Breguet elevated the craft of watchmaking to an art form that was the very antithesis of a production line of uniform pieces.

✧ ✧ ✧

When Daniels began work on his first watch in 1968, he was missing the hands-on guidance of an instructor. Crafts have historically survived in closely held, local traditions because of their need for personal contact and learning by example – practical knowledge can be enormously hard to translate into words. Daniels had to learn the complicated repertoire of watchmaking procedures himself, the thousands of minuscule manipulations that in sum become a practice. His close study of Breguet's techniques was as close to mentorship from a working practitioner as he was going to find in the 1960s. The rest had to come from the physical experience of living through tasks repeatedly, progressing from halting first attempts to quick, fluid expertise.

There were countless challenges to overcome. Components had to be fashioned precisely from metals and other materials, often with several operations required. Mechanical watches are made from incredibly small parts, and even tiny changes in dimensions or angles can have disproportionately large effects on the performance of the watch as a whole. If he spotted an issue, Daniels would remake a component, subtly assessing the qualities needed to find a more elegant solution. He had to think with his fingers, grasping and toying with parts to master techniques, finessing his fine motor control. It was a physical intelligence that grew over time. Being self-taught began to open up new possibilities.

Daniels' watches were the result of a skilful manipulation of everyday tools: a somewhat primitive watchmaker's lathe, pliers, wire cutters, screwdrivers, hammers and saws. Over time he invested in more sophisticated machinery and precision measuring equipment, but all of it was hand-operated. Daniels would often begin any more complicated work with a drawing, at a scale of up to fifty times actual size. He would cut out sketches of individual components with scissors, pin them to a drawing board and move them in slow motion to predict how they would work in unison. To fix something quickly, he would pen designs on a piece of paper to help reason through a mechanical situation. But most often

Daniels relied on seeing his work progress in front of him or visualizing it in his mind in three dimensions; rather than planning too much in advance, he preferred to keep his options open and introduce features as he went. He tested each finished watch for four months in various positions and at different temperatures – including in an oven and a freezer – to ensure it kept time to within half a second a day. Each watch was expected to run for 300 to 400 years.

Daniels realized that the core mechanics of the watch had not changed in centuries. The Swiss watch industry had continued adding complications to watches, but there had been no substantial innovations. He began turning his thoughts towards making his own contribution. The world's first quartz watch, which used an electronic oscillator to keep time, was released by Japanese watchmaker Seiko in 1969, and Daniels foresaw it coming to predominance. By the 1980s, the advent of solid-state digital electronics allowed battery-powered quartz watches to be made compactly and inexpensively. But the mechanical watch had historic and aesthetic qualities Daniels did not want to see disappear, and he was convinced there was room for it to live on. His attention soon turned to the escapement, the beating heart of a mechanical watch that had remained unchanged since Thomas Mudge invented the 'lever escapement' in 1754. The power created when we wind a watch is held in a mainspring, the release of which is controlled by the rhythmical ticks of the escapement. Ticking 600,000 times a day, a watch escapement's tiny components must be completely reliable for accurate timekeeping. Oil is smeared on the escape wheel teeth to ensure smooth running, but as this dries, flakes or evaporates over time, a watch eventually loses accuracy. Breguet himself had energetically attempted to fix the issue, investing twenty years in experiments before finally giving up.

Daniels took on the challenge himself and embarked on a project that would dominate his thoughts for the next twenty-five years. He filled his days making watch movements with experimental escapements, carefully testing different designs. The fruits of his labours all converged at 3 a.m. one summer morning in 1974, when Daniels awoke suddenly with a full visualization of what he wanted to do. He proceeded to quickly sketch it out, exploring his idea from various angles, buoyed with increasing certainty that he had found an answer. He had invented the 'coaxial escapement', the first escapement to provide force in both directions, self-start after winding and virtually eliminate all sliding friction. Daniels proceeded to file for a patent and was soon making multiple trips to Switzerland to present his innovation to major watch brands. Omega eventually decided to industrialize the coaxial escapement: it remains today the only, and superior, alternative to the lever escapement and has featured in over a million premium-quality watches produced to date.

Daniels found his time working with large watch manufacturers eye-opening. White-coated technicians worked at their computers using the latest computer-aided design (CAD) software. Omega's adoption of the coaxial escapement could only be confirmed after a prolonged study of computer designs and simulations. None of the hundreds of employees utilized hand tools or got close to the work in any way like Daniels. It became clear that a solitary workman at his bench had surpassed vast teams of engineers armed with the very latest computing and manufacturing technology. Daniels' physical, lived experience of watchmaking had given him an unparalleled understanding of the mechanics involved. Omega's technicians could zoom into exquisite detail and model improbably complex designs, but they lacked the hands-on know-how to coherently connect it all as a whole. Whereas Daniels could rely on instinct and hunches, able to visualize the entirety of a watch's workings in his mind's eye, Omega's team had to dissect his designs in meticulous detail, loading measurements and statistics into computer models to make sense of it all.

The danger with using software to design a watch is that a computer program establishes its own pre-set styles and procedures to work within, and it's difficult for a designer to remain alert to the limitations software can impose without their own practical knowledge to fall back on. Daniels handled real-world materials, either in his palms or via tools he directly controlled, and had total creative freedom to keep inventing. His long practice and ongoing submission to the physical realities of his materials had culminated in an unrivalled mastery and autonomy.

Omega's software engineers, on the other hand, were constrained to working within quantifiable parameters in a preordained system and experienced the essential physics of watchmaking at one remove, via their computer screens.

Computers may allow easily achieved perfection, smoothing out the edges for us, but when it comes to craft, the small traces of obvious handwork add to the beauty of an object. If one looks closely enough at the Space Traveller, it is possible to distinguish the faint lines and etches that Daniels cut himself. It makes one marvel all the more at his artistry. Crafting a handmade object carries risk at every turn: at any point it could be ruined. But it's the unique human decisions taken every moment that ensure the uniqueness of handmade objects and connect us with the individual lives of their makers.

Craft is a powerful way to transmute our thoughts into physical things as we organize our experiences and make decisions in the real world. When the work is done, the fruits of our efforts stand there unambiguously. And through the physical working process we can come to a deeper understanding of ourselves, our circumstances and the world around us. In the ability to make and look after our own things, there is self-reliance and a vindication of our own worth. Daniels' autodidactism propelled his life in a way that was anything but routine: his mastering of a craft was the very essence of self-transformation, an everyday process of learning and becoming.

Yet the physical difficulties he wrestled with to salvage a vanishing craft highlight how much our working lives have changed since. We simply don't handle or physically interact with things like we used to. When we work at our computers, our multi-sensory experience of the world flattens: we forgo the three-dimensional nuances of body movement for the complexities of pixels moved around on the screen. Sitting stationary, we primarily rely on our eyes as we scan images and information streams. The vast majority of body motion is highly prescribed: the constraints of a typical workstation today limit our bodily movements to the small area of a keyboard for typing and the confined actions of clicking and scrolling with a mouse. It's very easy to forget just how strange this is. Whenever we work online, we practically cease moving and depart our bodies almost entirely.

Watchmakers today use a Swiss-made CAD tool called Tell Watch for the complete design process, from research and development to final production. A 3D animation visualizes each step of the assembly process, even down to the tightening of the smallest screws. The time it takes to design and manufacture a mechanical watch has been shortened inexorably, and the commercial efficiencies gained naturally drive companies to restructure their operations accordingly. This software is relied upon today by Montblanc, Patek Philippe, Franck Muller, Chopard and many other premium watchmaking brands.

When watchmaking becomes a point-and-click process of assembling pre-existing parts and letting computer calculations silently work out the necessary fundamental physics, the human skill involved drops markedly. The exact understanding of each interlinking part of a watch that Daniels worked hard to gain becomes frozen in software code, and complex, extended procedures are collapsed to a simple menu option or a click of the button. Watchmakers are removed from the direct and immediate feedback on the job, the clinks and clanks when something doesn't quite fit in place.

The physical skills of George Daniels and the untold generations of craftspeople before him are being lost to posterity. The propensity for crafts and physical professions to see improvements in technique made over time and passed on from one generation to the next has diminished decisively. Does this matter? After all, we've never kept time so closely: the clock on our smartphones is accurate to within 50 milliseconds when connected to the internet. Improvements in CAD software today offer engineers unrivalled powers to design physical objects, watches included. From a technological standpoint, we've gained so much from digitization. Yet we've also lost unfathomable degrees of our physicality, and with it the grace and finesse of physical abilities that must be learned and honed over time. What is the importance of thinking with our bodies, and what do we lose out on when we stop doing so?

EMBODIED COGNITION AND SCREENISHNESS

It's fitting that George Daniels' pinnacle timepiece was named after the Apollo Moon landings, famous for their sheer audacity and reliant of course on very precise timing. While humans could not have landed on the Moon without the support of the Apollo Guidance Computers on board the command and lunar modules, the astronauts each had astoundingly dynamic personal skills, with a combination of flying abilities and engineering knowledge that would be impossible to find today. These top-level fighter pilots used to the cut and thrust of 1960s jet planes were armed with a comprehensive understanding of advanced physics and the mathematical permutations underpinning their flight-path; they also had a detailed grasp of the mechanical build of their spacecraft, down to the smallest of details. When the Apollo 13 mission went spectacularly wrong and a failed oxygen tank caused a cascade of life-threatening errors, the astronauts were able to deploy staggeringly brilliant fixes in ways only possible as a result of their intricate understanding of the technologies under their control. These moonshots happened at a rare moment in our past, when our full, physically embodied working lives were still intact but computers were just beginning to support us in new, profound ways.

At that time, the way we think was understood much differently than it is today, with the brain seen very much as a computational device, wholly separate from the body. Since the seventeenth century and the French philosopher René Descartes' work, there was a widely held belief that the mind and body were fundamentally separate in nature, with any physical sensations having to be interpreted in the mind before we could make sense of them. It was only in the 1990s that the notion of embodied cognition – that we don't just think with our brains but via our entire bodily experience – began to gain prominence and has flourished since. Cognitive science today holds that our motor system, perceptions and bodily interactions with our wider environment are as crucial to our fundamental experience of the world as is the brain itself. Interestingly, it's been in the field of AI and robotics that some of the most groundbreaking work has been done in this area. Early efforts in AI in the 1960s were naively optimistic, with predictions that machines would be capable of doing any work a human could do within twenty years. This plainly did not happen, and instead, work in robotics determined that reason-based calculations were enormously inefficient for negotiating the physical environment. It's only by mirroring embodied cognition principles that the most recent robots have been able to make pronounced leaps in capability that match more closely the ways we interact with the world around us. Yet paradoxically, just as science is making significant headway in discovering how physical action and sensory perception impact our thoughts, memory and skills, we're increasingly disconnected from our bodies.

There's a distinct reason why embodied cognition was misunderstood for so long, and equally why the profound changes to our working lives have been able to unfold without us readily recognizing their impact on us: we have a bewildering lack of mental awareness when we learn or unlearn physical skills and abilities. For any physical capacity that we gain, whether that be driving a car, mastering a sport or struggling with a DIY project, we imperceptibly get better as we practise, each time in ways that are enormously hard to pinpoint or articulate. Likewise, we often remain oblivious to the gradual decline of physical abilities until we attempt to perform the skill again, a phenomenon that could be referred to as 'physical skills blindness'.

Touch is one of the most fundamental of our senses and central to the human condition, and it's astonishing to think of the hours each day we largely abandon it at our workstations. We start our lives relying on touch to make sense of everything around us – children handle, test and prod everything they come across – and we continue to do so for the rest of our lives. Physical things are far more easily comprehensible to us. We can walk around them, pick them up and interact with them in innumerable other active, full-bodied ways. Screen technology, on the other hand, distances us from the world and the objects we find within it; anything we view or control on a screen is a representation, an image or graphic display designed to depict something that may or may not actually exist in the physical world.

When we work at our computers, our minds quickly adapt. The visual information on screen becomes our temporary reality, and our awareness of our wider surroundings dwindles to the faintest of consciousness. Our actions are led by the digital cues on display. Physical craftsmanship is altogether different. Vision remains crucial, but there's also an inescapable tactility: Daniels, for instance, would feel a watch case begin to take shape in a way he'd never have been able to plan on paper, taking moment-by-moment decisions led by the feel of a material in his hands. Scientists today claim we have as many as twenty-six senses – far more than the traditionally understood five. These include equilibrioception (our sense of balance), the vestibular system (which allows us to feel velocity) and kinaesthesia (our sense of movement). Our engagement with these senses is significantly limited when interacting with digital devices, as our physical contact is typically constricted to a mouse, keyboard, touchscreen, vibration alerts and the more recent haptic feedback integrated into smartphones. And whereas in the physical world there's an infinite range of movement, textures, pressures and temperatures – no one could say our sensory life is mundane – the variety of information we interact with at our screens, whatever its content, is mediated using the same basic controls.

Whenever an area of work or a job role is digitized, the end result is the same: real-world interactions are subsumed by the screen, and the physical skills required in a profession are superseded by reading and manipulating information streams. Architects, scientists and commodities traders, fashion designers, musicians and watchmakers: each of these seemingly different walks of life is being standardized into a curiously similar work experience. As software becomes increasingly indispensable, each job becomes progressively more sedentary, and the difference between careers lies increasingly in mere variations between software interfaces. Yes, the intellectual foundations and knowledge required for different professions remain vastly different and varied, but the *physical* day-to-day experience is largely the same. The work we undertake can have serious and dramatic physical results, but the worldly realities of what's being manipulated remain mediated underneath layers of digital abstraction. The net result is that we're able to arrive at phenomenally high levels of competence by working at a screen, but huge amounts of physical experience go missing.

The vast swathes of time we sit at our desktops cumulatively has an effect on us: we become ever more visual and less physical. Each hour at a computer is an hour of time we lose to interact with our physical surroundings. We've forgone innumerable other more active activities to make way for our digital endeavours, yet we've not felt a tangible difference. Physical skills blindness has prevented us from noticing the steady decline in our bodily abilities and the impact this has on us.

So what do we lose out on when we think less with our bodies? We can all picture a stereotypical 'bookish' person. They may have an air of refinement, but we might also imagine a frailer, less robust frame, dark circles under the eyes, reading glasses, a slight clumsiness. But what does a 'screenish' person look like? Their eyesight may also be affected, and if they don't match their screen time with exercise, so too is their physical fitness. But the prime characteristic of a 'screenish' person is more fundamental and nuanced: to be screenish is to lose a physical capability in life, a handiness. The more we work at our screens, the less able we become in other areas of our life. Conversely, the more we physically interact with the world, the higher the levels of coordination and fine-motor control we develop. One of the most visible demonstrations of this is the obvious difference between generations in our ability to fix things. Repairing the objects we're surrounded by forces us to fully comprehend them; we have to wrangle with their very workings to find a symptom and cause in order to fix them. Yet younger generations – and I include myself – are too often at a loss to ascertain why a light fixing, wall hanging or pipe has broken, much less how to mend it. We don't build things like we used to, drill holes or hammer nails: we turn our backs on all of this and face inwards to the computer.

Much of the digital work we do today requires a high degree of knowledge and skill. Vast volumes and complex iterations of data, together with fast-evolving software tools, mean no job function remains the same for long. At more advanced levels, intensive and prolonged education and training is needed. Mastering a new digital discipline involves many of the same challenges Daniels had to face in his work: confronting new situations, struggling with predefined features and rules, tackling restraints that curtail options and require reattempts. Digital work therefore has the potential to be as intellectually demanding as any physical craft. All the same, there are some fundamental changes manifesting in digital work that further threaten our capabilities.

Automation in the workplace has become a regular topic in the press, with continued debate on the extent to which jobs performed by humans will eventually be taken over by machines. Yet alarm at advanced AI taking command of almost all forms of intellectual work in the near future clouds a more pertinent and pressing issue: consideration of an intermediate phase – one which we are arguably in already – has largely been missing from public debate. We should be concerned about what is happening *right now* as our jobs are given over to robotic processes. As any job becomes increasingly automated, the person working in the role is forced to adapt to more programmed actions and behaviours: we ourselves risk becoming robots.

Deployed sensibly, automation has the potential to free us from mundane work to focus on more stimulating, complex tasks. But as machine learning has become more intelligent – and with the emergence of advanced language generation tools such as ChatGPT – sophisticated job functions until now untouched by standardized work processes are affected. AI-driven content-creation and editing, CAD tools that offer architects ever more elegant suggestions and deployments, intelligent systems that compare and contrast CT scans to diagnose cancer: all these reduce a skilled professional's responsibility to monitoring a screen or entering information into prescribed fields. The ways in which machine learning improves automatically through experience, gleaning insight from data and identifying patterns to make decisions, means that it is progressively surpassing humans' performance in various tasks. We're obliged to adapt our work, conduct and skills to the capabilities of the computers we increasingly depend on, and a job begins to feel gradually more stultifying. Not only has physical motion and interaction with the real work been replaced by static attention at a screen, now even non-physical, intellectual focus has been simplified and regulated.

In the 1930s, a typical craft apprenticeship was five, six or seven years; today it's normally three. Professions heavily laden with automated software are even simpler still. The training required for a large number of desk-bound jobs nowadays is very brief – sometimes barely days. The rush to adopt new software risks narrowing our perspective and degrading our abilities as the most inspired and meaningful work gets lost in the process. Software and automated workflows allow the potential for higher workloads and more advanced and complex end results. At times, this can elevate our work, freeing us to focus on final flourishes or new ways forward, but the programming behind any software is sequential and inevitably routine-led, and such a closed system constrains creativity. Our skills, and in turn, the things we create and build – from watches to skyscrapers – become standardized and homogenous. The very code that makes it possible for us to tackle higher levels of complexity reduces our work to choosing between architectures of alternatives: absolute blank-page imaginativeness today is far more elusive.

The final, fraught minutes before the first ever Moon landing were manually flown by Neil Armstrong as the world's population watched on TVs 400,000 km away. Today's astronauts – not to mention commercial airline pilots, or cruise-ship captains – share nothing like this freedom of command, bound as they are by layers of automation and computer-aided supervision. Truly invigorating work, on the other hand, presents us with the opportunity to exercise our own agency and autonomy and offers us the direct responsibility to use our own judgement. Rather than being channelled by other forces from afar, in a fulfilling job we can anchor ourselves in the real world and make deeper sense of it. Work that engages our mind and body can ground us and allow us to take control of technology, rather than submit to it.

RECLAIM YOUR CRAFT SKILLS

A multitude of studies confirm that craft significantly increases your overall well-being. The multi-sensory engagement and anticipated satisfaction of pursuits as varied as baking, gardening or furniture-making increase mood-boosting neurotransmitters and reduce stress hormones. Doing craft makes you feel good. It also improves your general cognitive and physical abilities. Basket-weaving and pottery can help people recover from strokes by re-establishing neural pathways and improving brain plasticity, and craft courses have played an instrumental role in occupational therapy since its inception in the late nineteenth century, helping people with physical, sensory or cognitive problems regain independence in all areas of their lives. Building craft into your life is a natural way to bolster your physical and mental health and resilience. It's also enormously fulfilling.

While digital technology is the cause of the degradation of physical and mental skills in many lines of work, it also presents some fantastic opportunities to find more craftsmanship in your life, not only as a hobby alongside your career, but also as part of your day-to-day work itself.

Craft hobbies and communities

The simplest way to get more craft in your life? Take up a new hobby. It's no coincidence that traditional pastimes such as knitting and home-brewing have seen a resurgence in recent years: craft hobbies offer the opportunity to fend off screenish tendencies earned on the day job and give us respite and recuperation from our work and consumerist lives. You might find a craft hobby that closely relates to or complements your working life, or choose one that's very different to act as a salve or a correction, whether that's jewellery-making, beekeeping, patchwork and quilting, car mechanics, or woodwork, to name just a few. At root, all these activities involve a fully focused practice and extended process of discovering how things work, with tasks taken on in their entirety. You can relish the difficulty and small signs of improvement and refuse to surrender to expedience; most often you're working with your hands.

Even bearing in mind the rejuvenation of interest in crafts of late, hobbies are in no way as prevalent as they once were: pastimes boomed from the late nineteenth century to the late twentieth, before going into a steep decline with the coming of the internet that caught the attention of millions of potential hobbyists before they had the chance to ground their interests in more real-world pursuits.

Take a few moments to investigate what you do most with your spare hours: list each of your hobbies and interests, and consider how much time you spend on each. Try to distinguish how screenish each of your pastimes is: a lack of physicality when you play computer games or watch box sets is quickly apparent, but you might be surprised to find a paucity of bodily skills in much of your downtime. Think back over the past three months and attempt to accurately log the number of hours you have spent on any craft hobbies or active pursuits that require physical and mental effort, learning and progressive improvement. Compare and contrast your screen-based and real-world pursuits and notice which take up most of your time. It can be revealing to see how much you associate yourself with certain interests but how little time you find to actually do them.

Put thirty minutes aside to also note down new hobbies you would like to pursue or any areas of interest that until now you have not found the time to explore further. Take into account your talents, interests and any new skills you would like to acquire. Consider your work and think of complements and contradictions: are there any hobbies that resonate with you that build on your working life, or others that present a total departure? It's best that any hobby you take up stems from your natural motivations: try to deeply question what you most enjoy doing, and what you would like to do more of. One hobby can absolutely be sufficient, but a number of personal pursuits can offer a more rounded opportunity to learn varied bodily skills that can be applied to other parts of your life.

Craft hobbies today are all supported by vibrant communities of practice for sharing and learning and are a fantastic way to meet like-minded people and gain hands-on skills. Dedicated websites, forums and chat groups connect disparate people around even the most niche hobbies and pursuits, while meet-ups and maker-spaces offer an opportunity to meet in the real world and work together in ways similar to the craft fraternities of the past. Craft communities can be an invigorating antidote to the alienation of much digital work seated at a screen and can become a springboard for something new, offering a window into how your working life can be different and altogether more rewarding. Run through your list of hobbies and see what communities exist in your local area – do any catch your eye?

In addition, much like Daniels' early watch repair work, fixing things is also an excellent way to wrestle with and make sense of the objects you use every day – by diagnosing a problem and determining how to resolve it, you're rewarded with a far more comprehensive understanding of something's inner workings. Try, where you can, to attempt to fix things yourself first, before requesting or paying for help. Take each breakage as an opportunity to learn and put aside a healthy block of time to tackle the challenge with a focused and fresh mind. There are plenty of online step-by-step guides to fix most commonplace household items, including seemingly impenetrable smartphones and laptops, and repair work, of course, is a natural precursor to more extensive DIY or build projects.

TAKE ACTION

- **List your hobbies and interests:** Distinguish how screen-based each one is and consider how much time you spend on them respectively.
- **Find some new hobbies:** Dedicate thirty minutes to considering any new interests you would like to pursue and how they might complement or conflict with your day job.
- **Find a maker-space:** Research local community craft groups and workshop spaces.
- **Fix things:** Try, where possible, to get into the habit of fixing things yourself around the home; to begin with, using online guides, tackle a few broken items.

Find craftsmanship on the job

Another option, naturally, is to change the way you work. Objectively evaluate your current role: how screen-based is it, how automated?

The 'Motion' chapter suggested tracking how sedentary your daily life is. Using the same technique, jotting down notes with pen and paper, take a week to log where and how you spend most of your time in a working day. Be alert to repetitive or mundane tasks: monitor how much time you spend at a screen and whether any task involves any physical elements. If so, are they nuanced and skilled? For each task area, on a scale of one to ten, honestly evaluate the level of intellectual effort required from you. At the end of the week, take a step back and try to coolly evaluate if your work is sufficiently physical and mentally demanding to make you feel fulfilled. If not, why not: what are the root causes?

It might be possible to find ways to incorporate more physicality, creative work or autonomy into your current role, or you might see that a side-step or promotion could enable this. A more involved option, of course, is to reskill and pursue a new occupation entirely. Natural alternatives for employment tend to be complementary to your current industry and skillset or might stem closely from a passion, interest or craft hobby.

Societal shifts over the years mean many view trade jobs such as electrics, plumbing or carpentry as less intellectually challenging or rewarding. The opposite is often the case. There remains as much demand for trade services as ever before, and remuneration can be as good or better than many office jobs.

Considering a new career path requires a clear-eyed view: look past the societal valuations of a profession and try to get a realistic picture of what your current working life consists of, and then of how the day to day in a different job would be. In the chase for the latest digital opportunities or white-collar office work, more traditional and physical job roles, which are often both challenging and fulfilling, are often forgotten. The array of jobs on offer today with flexible hours also opens up opportunity. Combining part-time jobs, for instance, is a great way to create more breadth in the intellectual or physical skills you develop, and widens your potential routes to employment at the same time. By thinking creatively about the different job options available to you, it can be possible to reduce the hours on your current day job and the corresponding reliance you have on it financially. Research widely and think daringly about what you might prefer to do as a career, and the practical steps you need to take to make it happen. Investing in some sessions with a coach is a great idea, as is volunteering or work shadowing.

TAKE ACTION

- **Evaluate your current job role:** Track how and where you spend most time in the day, noticing repetitive or mundane and screen-based tasks.
- **Ask hard questions:** Consider honestly whether you find your job sufficiently physically and intellectually demanding. Is there something you would prefer to do instead?
- **Consider your career:** Investigate potential career side-steps, promotions or new occupations entirely that could allow more physicality, creative work and autonomy.

Craft entrepreneurship

A riskier, though perhaps even more rewarding, way to integrate meaningful and craft-based tasks into your working life is to strike out on your own. The job market's close alignment with wider economic and technological changes makes finding roles that have not been superseded progressively harder. Although entrepreneurship is also at the mercy of the market forces of supply and demand, starting a new business offers total flexibility to set working processes for yourself, tackle screenishness and remove the current constrictions of your working life. Self-funded microbusinesses in particular are nimble enough to cater to even the most niche of interests and offer scope for highly focused product offerings and delivery mechanics. Successfully managing a startup requires an integrated view, from overall strategic direction to the detailed workings at each stage of production – the very opposite of so many roles today that focus on a limited number of tasks in dislocation from others.

Nestled in one of the archways of Camden Market in London is the Camden Watch Company, a business very much of this nimble entrepreneurial mould and one of the freshest faces in contemporary watchmaking. Anneke Short and Jerome Robert started out in 2014, offering a small selection of watches named after local bus routes. Their watch design and prototyping make use of the latest CAD software and is inspired by machinery and architecture in the vicinity, with colours and small details drawn from bridges over the connecting canalways. A range of automatic watches use mechanical movements affordably sourced from a Japanese company called Miyota that kinetically power themselves from the motion of a wearer's wrist.

Aside from the manufacture of separate watch parts, Anneke and Jerome manage every aspect of the business themselves, from product design and assembling to marketing and retail, and Jerome personally repairs any damaged pieces. By making the most of technologies available today, they are able to release small production runs of unique watches at affordable prices, and rapid prototyping allows ideas to be quickly turned into working reality. The craftsmanship is not at the same level as Daniels', of course – these are everyday watches, not one-off artisan pieces – but there remains an intrinsic physicality to the work involved, and plenty of scope for finer workmanship at higher price points. There's also skill and ingenuity required at each step in the supply chain of the business. Anneke and Jerome show that by confronting technology with the same curiosity as traditional craftsmanship you can make it work for you in new ways. The Camden Watch Company's individual pieces are not merely gadgets, they're emotionally engaging and enduring objects that derive directly from their historic surroundings. They demonstrate that craft knowledge can be applied to humanize technology and create things that resonate with ordinary people, not just in gallery showrooms or at out-of-reach prices.

The economics of digital technologies are making companies like the

Camden Watch Company possible across most industries as intensive testing of software settings and manual adjustments to underlying code make it possible to fluently adapt digital tools and experiment at will: one-of-a-kind products can be created that would be impossible any other way. It's feasible again for craft fraternities to re-emerge from networks of interconnected workshops running small-batch and short-run production, so craft entrepreneurship today doesn't have to be a solitary pursuit. George Daniels might be amazed to see that the future for the mechanical watch, and thousands of other crafts, looks decidedly bright indeed.

TAKE ACTION

- **Do your homework:** If you are serious about quitting your day job, look closely into craft entrepreneurship opportunities that relate to your current skills, hobbies and interests.

Chapter 9

Memory

SHAKESPEARE'S PLAYERS

In Shakespeare's time, the profession of acting was markedly different to what it is today. Theatre was not yet the commercial enterprise it would later become, and a company of actors – at that time called 'players' – would rely on wealthy patrons to help fund their plays. In the 1500s, productions were initially performed privately for an invited audience at court and then toured to taverns, inns and even bear-baiting arenas in the provinces. Later in Shakespeare's life, more dedicated playhouses were built. A dozen or so actors were responsible for performing a dizzying number of plays – often as many as six different productions in a week, with a new show launched each month – and these were staged in varying rotation throughout the year. It was rare for an actor to play the same role two days in a row, and even though a company would stage performances most days of the week, even the most popular roles were only played sporadically.

Players therefore had to keep an assortment of lines across a wide body of plays fixed in their minds continually. They also had to brush up on new lines very quickly: the Lord Chamberlain's Men company – which became the King's Men on the accession of James I in 1603 – had Shakespeare as its playwright for the majority of his career, and, on one occasion, barely had a day to revive the defunct *Richard II* for a last-minute performance during the time of Essex's rebellion. In addition, it was rare for a player to receive a full script of a play, as printed materials at the time were extremely scarce: there was certainly no rote memorization of text. Whereas professional stage actors might nowadays spend weeks or even months memorizing a part, the time-pushed players in Shakespeare's day had to rely on other, more innate memory skills to assimilate their lines. As remains the case today, drawing a blank on stage was an experience to be avoided at all costs. Its potential for distress is perhaps best captured by the great eighteenth-century Shakespearean actor Charles Macklin, who in his late eighties froze one night onstage and turned to the audience to apologize for what he described as 'a terror of mind I never in my life felt before', one which totally destroyed his 'corporeal as well as mental faculties'.

So, how did Shakespeare's players manage to remember their lines across multiple plays and without printed materials or weeks dedicated to rote memorization? The ability of humans to remember vast numbers of lines in theatre or song in fact dates back to some of the earliest accounts of civilization on record, and scholars over the centuries have debated how the bardic tradition produced Homer's the *Iliad* and the *Odyssey*, both dating from the eighth century BCE, prior to the introduction of alphabetic writing in Ancient Greece, and totalling over 15,000 and 12,000 lines respectively.

In the 1930s, the American classicist Milman Parry made a fascinating discovery about how bards or troubadours across a variety of cultures throughout our past have been able to recite such a large quantity of material. In his search for surviving oral cultures – in which individuals still performed lengthy, complex recitals of stories and songs from memory alone – he happened upon a remote area of Yugoslavia (now part of Serbia and Montenegro) and met Avdo Međedović, a poet and farmer who could still sing an assortment of traditional folktales – including one which was over 13,000 lines long.

Parry's visit happened to coincide with wider availability of the first portable electronic recording devices, and he made his own modifications to a Bell Edison phonograph so that his recording sessions could be extended indefinitely – Parry found it was important not to disrupt Međedović once he was in full flow. One of Međedović's performances of a song took up over sixteen hours of audio recording, made in one sitting. Međedović had never learned to read or write, but he was enormously proficient at following the distinct rhythm and structure of a verse form. He performed with a gusle, a single-stringed instrument played with a bow, and sang clearly and movingly.

In Homer's time, performances were delivered in dactylic hexameter – a metric scheme which creates a natural rhythm and flow to pull the listener (and also the performer) along. Performances of the *Iliad* and the *Odyssey* would have been accompanied by a type of lyre called the phorminx, which singers played at festivals and courts. Parry discovered that the ordering of text as rhythmic verse closely fits the natural language-processing abilities of our minds and creates a structure for us to more easily form memories and recall specific lines.

It is very difficult for us today to fully comprehend the extent to which we relied on our own memory in the past. Physiologically, we are virtually identical to our ancestors, but the ways that we inhabit our own minds are very different. Today, we primarily store our memories outside of ourselves – in books, photos and museums, and, increasingly, across a multitude of digital formats – but for the majority of human history, we relied on our own natural recollection of events to establish a shared culture and to transmit the virtues and values that we held dearly. This was how we preserved the things we found to be most important, and it was by forming and passing on oral stories and folktales that we fought against our transience and mortality, ensuring records of our exploits could live on.

Our first *external* memory aids were painted on the walls of caves, carved on pieces of wood or held in the form of the physical artefacts that we created, but with the invention of writing, first in the logo-syllabic script of cuneiform and then eventually, in Europe, in the use of a more versatile alphabet, there was a seminal shift in the complexity of information we were able to hold externally. Quite soon, the old techniques of Homeric bards were no longer adequate to transmit the growing intricacies of a textual culture, and over time the prime function of oral performance of story and songs changed from documenting the past to entertaining.

Parry noticed that Međedović, within the framework of a verse form, would reconstruct his own version of a song each time: one scene that was originally related in 141 lines was expanded by Međedović to more than a thousand. Parry argued on this basis that although the *Iliad* and the *Odyssey* have a fixed form today, this is only because they were written down at a later stage; for centuries prior they would have morphed and developed as different performers evolved their own renditions. Homer's work is understood today not to have been that of an individual poet but rather an amalgamation of work by different bards. The *Iliad* and the *Odyssey* could well have started taking shape as early as 2000 BCE, a full 1,200 years before they were finally recorded on the page.

Shakespeare also wrote in metric lines, in iambic pentameter, and as with Homeric metre, this natural rhythm of verse, which is in fact very close to how we speak in everyday life, helped players onstage to remember their parts. Yet this does not quite explain how his actors remembered so many lines: by Shakespeare's day, writing was not only commonplace but also highly developed as a creative medium in its own right, and expectations in terms of fidelity to a text had changed. Although lines were not kept to quite as rigidly as we have come to expect today – players had some freedom to substitute words within the metrical framework and narrative thrust of the play – there was by no means the level of flexibility that Međedović, or any other storyteller from the ancient bardic tradition, would have been accustomed to. Shakespeare's verse is immeasurably precise, and its final form is a product of quite deliberate intention. Players were expected, therefore, to achieve as close a rendition as they could.

Medieval scholars distinguished between '*memoria rerum*', the memory of things; and '*memoria verborum*', the more precise memory of words. They found that memorizing specific sections of text was particularly difficult as it did not fit so readily with the spatial and visual basis of our memory and imagination. When we remember something, we recreate a scene in our minds, and we have evolved to retrieve our past moments using the same cognitive faculties with which we perceived them in the first place, in particular that of vision as we run through memories and scenes again in our mind's eye. If we take ourselves back to any dramatic moment in our past, we inevitably step back into our own shoes. Even when recounting a major piece of news that we read on our phones or saw for the first time on TV, we mentally place ourselves again in the physical situation we found ourselves in when receiving the news, and rely on our sensory recall to run through it all once more. Of course, when we pay more attention in the first place, we can later marshal more sensory memories, making it easier to flesh out our recollections. In contrast, committing large sections of written text to memory, removed from a multi-sensory, lived reality, is one of the hardest mnemonic challenges we can face.

Of all the differences between theatre production today and in the early modern era, it is the players' reliance on individual cue-scripts that would have had the most impact on their recall. Actors were given a scroll that contained only their lines and cues for entering the stage: they never saw a whole manuscript of a play. This scattering of individual parts between the cast – without anyone being able to properly study another person's role or lines – stitched a play together in a remarkably economical way. Each actor was given only the bare minimum guidance needed, and the cast was then thrown together onstage. Between scenes, the cast would collect backstage around large manuscripts called 'plots' hung prominently on the wall. Only seven such plots survive today. Although they offered the only opportunity the players had to see a play in its entirety, the information they display is surprisingly scant. Each new scene is marked clearly with heavy underscoring, but the only other directions consisted of characters' stage entrances and exits; beyond that, actors had to work things out for themselves. Players were trained to listen out for one- or two-word cues (which tended to be unusual, memorable words) from their fellow actors, and took to the stage with little understanding of what was going to happen next.

The sparseness of the sixteenth-century stage – a simple marked playing space with no set or lighting – likely helped an actor to concentrate and closely follow the unfolding drama. Being thrown blind into a new scene sparked a natural spontaneity and energy – it made being onstage feel more like a highly charged, real-life encounter than a staged performance; players learned to live in the moment and to participate fully in the play. More than any other technique or trick to remember lines, this heightened alertness and increased attentiveness was the prime facilitator of the phenomenal memory of Shakespearean players. By getting as deeply into character as they could, and by intently following the dialogue, players would inhabit their role to such a degree that instinct and intuition would lead them just as much as any line recall. Theatre, of course, relies on the physicality of an actor's performance to get a story across, and players would closely attend to the movement of other bodies on the stage, using eye contact, gesture and the slightest pauses of breath as prompts for what should happen next. Through these techniques, they developed a deep understanding of what was unfolding in the play, and actors chose their words not only from their own font of memory but also in direct correspondence with the events onstage. Quite simply, the more the players paid attention, the more they remembered.

The memory abilities of Shakespeare's players were by no means a rarity at the time. We humans used to invest prodigious portions of time training our memory. History is replete with accounts of books recounted verbatim or the names of soldiers in vast armies rattled off in order, of conversations full of quick-fire ripostes or peppered with countless facts or figures. Much of our time was spent committing items to memory or calling them forth.

Memory training, in fact, was a centrepiece of classical education. Students were taught not only what but *how* to remember, and there was a vital distinction made between natural and artificial memory. Natural memory is enmeshed in our minds, and relates to how we think and the connections we make between our learning and experiences – this is what Shakespeare's players called upon onstage. We draw upon our natural memory capability when we fully immerse ourselves in something, and it's also how we improve our skills, building up layers of expertise, taking in details and understanding them more fully by assimilating them with our other experiences.

Artificial memory is assembled on top of our natural memory as architecture built to hold extra information, outside of the everyday workings of our mind. Ancient Greek and Roman artificial-memory techniques, which survived well into Shakespeare's time and beyond, relied on creating 'memory palaces' in our minds to hold mental images of things we wanted to recall later by placing them within an envisaged space. Although this allows us to retain isolated details, it's not the same as the connecting webs of memories we create naturally, and there is the potential with artificial-memory training for a person to regurgitate facts and figures without a full grounding of knowledge behind them. Yet the artificial memory-palace technique, when combined with natural memory and thought, can be incredibly powerful. It allowed Roman orators to speak eloquently for hours and enabled medieval monks to retain reams of insights from readings; it was also a likely practice used by Shakespeare's players to learn their lines, although it was not as important as the vibrant, lived moments onstage as they paid close attention to the drama unfolding around them.

MEMORY THEATRE

The first-century encyclopaedia, Pliny the Elder's *Natural History*, is the largest single work to have survived from the Roman Empire. Among its entries, it lists some of the most exceptional memories known at that time. A Lucius Scipio is reported as having memorized the names of every person living in Rome; King Pyrrhus's envoy Cineas could apparently recount the names of all the individual senators in the city within a day of his arrival there; and the renowned orator and lawyer Hortensius was able to recall the names of all of the people involved in his past cases and the amounts of money in question each time. Not all of Pliny's facts or figures can be trusted, of course, but the variety of anecdotes about the capabilities of human memory is itself revealing. Most classical writers seemed to presume that memory techniques were so well known that they did not need to be described in detail. If it were not for a short, anonymously authored book called the *Rhetorica ad Herennium*, written between 86 and 82 BCE, the memory-training methods followed in Ancient Greek and Roman times would not have survived until today.

The *Ad Herennium* ascribes the invention of these ancient memory techniques to the Greek lyric poet Simonides of Ceos, who, upon standing in the fresh rubble after the collapse of a great banqueting hall in Thessaly, realized that if he closed his eyes and reconstructed the building in his imagination, he could easily remember where each of the guests at an earlier dinner had been sitting. Simonides then reputedly worked out that he could place other people – or indeed anything that came to mind – in the same positions around the banquet table, and that, in so doing, he could call upon his spatial memory to mentally arrange items to remember later. The *Ad Herennium* takes only ten pages to explain how to create a space in the mind's eye and then populate that imagined place with images of things to remember. This simple trick of spatial positioning that the Romans called the method of *loci*, and which, over later years, evolved to become known as a memory palace, was the foundation for an 'art of memory' that blossomed through the medieval era in particular, and continued to be advanced in Shakespeare's day.

Although considerable improvements have been made in the art of memory in the intervening two and half millennia since Simonides's reported discovery, the underlying principles have remained the same. Contestants who compete in memory championships today also use the same techniques, including Mahavir Jain from India, who recently memorized all 80,000 words and 1,500 pages of the Oxford Dictionary and could give the exact page number of any entry. When we visit a new place, we find it easy to create a mental note of how things relate to one another, and if it is a room of a house, the exact dimensions and arrangement of its contents. Although we do not realize it, spending just a few moments taking in what we can see in a space can amount to a colossal amount of precisely recorded information. What Simonides recognized – and what countless others have relied on through human history – was that the tremendous powers we have for spatial memory could just as easily be applied to any other form of knowledge. Natural navigation skills show that humans are highly adept at learning the features of spaces, and civilizations such as those of the Australian Aborigines, or of the Apaches in the American Southwest, independently invented similar spatial memory techniques, using the local topography to embed their own cultural memories.

For the majority of humanity's past, a strong memory has been seen as one of the most esteemed personal abilities and virtues. More than its everyday utility, we have most revered the potential a honed memory holds for an internalization of a whole universe of understanding. The awe that people reserved for those with impressive memories continued on from Ancient Greece and Rome – where memory was most readily employed to speak at length in public – to the medieval era, where memory was applied to deep religious and philosophical study. But it was during the Renaissance and Shakespeare's day that the art of memory reached its zenith. The explosion in available information at this time – as a result of efforts to revive and surpass the ideas of classical antiquity, and then as a compounding consequence of the invention of the printing press – led to renewed endeavours to broaden the versatility and accuracy of the art of memory so that it could more comprehensively accommodate the growing canon of human knowledge.

The Dominican friar Giordano Bruno published a book in 1582, *On the Shadows of Ideas*, which for the first time suggested that a dynamic mnemonic device could be used to turn any word into a unique image. He exhaustively devised a series of concentric wheels that could be pictured in the mind; by using the imagination to visually move and spin them, it was possible to create any combination of letters from the alphabet, and then to connect words with a whole catalogue of symbols denoting different actions and circumstances. By committing these rotating, algorithmic combinations of letters and images to memory, Bruno found that he could create a repository of knowledge that could be controlled and calibrated at will. This discovery that memorized images could be added together in any number of combinations, and animated in the mind with the deliberate use of human imagination, was a huge leap forward. Rather than just using memory techniques to store away information for retrieval later, Bruno arrived at the discovery that computational memory could be used to create entirely new sequences of information – a phenomenon we rely on today to process and utilize the agglomerations of data held on our digital devices.

Bruno's inventions were very much a successor to that of Giulio Camillo, an Italian philosopher who had the epiphany of making a real, wooden construction of a memory space. Camillo secured financial backing from an assortment of noted individuals, including King Francis I of France, and deployed it to build his own 'theatre of memory'. This intricately built memory palace was shaped like a Roman amphitheatre, but with the viewing experience turned around: rather than having spectators sit in seats, it was designed for a person to stand onstage and look out at the surrounding theatre. Paintings were placed on seven round tiers of seating, and rows of drawers on the undersides of each seat were packed full of cards that were intended to contain the sum total of all human knowledge. Scale models were presented in Venice and Paris, but the finished structure was never built, and Camillo saved it for posterity by quickly dictating a final description on his deathbed. The English philosopher and mathematician Robert Fludd took this idea of a memory theatre and, combining it with Bruno's calculative zeal, elevated the art of memory to its highest reaches.

It was not until 1599, late in Shakespeare's career as a playwright, that the Globe Theatre was built on the south bank of the River Thames. The Globe was the most impressive of the playhouses that were cropping up across London at that time, and it was the most impressive. The sign at its front supposedly depicted Hercules carrying the world on his shoulders. Shakespeare's memorable metaphor from *As You Like It* – 'all the world's a stage, and all the men and women merely players; they have their exits and entrances, and one man in his time plays many parts' – was grounded in reality. The Globe housed an auditorium that at last relieved the players of the makeshift conditions of their stage performances. Built in the style of the Ancient Roman architect Vitruvius, its circular edifice and the square stage and entrances inside were designed to suggest a human world in miniature.

When Fludd set out his own memory theatre, he based it on the Globe.

In 1619, just three years after Shakespeare's death, Fludd published his own elaborate memory system in the steadfast belief that it could be used to gain an integrated, fully comprehensible view of the workings of the universe, and everything that exists within it. In his detailed treatise, *The History of the Two Worlds*, which he dedicated to his patron King James I, Fludd makes the final recorded attempt to devise a means for a human to collect the entirety of knowledge known to civilization in the fathoms of their own mind. He relies on a recommendation made in the *Ad Herennium* against the use of fictitious places for the art of memory, which might impede the original clarity and strength of any recollection, and transplants Camillo's memory theatre to inside the Globe.

The later forms of playhouses in Shakespeare's day had paintings of the 'heavens' on the ceilings above the actors as they performed on stage. The images of our solar system and the wider cosmos portrayed on the ceiling of the Globe Theatre, the King's principal playhouse, would likely have been the most embellished and refined. Fludd lays out a scheme for prolific memory recall with a visualization exercise: by imagining standing centre stage at the Globe and looking out at the auditorium in just the same way Camillo intended, he allows the possibility of glancing above to be prompted by the depictions of the physical laws of the universe. Fludd was as much a chemist and lab technician as he was a creative thinker, and his attempts to ground humankind's understanding of the world were very much of his time. He set out staggeringly comprehensive schemes of symbols and imagery to hold in his memory theatre and employ generatively in the mind in new combinations, but in the end, his colossal efforts to amass all human knowledge became too much for one person to handle. His ambitions, though, influenced his contemporaries to arrive at a more empirical and mathematical means of recording information and, in consequence, to the very beginnings of the scientific and technological revolutions.

The seventeenth-century German scientist and mathematician Gottfried Leibniz began his own work on the art of memory in the same ways as Bruno and Fludd, but he became one of the first to swap images and symbols for numbers. In the same extended search for a combinatorial method to make sense of the expanding volumes of information being collected to measure the world, Leibniz arrived at his inception of calculus, which was one of the earliest successful attempts to create a fully flexible language to express algorithmic data, and one that is still used in any branch of science or computer operations today to mathematically model complex, changing series of information, including AI systems such as ChatGPT. Other, more computable ways to record the world around us began to replace the art of memory, and in 1620, just a year after Fludd revealed his memory theatre, the English philosopher Francis Bacon set out a foundation for a new scientific method, gathering and analysing data from direct experiments and observations. We soon began to store information in more quantifiable forms, outside of our own minds.

The profound computer memory we can access today is a result of an extended lineage of human inventiveness and fine accomplishments of technical engineering. Digital technologies and the internet have been able to do what Fludd hoped for with his memory theatre: to hold the entirety of human knowledge collected to date. Yet rather than one mind orchestrating these contents, a significant portion of the global population now has access to an unprecedented wealth of knowledge, giving us an unrivalled power to understand the world and to create further new technologies and realities. Without care, though, when we over-rely on digital devices as memory repositories, we risk become passive spectators, merely watching tremendous feats of external memory rather than performing our own.

Digital devices rely on two distinctly different types of memory. 'Storage' refers to the space used to hold information so we can access it again later, such as hard drives or solid-state drives. This allows for the long-term retention of data, similar to ancient techniques devised by Simonides; modern storage devices, though, have astonishingly high speeds and capacities compared to their historical counterparts. 'Random access memory' (RAM), on the other hand, is the function most associated with computer memory and is responsible for the work being done at any one time: when we power up software or load a new web page, it all happens within the RAM, and the more 'memory' a device has, the more tasks it is able to handle. This distinction between the two types of digital memory that we use today was in fact discovered by the likes of Bruno and Fludd, who realized that stored information could be used in ever more creative and powerful ways when combined with working memory.

As it turns out, our own natural memory works in a very similar way to computational memory. Cognitive psychology holds that we have both a long-term memory capacity – whereby we can store high quantities of information for later use – and working memory, which we use to perform any cognitive task. A single human brain has an astoundingly large long-term storage capacity: we can hold as much as 2.5 petabytes of data in our minds: that's 2,500,000,000,000,000 bytes or the equivalent of 500 billion pages of standard printed text! Humankind has continually proven that when we apply ourselves, we can save a phenomenal amount of information in our heads – more than we could ever actually need. The chief difference between human and digital memory lies in how limited our working memory capacity is: whereas the speed of computer operations today allows RAM to run exceptionally high numbers of tasks in unison by interleaving them in fast, combined sequences, studies over the years have shown that humans can only process as few as four to seven different chunks of information at any time, depending on the type of work that we are doing.

As Shakespeare's players found, our memory is fundamentally tied to our attention: by living in a role as naturally and attentively as possible, an actor has far more chance of cementing lines in their long-term memory. We need to focus our mind on a task before we can take it in fully (there simply is no other way), and when we do, the operations of our mind are most often prevented from doing anything else, simply because, as we go about the task, we use up the processing capacity of our working memory. Consider, then, what happens when we are distracted by our digital devices – it follows that our memory capabilities are at risk. To really remember something, we need to actively switch between our working and long-term memories; when we are stuck in a more passive or distracted mode of attention, we typically activate just our working memory.

A study by University College London in 2022 showed that using smartphones to remember important information could actually improve our recall, by prodding our memory as needed, and freeing us to recall more important things too. The memory stored on our devices works in the same way as any artificial memory system: it extends the places that we can store things that we need to recall later, and in this way, digital technology of course increases the amount of information we have access to. But the study also determined that when the smartphones were taken away, people were most likely to forget the information that they deemed of highest importance and had saved on their devices.

Our memories shape us and become a part of who we are. When we think of new ideas or come up with solutions to problems, we draw deeply on our memories and thought. This happens most often in our quiet moments of introspection and undivided attention. It follows that if memories and key information are not held in our own heads but rather on a device, we cannot use them in these moments of contemplation. Outsourcing memory to devices therefore impacts negatively on our capacity to think.

Until fairly recently, most psychologists believed that our brains functioned as high-fidelity recorders, but in actual fact, our memories are nothing like the information neatly stored away in folders on a disk drive. Rather, they are bound together in a complex web of associations that in itself is a reflection of the brain's physical structure. The human brain is primarily made up of neurons, and it is the connections, the waves of electric current passed between them, that count. One neuron on its own cannot amount to much, but when the 100 billion neurons in a human brain function together – with each individual neuron linking to as many as 10,000 others – our minds are capable of making 1,000 trillion different connections. Our memories consist of patterns of association between these multitudes of links: every sensation that we remember, or thought that crosses our mind, alters these connections and physically changes our brain in ever new ways.

One of the prime reasons the art of memory was so keenly studied in monastic traditions in the medieval era was the realization that the more fully we memorize something, the more we can use it to think flexibly and generatively and create ourselves anew. This nuanced understanding of the positive interplay between our memories and imagination showed remarkable foresight, as it is precisely the finding of cognitive science today: when we remember something we recombine multiple sources of information from the wide array of associate links in our brains, and the new thoughts that we have stem from the past experiences we have gained. Our deepest connections are the ones we have lived most intensely, either through the full range of human senses or by repeatedly working away at a problem to frame it from many different perspectives, and it is this deep-seated experience that allows for intuition and natural, multi-faceted understanding. This is something that simply cannot be matched by any quick search or scan of text on a device. (Indeed, it has only been since attempts at forging artificial intelligence have progressed from using sequential lines of code to employing massive data sets and pattern recognition that complex machine learning has become possible.)

Digital memory aids are the modern-day equivalent of the vast artificial memory systems we used to hold in our minds. We are hugely fortunate in this regard. After all, building and maintaining our own artificial memory is phenomenally hard work, and the power of digital memory outmatches that of any memory palace, no matter how ornate. But the pervasiveness of digital memory is also beginning to supplant much of our natural memory too – and it is only by using our natural memory together with artificial or external memory that we can maintain and enrich the connections in our own minds.

Memory plays an essential role in the human condition – a topic returned to regularly by Shakespeare himself – so when we relinquish our natural memories to computers, we are losing vital aspects of ourselves. Luckily, our natural memory skills can be developed with use and practice. By more attentively focusing when taking in new information or experiences, we can regulate the depth, clarity and strength of any later recollections. Decluttering our sensory environment – in particular, removing digital distractions – helps us ensure that our initial perceptions are more vivid and then easier to recall. Our memories are sustained by use and intelligent association, so by calling forth our own recollections more regularly, we can increase our visualization powers. Identifying when digital technologies result in our natural memories being underused – when we over-rely on photos to capture moments, for example, or when we too quickly pull out a device to note something down – can help us build better habits to establish clearer memories that stay with us for longer. Often the best memory technique is just to jump back into the life carrying on around us.

When we improve our memory, we enhance our minds. It not only heightens our ability to pay attention and helps us focus for longer periods of time, but we also become more adept at making our own, creative leaps of thought and arriving at deeper, more refined levels of comprehension. Its impact on our personal perspectives on life cannot be overstated – our memory really is our world. Whatever we find ourselves doing in life, any contact or interaction that we make is illuminated by our inner thoughts and recollections. Developing and sustaining our own memory with mentally stimulating activities is the most direct means we have to enrich our mental acuity in day-to-day life and may even help reduce the risk of Alzheimer's or dementia.

Memory is just like any physical attribute that we might train – our strength, endurance or agility, for example – and without regular practice, it too can decline with lack of use. The phenomenal amounts of text, images and videos we encounter or leave behind online have a negative impact on our memory skills. When we put our labour into managing and filtering a constant slew of information and task digital memory with taking on the burden of our own natural memory, we invest less in forging our own individual persona. And, while we might spot the small memory lapses that seem inevitable in our busy, digital age – forgetting someone's name, or an important birthday, say – it is not always straightforward to detect the longer-term effects of our reliance on digital memory. The good news is that this can be fixed: you can continue to enjoy the benefits of digital technology while also honing your own natural memory.

STRENGTHEN YOUR MEMORY

Memory is a natural extension of your attention. To form any memory, you must encode and store it in order to retrieve it later, and of these three processes, how your mind initially encodes an event is the most critical. The more vivid your first impression, the longer lasting your memory of it will be, so when you properly attend to something, you dramatically increase your chances of remembering it later. Any form of memory training relies on this fundamental premise. Sensory memory is particularly important: the more you live within the physical sensations of your sight, sound, touch, smell and taste, the more your brain's initial impression of an experience will resonate with you later. Emotions also play an integral role – your memory will significantly improve if what you are trying to remember is connected with something eventful or if you find it stirring or thought-provoking. But there are also a few other methods you can try to increase your levels of recall.

The art of attention

When something is important to you, make sure that you live it as attentively and as fully as you can. Try to avoid the distraction of passing thoughts and put yourself as directly as possible into the experience. Some occasions in life, such as your wedding day or the birth of a child, are obviously remarkably rare and hence memorable, but other bright, luminous moments can quickly pass you by. Even instances of startling beauty might only hold your attention for a brief spell, yet how many supermoons, cloud inversions or night skies unspoiled by light pollution are you truly likely to witness in your lifetime? When a fleeting moment of deep personal resonance next arrives, use your natural interest to help keep you absorbed: observe the small details, moving your focus from one thing to the next, and try to build as rich and definitive a memory as you can. Be aware of your feet nestled within your shoes, or of the smooth palm of a hand held within your own, and focus on the distinct physical feeling of being there. Pay particular attention to your surroundings, as a strong sense of the space you are in will help you to recall it all again later.

Fostering a depth to your perception can soon become a healthy habit, and with practice, an increasingly normal way to live. The more you are able to pique and sustain your interest in something through open curiosity, the more detail you will take in, and the longer your memory of it will survive.

TAKE ACTION

- **Turn on your curiosity:** Home in on small sensory details to help build a richer, more vivid memory of an experience you want to remember in the future.
- **Search for intelligent connections:** Deliberately make connections between memories and ongoing experience to more deeply embed both in your mind.

Consolidate your memories

Take yourself back to this time last week. How much can you remember about what you were thinking or doing? Even events that happened only yesterday might not seem very sharp if you were not paying close attention to them at the time. In addition to being more attentive to the present moment, taking the time to consolidate and organize your memories afterwards can also help improve retention.

Spending just a few moments deliberately running through events that happened earlier in the day significantly helps you to more thoroughly embed your memories. When you mentally revisit events, you reinforce them by engaging your attention and working memory. Keeping the routine of writing in a daily diary in which you review – and interrogate – your recent memories is a great way to do this. Telling an anecdote helps memory too (after all, stories are the main way we humans have held on to our thoughts throughout history), and daily or weekly phone calls, emails or letters sharing news with a friend or relative can also be a great way to consolidate and cement your memories.

The more deliberate you are, the better. And with practice, even just a few minutes each night spent mentally reviewing the day's events can have a profound effect on the accuracy and levels of detail that you can recall later.

TAKE ACTION

- **Keep a diary for a month:** Put aside time every evening to run through the day's events again in your mind and write them down.

Protect your attention

Your limited working memory capacity does you a great service. The fact that you can only think about a few things at a time plays a critical role in filtering the world for you – otherwise, you would be drowning in inconsequential information. Most observations that you make last only a split second, and they pass through your mind without you needing to hold on to them. But when something important happens, you have to register it more fully before you have any chance of encoding it and storing it away, and it pays at these times to be more conscious and careful about how your working memory is being used.

To form a vivid memory that has sufficient clarity and detail to connect with other associations in your mind, you need the time to work through something properly, and if you are focused, all of your working memory will be activated as you go about it. But it doesn't take much distraction to seriously inhibit your memory capacity. Once your attention is stolen elsewhere, the chain of connections that your working memory was processing instantly gets broken, and it typically takes a lot of mental effort to pick up where you left off. Usually, the memory that you were building in your mind is never completed, and the chances of it embedding fully with your other thoughts is much reduced. You can spot the disorientating and jarring feeling when this happens: your mind jolts as it is removed from whatever you were engrossed in, and it can take a few strained moments to adapt to the new circumstances grabbing your attention. Perhaps your temper even flares. Watch out for these moments in particular, as they're invaluable indicators of the times in your day when you most need to protect your attention.

Whenever you are trying to focus attentively, be very wary of other calls on your working memory, in particular when you are striving to learn something new or to cement something in your mind for later. Quiet working environments really do help. When you are processing information, particularly in text-form or as spoken words, you often rely on a 'phonological loop' to repeat things over in your head until you understand and assimilate them. This is the same loop that might get filled with a catchy tune or other repeating thoughts you have throughout the day, but in times when you are really focused on something, it allows you to process and move information between your working and long-term memories.

TAKE ACTION

- **Observe your irritation:** Note when a sudden interruption or distraction triggers undue stress and consider how you can protect your focus at times like these.
- **Try noise-cancelling headphones:** Borrow a pair to use in a busy setting when you need to focus and notice any differences to your attention.
- **Find a more secluded spot:** Seek out a convenient place to work at the times when you need full focus.

Look out for what most readily distracts you day to day – particularly the interruptions that most aggravate or discombobulate you – and have a careful think about what steps you can take to better protect your attention at these times. In busy, bustling settings, noise-cancelling headphones really can help protect the functioning of your phonological loop. Failing that, it often pays to simply remove yourself and seek out somewhere more secluded – libraries are usually a far better option for deep, focused work than a crowded cafe or open office, for instance. When you really need to ruminate and think through something, often the best option is to take yourself out for a walk.

Train your working memory

In 2008, two neuroscientists completed an academic study that proved it is possible to improve your working memory – but not in the way that you might expect. It turns out that regular memory training does not increase the capacity of your working memory to hold more items in your mind at any one time; instead, you actually get better at *reducing* your capacity – at least when it comes to irrelevant information that interferes with your task at hand. With practice, you can improve the ability of your working memory to quickly disregard digital and real-world distractions or other thoughts so that you can more fully commit your mind to whatever you might be focused on.

You naturally train your working memory in this way when you set about any complicated, cerebral task. Reading fiction in particular gives your working memory a fantastic workout: as you get engrossed in a story, and leaf through from beginning to end, you have to hold a tremendous amount of detail in your mind about the various characters and plot developments. One of the first signs of early dementia can be that a patient stops reading fiction, as it simply becomes too difficult. Testing games of logic, such as chess, bridge or Sudoku, are also excellent at forcing you to hold shifting amounts of information in your memory; and equally, computer games that require your dedicated focus and logical precision of mind can help. Closely following instructions – whether it be to build a flat-pack piece of furniture or cook a more complicated food recipe – also tests your working memory in enormously healthy ways.

You can easily spot the moments when your working memory is being tested sufficiently. When you next set out on a complicated task, watch for when your mind seems to stall or empty; this mental exhaustion can often feel quite exasperating, and there can be an inclination to stop, or to try to get help. But these breaks in your working memory are useful indications of areas where you can improve, and it is only by pushing on with a task that you can stretch yourself and train your mind to more closely follow the steps you need to take.

TAKE ACTION

- **Pick up a novel:** Observe how the unfolding narrative tests and strains your working memory.
- **Look out for when your brain stalls:** Notice the uncomfortable moments when your mind seems to empty and fluster; focus on making decisions that will best help you progress.
- **Test your working memory:** Try to list, remember and rank the chapters you have read of this book.
- **Try daily memory exercises for a month:** Dedicate ten minutes each day to working-memory exercises.

If your work is very numerical or text-based and you regularly have to rely on your own abilities to process high volumes of information, it is most likely that you are already training your memory daily. Yet whatever your work situation, there is always room for improvement. One rewarding way to build memory capacity is to seek out new projects or weekly chores that mentally test you on a regular basis and oblige you to hold things in your mind as you go. You can also do daily exercises, and if you are serious about training your working memory, these can quickly yield noticeable results. You can easily find memory tests and exercises online – in essence they all involve you holding an increasingly complex amount of information in your mind and sorting through it in different sequences. Here's one to get you started: try to list the titles of the chapters of this book that you have read up until now, and, in your mind, place them in alphabetical order by title. Decide on the most important thing you learned from each chapter, and then rank each of these in your own order of importance. You will notice that you have to work much harder for the last two steps: this is exactly the level of mental exertion you need to develop and sustain your working memory.

Make digital memory work for you

Photos or videos are not the same as your own recollections. Any digital memory of your past only serves to stimulate mental recall. But you may have noticed that photos can somewhat take over your personal history: when you picture a time in your past (particularly one that was well-photographed), often the images that surface in your mind are the photos that were taken, rather than the wider variety of events that actually took place.

Digital memory does a useful job computing high quantities of data to give you precise answers. This is an undoubted advantage, and there is so much that would simply be impossible today without digital processing capacity. But when digital memory and computing power begin to supplant your own memory abilities, your personal intelligence is at risk.

If you find that you cannot always trust your memory, or that you struggle with tasks at times that you know should not be too difficult, digital memory use is most likely already affecting you. Natural memory is designed to support you in everyday life: in the conditions human beings have lived in for most of our past, the trials of daily existence would have been sufficient to keep your memory in good shape. But as digital technology – most of the time very usefully – wraps around so many of the moments in your life, the number of occasions when you are forced to rely on your own memory abilities has inevitably decreased. Adapting the ways you use technology can help, and the suggestions covered here will help you get your memory back. It is also important to keep in mind the very close connection between your navigation skills and your wider memory abilities – training your competence at wayfinding alone will give your memory a very noticeable boost.

That said, this does not mean you need to go to great lengths to limit your interactions with the digital memory that underpins so much of our culture. Remember that people in the past would have spent days, weeks, months or even years of their lives committing things to the artificial memory spaces they created in their minds; whereas you have the internet or AI chat tools, external memories of vast scope and power, ready for you to use for whatever pursuit you might like. What is most important is the mental dexterity and nous to make the best active use of digital memory, and you can achieve this by keeping your mind sharp in other ways.

Training your own working memory is the first and most vital step, as all your mental abilities spring from there. Getting into the habit of taking time away from a screen can be a great help when you are reading a lengthier article or digesting some complicated information – by trying to recall the key points without referring back to the source, you strengthen your working memory and significantly improve your chances of recall later. While passive browsing and unconsidered consumption of text does not give your brain the chance to form stronger connections, actively applying information that you find online to real-life situations or projects helps solidify concepts in your memory. If you want to memorize something specifically – perhaps you are learning a new language or preparing for an exam or presentation – so-called spaced repetition software, of which there is a variety online, can create flashcards with information you want to remember and also optimize the intervals and repetitions of viewing these to increase your retention.

Taking on a hobby which requires you to exert mental energy to assimilate something new without using digital memory is also an excellent way to keep your working memory sharp and help protect against the detrimental effects reliance on digital memory can have on your abilities.

TAKE ACTION

- **Gauge your own memory ability:** Do you trust your memory? How often does it fail you? And do you think it could perform better?
- **Work on your navigation skills:** Training your wayfinding abilities will also improve general memory.
- **Keep your mind sharp in other ways:** Take on a new creative project that does not rely on digital memory, and use it as a fun way to hone your memory skills.

Chapter 10

Dreams

OUR TRUE INWARD CREATRIX

Late in 1797, Samuel Taylor Coleridge awoke from a dream and wrote 'Kubla Khan', one of the most famous poems in the English language. Earlier that day he had taken a long walk along the North Devon coast. According to the unique preface that precedes the poem, Coleridge stopped for the night at a farm and drifted off to sleep while reading about Kublai Khan, founder of the Yuan dynasty of China, in a book of travel writing by English clergyman and geographer Samuel Purchas. In the preface, Coleridge introduces the poem as a 'psychological curiosity', a momentary record of the succession of images encountered in a dream. He describes the lines as being entirely created in his sleep and wholly formed when he woke up, ready to be written down. The poem begins on firm grounding – 'In Xanadu did Kubla Khan / a stately pleasure-dome decree' – based on the last sentence Coleridge read in Purchas's book, then, in a heady rush of rich imagery, swiftly follows the flow of the 'sacred river' Alph through 'a deep romantic chasm' and 'caverns measureless to man' until it reaches the ocean and 'a sunny pleasure-dome with caves of ice'. Reading the poem feels undeniably like entering a dream, and it survives today as a revealing glimpse into how our minds function when we sleep or daydream.

Coleridge had been reading widely that year. He had moved to Nether Stowey, a small village at the foot of the picturesque Quantock Hills in the southwest of England, and had committed himself to intensive study in preparation for his writing. His close friend and fellow poet William Wordsworth had also rented a house close by with his sister, Dorothy, and much of their time was spent in conversation on long walks, often discussing the fruits of Coleridge's reading, across an exceptionally varied array of topics. The late eighteenth century was a time of exploration and discovery, with travellers reporting on their adventures in lengthy, evocative books. Coleridge read these with particular intent, busily noting down findings in his commonplace books or carefully annotating a book's margins. Although not long, some critics claim that 'Kubla Khan' draws on more bibliographical sources than any other English-language poem. Numerous studies postulate the multiple literary origins of Coleridge's rich, earthily exotic scenes, and these investigations shed light on a complex web of associations, in other words, Coleridge's memory.

It was during this time that Coleridge produced much of the poetry for which he is most remembered today, including *The Rime of the Ancient Mariner* and 'Frost at Midnight'. Later in his life, he succumbed to problems with opium addiction that stood in the way of his reading, writing and creative process, and, with regret, he often looked back to this formative period when his talents and ideas had once come easily to him. Coleridge was a daydreamer, and he developed an early ability to apply his imagination to whatever situation he found in life. In particular, he was constantly searching out and noticing new things – in his words, 'picking flowers from the galaxy' – before drifting off into his own mind to form deeper connections and complex impressions of his experiences. To explain the action of the human imagination, he frequently evoked the image of an electrometer, a tiny piece of delicate gold foil held within a glass vacuum that responded to the minute fluctuations of electrical charge in the outside world. For Coleridge, the ability to create within one's own mind was the most potent skill humans possessed, and the prime agent of all perception, our 'true inward creatrix'. His move to Nether Stowey was part of a deliberate rejection of a more conventional literary or journalistic career, a striving for a new form of self-sufficiency, with time for inner growth and, he hoped, more original thought.

Throughout his life, Coleridge subscribed to the notion that poetry was pure imaginative force: it relied on the power of an individual mind to use text to conceive animated thoughts, and to invent and employ entirely new forms; poetry was able to elicit clear, rich visions, sweeping a reader or listener along with the shifting imagery that forms in the mind's eye. Coleridge, very perceptively for his time, mooted that the ways our eyes 'make pictures when they are shut' relied on the same imaginative capabilities we have to recount memories or envision new, future scenarios. He paid extremely close attention to his own internal experiences and noticed that in his private moments he spent just as much time playing out different visual scenes in his mind as he did registering anything new in the outside world. Indeed, in many of our most solitary or private moments, we are at our most creative, and when we revisit moments in our past, we often refashion them in quite fantastic and unexpected ways without rules or limits to restrain us.

Coleridge's most innovative leap was his realization that this waking visual relay exists in a similar form when we sleep. In our daily lives, whenever we have a new thought, or encounter something that demands closer attention, a flowing sequence of mental imagery overlays – sometimes distractingly – whatever else we might be doing. When we dream, the same internal vision creates evolving scenes, but this time they command our entire focus. Coleridge saw a natural relationship between our waking moments and the different states of sleep that we pass through. He recognized that at any moment in life – whether we are fully awake or fast asleep – our unconscious mind plays a tremendously powerful role in generating what appears in our mind's eye and informs many of our most creative and inspired moments. He cherished the liminal moments between wakefulness and sleep, and found that at these fleeting intervals he could tap into an almost limitless resource of creative thought.

Since its publication, 'Kubla Khan' has become a go-to example of the power that poetry, or any other creative work, can hold over us, and also of the way in which our dreams can shape our memories and lives. In demonstrating how our minds create and develop new ideas, Coleridge revealed the formative function our sleep in particular can have in offering us fresh thought and new perspectives. Coleridge wrote extensively, most copiously in his own private notebooks, but also for magazines and newspapers as well as his own published books. Yet it is 'Kubla Khan' – only some 350 words long – that most powerfully represents the importance of some of our most intimate and private moments, particularly in the stages between sleep and wakefulness, and shows how dream states can support our creativity.

The reasons why we sleep and dream were for a long time disputed, although it is clear that there must be advantages to spending one third of our lives removed from events in the outside world, otherwise we would not have evolved to do so. In only the past twenty-five years, a series of neuroscience studies have shown conclusively that sleep supports almost all of our bodily and psychological processes, from the regeneration of our cells and the calibration of our immune system and metabolism to our emotions and our outlook on life. More than diet or exercise, sleep is the key determinant of our health and well-being. Without it, we would die. Indeed, its essential function is obvious if we miss any large portion of rest: we very noticeably become physically and mentally impaired.

One of the clearest findings neuroscience has unveiled in recent years has been the multitude of ways in which sleep controls our memory and creativity. We alternate between two quite distinctly different phases of sleep each night – non-rapid eye movement (NREM), when we move from a light sleep into a deep slumber, and rapid eye movement (REM), which usually begins after around ninety minutes and is when we do most of our dreaming. Over the course of a night, we progressively spend more time in REM, and we fill the second half of a night with most of our dreams. We relive experiences in our lives when we dream, and by combining different associations in fresh, new ways, we remodel and update the neural circuits in our brains. This primarily helps us manage the finite storage we have available, prioritizing what is important and discarding what can be forgotten. Through the process of dreaming, REM sleep strengthens connections in our minds and forges new ones, whereas during NREM phases, unnecessary information is weeded out and remaining impressions are transferred to our long-term memory. In sleep, we prune and shape our minds, and the changes are carried through into our waking hours.

Over the course of some forty years, Coleridge regularly recorded his dreams and different states of consciousness in his notebooks; on many occasions, he can be seen in his notes to have awoken with a sentence or an idea in mind, scribbling it down in haste to try to save it. He most often wrote his dream records immediately after waking, but sometimes he delayed for hours, days or even weeks. The entries in which he captured his dreams right away are concise and clipped – he jumps straight to the essence of what he was experiencing and gets it succinctly down on the page, even inventing new words to encapsulate an image, or relying on numerical code. If he returned to a dream later, he more often struggled to grasp what had happened and would try where he could to reclaim a certain thought or feeling. He suggested that memory and new imaginative ideas were most powerfully awakened by the occurrence of a whole mood or state of being, most notably when it repeated or resembled a previous one. He found that powerful emotions underpinned a lot of his dreams, and it was these emotions that stimulated memories to resurface.

When we are in NREM, the neural firings in our brain unite in an astonishing coordination of mental unity: our cerebral cortex, which plays a central role in attention, perception, awareness and thought, relaxes into a deliberate, default mode and an almost hibernating state. In REM, the situation reverses. We are often more attentive when we dream than in our waking hours – some parts of the brain are up to 30 per cent more active – and electrical brain-wave activity is typically of an elevated, but nonetheless very similar, form to when we are awake. This is exactly what Coleridge found: the images he recalled from his dreams were more vivid than many of his imaginings in everyday life, and he deduced that this was a direct result of the exclusion of all outward impressions on our senses when we dream.

In REM sleep, we watch our own private theatre of memory, with no distraction or interruption, except for when we are suddenly woken, and we see different events of our lives combine in ever-new sequences and associations. The amount of time that human beings spend dreaming is markedly different from other primates – whereas we sleep for eight hours a day on average and other primates sleep for a far longer ten to fifteen hours, we manage to pack in far more REM: typically 20 to 25 per cent of our sleep is spent dreaming, while for other primates it is just 9 per cent. This is another fundamental way in which we are unique in the mammalian world: no other species spends as much time as we do consolidating our memories in our sleep or fine-tuning the connections in our brains.

Neuroscience today confirms what Coleridge intuitively believed: when we dream, we take our most recent experiences, freshly preserved by our NREM sleep, and begin colliding them with other memories from the whole backstory of our lives. As in a chemical reaction, our memories combine together to form new ideas. When we have a good night's rest, we solidify our learnings from the day before, and the vast associative networks of memories that fire in our minds during REM sleep create new links between entirely unrelated experiences. This is exactly what happened to Coleridge when he fell asleep at the farm. As he entered a deep sleep and then began to dream, his mind took his most recent experience of reading about Kublai Khan and Xanadu and spliced it with a mix of other thoughts and images.

Numerous academics have scrupulously studied Coleridge's notebooks and annotations in books from the same period and argue that the reading that informs much of the poem spans four continents: it seems Coleridge may have been influenced by travel writing about Asia, Africa and North and South America, and by the work of Ancient Greek writers Plato, Herodotus and Strabo; by Seneca's and Virgil's writing from Roman antiquity; and by seventeenth-century English poet John Milton's *Paradise Lost*, among other sources. Yet there are also lines in the poem for which no literary source has been uncovered; these more likely stemmed from Coleridge's wider reading or his walks and lengthy discussions with Wordsworth, but also from a deep haul of his unconscious and his life experiences up until that point. When he woke up, the lines of the poem flowed quickly and easily from his pen.

History is full of accounts of resolutions arrived at after a good night's sleep, or of entirely new ideas surfacing upon waking, such as George Daniels' vision of the coaxial escapement. The periodic table of elements was conceived in a dream after the Russian chemist Dmitri Mendeleev fell asleep wrestling with a pattern he had found in atomic weights: he woke suddenly, visualizing a table where all of the constituents of the known universe fell into place, and proceeded to write it down. And it was also only when fellow chemist August Kekulé dozed in front of the fire and dreamed of a snake eating its own tail that he succeeded in determining the ring structure of the chemical benzene. Author Mary Shelley famously hit upon the form and narrative of her novel *Frankenstein* after waking from a particularly frightening nightmare, while Charles Dickens's essay 'A Sleep to Startle Us' describes how he would also often awake from his dreams with a storyline or characters, including Ebenezer Scrooge of *A Christmas Carol* and Miss Havisham in *Great Expectations,* well formed in his mind. Classical composers Brahms, Puccini and Wagner were all reportedly in sleep states while arranging some of their best-known compositions, and many songs in the contemporary canon of popular music have also arrived in dreams: Paul McCartney settled on 'Yesterday' and 'Let It Be' just as he woke up; and Keith Richards of the Rolling Stones created the opening riff to 'Satisfaction' while fully asleep.

Studies by neuroscientists have confirmed that when we sleep, our restricting sense of judgement is removed so that ideas and thoughts can collect and influence one another in unforeseen ways. Additionally, our problem-solving abilities significantly improve in the moments just before we enter deep sleep, although answers to problems commonly take a while to surface and require our awareness and attention on waking.

Perhaps the most famous inventor who relied on sleep was Thomas Edison. Rather than wait for the serendipity of a dream to help him come up with new ideas, he deliberately took naps when he was struggling with a problem. He would allegedly take a rest sitting at his desk, and place a pad of paper and pen on the armrest of his chair, ready for when he woke up. But to be sure he caught the exact moment as he drifted into a deeper sleep, he would hold steel ball bearings in his hand. The muscles in his hands slackened as he fell asleep, and the balls clattered into pans on the floor to shock him back awake to rethink whatever challenge he was tackling.

Edison's most renowned invention was the light bulb, so it is ironic that today it is artificial light – particularly in the form of the tiny pixels that light up our screens – that most often prevents us getting the sleep we need, or using it in the best way to inspire our creativity. Numerous recent studies outline how damaging the disruptive effects of technology can be to sleep. In particular, the close proximity of our phones creates in us a tendency to remain online, even in the last moments before we fall asleep and typically within minutes of waking. By limiting screen use in the mornings and evenings – and better yet, removing devices entirely from our places of rest – we can protect our sleep and create space to fully experience the transitional moments when we awake from our dreams, strengthening our memory and expanding our thinking.

'Kubla Khan' closes with a final section that was written later by Coleridge, when he could no longer recapture the intoxicating burst of images delivered so easily to him upon waking that evening at the farm. This final stanza is less lucid and free-flowing and feels more premeditated. Coleridge explains in his preface that his process of quickly writing down the lines of the poem upon stirring from his dream was interrupted by a person on business from Porlock, a nearby village – the poem, he claims, would otherwise have been 200 or 300 lines long. As Coleridge experienced, our creative powers can so easily be hijacked. These days, of course, we are constantly interrupted by business, usually delivered via our phones, and our transient dream states – sources of such creativity – as well as sleep itself, are often the casualties of our constant connectedness.

A WILLING SUSPENSION OF DISBELIEF

Later in his life, and after some tortuous periods battling opium addiction and a total collapse of his health, Coleridge published his *Biographia Literaria* in 1817, an autobiographical review of his work to date, and a meditative look at the shaping power of the human imagination. Within it, he revisits his collaboration with Wordsworth and the origin of their

Lyrical Ballads, a publication that secured Coleridge's early fame and ushered in a new era of Romantic poetry, and in which he wrote his most famous description of the imagination at work on the reader's mind: 'that willing suspension of disbelief for the moment which constitutes poetic faith'. Ever since, the phrase 'willing suspension of disbelief' has been used in relation to the capacity a creative work has to directly control the thoughts and imagery that we hold in our mind. We can use our imagination to create, but we also quite willingly offer it up to interpret others' creations.

Part of the mystery of dreams that most intrigued Coleridge was their continued novelty. He was deeply aware that a dream totally possesses us and that, in the majority of our dream states, we cannot control the sequence of events that unfold. In studies of his own dreams, Coleridge found them to be of a 'streamy' nature, with their own quite distinct feeling of continuity; and they always appeared quite real, even though the events that unfolded often seemed irrational or incoherent in retrospect.

Coleridge frequently referred to his own dreams as stage dramas, complete with their own characters and settings, and unique time and spatial conventions. He was a keen enthusiast of theatre and played a central role in reviving the plays of Shakespeare, whose popularity had waned in the years since his death. Coleridge's extensive writings and public lectures on Shakespeare explained the complex beauty of his work in a way that made it accessible again to a mainstream audience, and this resurgence of interest helped secure the renown of Shakespeare's work that continues today. Coleridge's close acquaintance with his dreams, together with his detailed study of Shakespearean theatre, allowed him to arrive at his own unique conclusion that both dreams and stagecraft direct our attention and thoughts in fundamentally the same way. To be fully swept away in the theatre, we not only have to suspend our disbelief but also largely forgo our own perceptive control – in just the same way as when we dream.

For Coleridge, one of the key differences between when we are asleep and when we are awake is that our dreams can have the most fantastical or comically bizarre circumstances, yet we accept them at face value.

Coleridge found the same forces to be at play whenever we read a novel or watch a stage drama: as a plot develops, we adjust to the events that take place and accept them in good faith, even though we might find their occurrence in everyday life unrealistic or perplexing. Coleridge suggested that we gradually choose to be deceived when we immerse ourselves in something that has been created by another person. For him, the true circumstances of stage illusion rest on a steady surrender of our autonomy: the longer we stay within the narrative world created onstage (so long as our experience is not punctured by an obvious plot-hole or distraction), the more we accept what we see and settle within the experience.

Coleridge's river or stream is an apt illustration of how our attention moves effortlessly from one thing to the next without conscious control, much like water following the path of least resistance and drifting downstream due to gravity. Attention also has its own natural flow, and unless we make an effort to control its course, it moves according to a number of preset psychological modes. Our attention is led more by our predispositions and encounters with the outside world than by our own conscious control. Every slight shift in focus not only steers our eyes, ears or thoughts but also guides our entire perceptual apparatus, including our conscious awareness at that moment and the changing mental pictures in our imagination.

In the absence of something prompting our attention, we have a natural tendency to let our minds wander. Research has found that we spend as much as 50 per cent of our time each day focusing on something that is entirely irrelevant to whatever we might be doing. With freedom, our attention finds its own inclination to go where it wants, and cognitive research suggests that our daydreams are not at all as passive as when our attention is taken from us. In fact, when we become lost in thought – or, to another person, seem absent-minded – we place a block on our senses for a time. If something important happens, we quickly revert back to attending to the world around us, but otherwise, we point our attention inwards. The images that cycle through our mind when we daydream are guided by some of our deep concerns and desires, many of which we may not readily recognize. Cognitive scientists today classify daydreams as a form of active attention, and although, during daydreaming, we are largely unaware of outside stimuli for much of the time (much like in many of our other kinds of dream states), studies have shown our brain activity to be very similar while daydreaming to when we are intently focusing on an active task.

Daydreaming plays a vital function in reframing our thoughts and recalibrating our habits of mind. Research studies have found our daydreams to perform many of the same functions as REM sleep; we consolidate our memories when we brood on different topics in the day, and as we realign our thoughts and views, we inevitably adjust our personal perspectives.

Suspending our disbelief when we enjoy a play or film is often congenial and illuminating in its own way as it leaves us open to new, unexpected experiences. But there are other instances in life when the effect can be more negative, and even damaging psychologically. Coleridge noticed that when we forgo conscious control, it can even disturb our personal identity. Although he distinguished different levels of loss of personal control when we sleep, daydream or become transfixed by things in daily life, he also noticed that at times when awake we can act just automatically as if we were deeply asleep. Throughout his life, Coleridge proposed that there was an intimate connection between the ways in which we dream and our waking lives, in particular the ability we all have to drift meaningfully and freely in and out of reverie. He pondered a question that resonates today: if our mind has the potential to be led automatically by external prompts and ideas, how does this affect our personal autonomy and the directions we are able to take in life?

Recent advances in neuroscience have shed light on why we are likely to become so immersed in stage dramas, novels, news feeds or videos. All of these engage the prefrontal cortex, the area of the brain responsible for our decision-making, reasoning and attentional control, and which is also implicated in imagination and mental simulations, whether self-directed or prompted by external sources. Studies have also found that the same executive functions of the brain are involved in narrative comprehension, specifically when constructing a coherent mental model of a story. The amygdala, a separate brain region involved in processing emotions, has been found to be active not only when someone is dreaming but also when they are watching emotionally charged theatrical scenes. Both experiences appear to tap into the same neural mechanisms for emotional processing.

Compare the amount of effort that goes into creating a blockbuster television series – the years developing a script, the hundreds of people on set, the months of painstaking work using the latest camera and computer-editing equipment – with the ease with which we can settle down to watch an episode from it. The same can be said for most of our everyday digital experiences. Merely showing a digital ad to a single person can emit half a litre of carbon dioxide into the atmosphere. It is typical for digital technology companies today to employ hundreds of thousands of people, and the volume of work that goes into maintaining a major social-media platform, search tool or web app is staggering, particularly if we again contrast it with how simple it is to consume the final result. The World Bank estimates that the digital economy contributes more than 15 per cent of global GDP: this is a phenomenal volume of enterprise and individual thinking minds, the majority of which are committed to capturing people's attention and directing it in preformulated ways.

Many of the multimedia forms that we take for granted as normal today – film and TV in particular, but increasingly the multitude of captivating forms of content that we find online – compete with our own dream states, most notably our daydreams. Studies have found the mental activation and cognitive reports from people watching a film, TV programme or video stream to be most similar to when we are idle or daydreaming; and uninterrupted, extensive TV viewing has been deemed to be a particularly receptive state. It's quite typical to seek out these pleasant modes of semi-consciousness for a time to escape from the troubles of the real world, and to use them as a means to create a new one. Many of the conventions of film scripts and TV programmes, such as cliffhangers or plot twists, are deliberate ploys to maintain that state of mind and keep us watching until we have 'completed' the experience. Digital technology has evolved in similar ways to keep our attention – the autoplay functions on streaming platforms that trigger at the end of any episode are perhaps the most visible example of this.

It is not only when we watch video content for hours at a time that we become less guarded and more suggestible. One of the prime features of contemporary life is the burden of a permanent, low-level attentiveness that our different devices demand throughout large stretches of our waking lives. Online, we typically fall into a meandering drift – we browse, click and scroll through reams of different pages, images and videos, often stopping only briefly as we go, and the standardized ways in which we typically respond make for an historically unprecedented mix of diffuse attentiveness and semi-automatism. It is a dream mode, not at all unlike our REM sleep or our daydreams, but the direction of its contents happens outside of our heads. We might be aware of some of the times when we allow our actions to be led by our devices, particularly when we are tired, but there are many other occasions when we are simply oblivious to the ways in which our behaviour is being regulated by external forces. Both daydreaming and dreaming are associated with the activation of the default mode network (DMN), a network of brain regions linked to self-reflection, mental stimulation and social awareness which are active when the mind is not focused on the external world. Two recent studies, one by the University of Copenhagen and one by the University of California, have found that browsing activity on digital devices is also associated with increased DMN activity.

Dreams play a role in our emotional processing, helping us make sense of our experiences and regulate our feelings, so when digital experiences resurface in our actual sleeping dreams – and academic research suggests that activities such as playing video games can influence dream content – our digital experiences become integrated into our memory networks, influencing how we remember and perceive events, which can affect our decision-making, beliefs and attitudes. Research on the full extent of the impact on dreams, memory integration and emotional processing is still at a nascent stage, but there is a distinct likelihood that digital experiences contribute to cultural or confirmation bias, influencing how we remember and interpret information, particularly when we spend extensive periods of time online. In addition, as the boundary between our authentic experiences and the virtual world presented by technology becomes increasingly indistinct, our sense of time and our ability to distinguish between real and fabricated events can be compromised, leaving us more susceptible to manipulation and misinformation.

Boredom can be a catalyst for many of our more interior, searching moments: when we are idle, we are at our most receptive. Daydreams in many ways can be a form of resistance – somewhere we can go to in our minds to retreat from the world and make better sense of it for ourselves – and they can help us withstand the more adverse effects of so much of the routinization and coercion of thought in modern-day life. When we go online because we are bored, a digital experience takes over the time that might otherwise have been spent daydreaming, making us more liable to being influenced by external input, which threatens our personal identity.

It is important to acknowledge that the incredible imagery in Coleridge's 'Kubla Khan' may have been heavily influenced by the poet's opium use. He would take it as laudanum, a drink dissolved in brandy, and he had a dose that night at the farm. By 1804, when he had moved to the Lake District, he found himself battling a serious addiction, and towards the middle of his life, he made a serious effort to finally break off his dependence.

Although we might not be aware of it, the technology through which we encounter visual imagery can also prove to be damagingly addictive. Just as opium provided relief and vivid creativity for Coleridge but ultimately led to harmful addiction, an over-reliance on TV, online videos and other digital experiences as a form of escape can result in issues such as inattentiveness, poor mental health, weakened relationships and other negative consequences in the long run.

'Kubla Khan' has continued to inspire popular culture today, perhaps most prominently *Citizen Kane* – routinely voted the greatest film of all time – in which the enormous, luxurious estate named

Xanadu, built by Charles Foster Kane, a newspaper mogul, becomes a kind of gilded cage for its creator. The *Oxford English Dictionary* now defines Xanadu as a false paradise and place of magnificent excess that serves as a cautionary tale.

Might the internet be today's Xanadu, a place of fantastical imagery that threatens to imprison us? Online, and increasingly with virtual and augmented reality technology, we can conjure almost any vision, travel to new worlds, and see spectacles that would be impossible in the real world. However, as Coleridge discovered in his dependence on opium, such artificial manufacture of daydreams can come at a substantial cost. When we replace our idle, natural states of daydreaming with online stimulation, we forgo mental restoration and clarity and risk our thoughts and emotions being influenced without our awareness. How, then, can we protect our sleep and natural daydreams, which help ground us in our real-world lives, memories and identities?

MAKE ROOM TO DREAM

Research has shown that excessive screen time can impact on your sleep, and poor sleep can negatively affect your cognitive functioning – including attention, memory and decision-making, the facilities you rely on to evaluate the credibility of information and discern fact from fiction.

With a healthy sleep routine, you should spend two hours each night dreaming during REM. Cognitive scientists have found that daydreaming for around 30 to 50 per cent of waking hours is normal and considered healthy for most individuals; but if you're anything like the average adult in the United States, who typically spends 75 per cent of waking hours interacting with media and devices, there's little time left for your own daydreams.

Understanding how human beings have made more space and time for sleep and daydreaming in the past, you can more easily make changes to improve the quality of your own. Being more attentive to the different states of consciousness that you pass through each day is a great way to begin.

Sleep hygiene

In sleep-research circles, the term 'sleep hygiene' encompasses the natural habits and practices you can follow for a good night's rest. Sleep is one of the last activities in modern life that remains roughly in sync with the daily rhythms of solar light and darkness; but, of course, artificial light and screen technology have profoundly shifted sleep patterns compared to those of previous generations. Electric light has been one of the most fundamental lifestyle changes for human beings, and one of course that you'll be fully accustomed to. You can continue to enjoy the freedoms you have over your ancestors: most notably in the winter months, when life really did used to grind to a halt in the evenings. But there are a few steps you can take to protect your rest so that it matches more closely the ways that the human body has naturally evolved to sleep.

For the vast majority of humans that have ever lived, very few activities were possible once it was dark. A naked flame was the most light that would have been available, and there was little to do after dusk. Oil-burning lamps were the first significant invention to change things – the earliest known examples date back to Ancient Egypt, Greece and Rome – and the first street lighting was installed in London during Coleridge's lifetime. Yet it was not until Edison built the first commercial power plant in New York in 1882 that humans' access to light at night fundamentally altered. Your eyes can take in a light spectrum that encompasses the shorter violet or blue wavelengths, and longer ones of yellow and red. Sunlight is a powerful blend of all of these wavelengths, and your brain notices as soon as it disappears. When it gets dark, the pineal gland at the back of your head releases high quantities of melatonin, signalling to your body that it's time for sleep. But artificial light – even if it is just a bedside lamp dimmed to a low lux – fools your brain into believing that the Sun has not yet set and delays the melatonin that you need to fall asleep.

In 1997, a trio of Japanese engineers produced blue beams from a semiconductor and went on to create the first bright white LED, creating an entirely new form of artificial light. Laptop, tablet and phone screens are all LED-powered, and they're another way that we trick our minds that it's still daytime. All of the extra illumination that you receive from your home lighting, and from the screens that shine brightly in your face, wind back your internal clock by as much as two or three hours each night. It's only when you turn out your bedside lamp that your body begins to get the levels of melatonin that you need for the onset of deep sleep, and if you struggle to drop off, it is most likely because your melatonin has still not reached peak concentration.

Using a screen just before sleep has been found to cause a significant loss of REM sleep, and you will feel less rested and sleepier the following day. The neuroscientist and sleep specialist Matthew Walker suggests that you can suffer from a 'digital hangover effect', a ninety-minute lag in your rise in melatonin levels that lasts for several evenings after you stop watching screens late at night. Screens also stimulate your mind when you would be better winding down. To remove the temptation to use a screen in the late evening, the easiest way is to clear away any gadgets or screens from your bedroom: buy an alarm clock with a non-lit screen, if you need one, and make your sleeping quarters a place where you can retreat from digital life.

TAKE ACTION

- **Keep your bedroom screen-free:** Remove any TVs, laptops, phones or other screens from your place of rest for one month and see what effect it has.
- **Set an alarm to start your bedtime routine:** Factor in eight hours' sleep as well as enough time to drop off and wake up naturally.
- **Turn off your morning alarm:** Test waking naturally for a week without an alarm and notice any difference in how you feel.

It's quite normal to take half an hour or so to fall asleep, so try not to worry if sleep does not come right away. The most important thing is to give yourself the opportunity to get your full eight hours. (Studies suggest that it's very rare to need less sleep than this each night, and if you regularly get just six or seven hours, it will affect your health and well-being over the long term.) One excellent habit is to set an alarm for when you need to go to bed, rather than setting it for when to get up, so you can plan in the time you need to pass through all sleep states and wake up refreshed in the morning. A morning alarm suddenly spikes your blood pressure and heart rate, and if you can avoid using one, it is far better for you. Waking naturally allows you to get all of the REM sleep you need, and you can enjoy a pleasant series of dream states at the start of each day.

A second sleep

The historian Roger Ekirch made a fascinating discovery when he was researching a book on the history of nighttime and consulted the UK's National Archives – a maze of shelves filled with ancient vellum and manuscripts dating back over 1,000 years. He noticed, from the late Middle Ages to the early modern period, increasing references to people 'double sleeping', and of taking a 'first' and a 'second sleep' each night; when Ekirch expanded his search to include online databases of other written records, he uncovered how widespread this way of sleeping truly was: in Italy, a first sleep was the '*primo sonno*', in France, the '*première somme*' – and evidence of this could be found in countries around the world. People would typically go to bed at a normal time, but then they would often awake and get up in the middle of the night, a time that was known as 'the watch', and was most commonly filled with light tasks or chores. The philosopher Henry David Thoreau placed a pen and paper under his pillow and wrote in the dark when he awoke; the Buddha is reputed to have attained his enlightenment during a night watch.

As you get older, your sleep tends to naturally break into the same pattern, and from the age of fifty, many people revert to this historic custom of getting up in the night for a while. Yet waking regularly in the middle of the night can be a cause of anxiety or concern for many, and can be readily labelled as insomnia today. Sleep science has arrived at a recent consensus that the 'monophasic' sleep patterns most people adopt in the industrialized world are not our most natural mode and that 'biphasic' sleep can offer distinct benefits. So when you next wake up in the middle of night, try to settle into the experience and consider it part of your daily rest – it's also a unique opportunity for some contemplative time alone. Avoid screens and switching on any lights if you can; instead, relax into your thoughts and aim for a sense of calm. It's a time when you can be most receptive to new ideas, and one of the few times in the day when there are no distractions. Take Thoreau's lead and keep a pen and paper by your bed: if you feel inclined, write down any observations or thoughts.

Historically, in colder climates with long dark winters the two sleeps have been taken at night, whereas in warmer settings, a midday siesta has often replaced a first sleep. If you work from home, taking a nap in the day can be a fantastic way to get time away from your desk and to give reprieve from the pressures of always being online. Daytime naps have been proven to improve alertness, cognitive performance and mood, without causing extended grogginess. You have a 'post-prandial alertness dip' mid-afternoon that has been found to be a normal part of the daily rhythm of human life; this is the perfect time, if circumstances allow, to listen to your body and have a rest. A nap can help you consolidate your memories, as long as you take at least twenty minutes to sleep, and can be an excellent boost when you're working on a complicated project or trying to learn something new. If you have lost out on sleep the night before, napping can also help dispel some of the exhaustion you might be feeling.

While the twenty-minute 'power nap' is often suggested as ideal, there is also growing evidence that a longer nap of around an hour can be more restorative if you time it correctly. Experiment to find what works best for you – try different lengths of time and notice how you feel afterwards, as it's best to wake up at the end of a sleep cycle. Be sure not to nap after 3 p.m., as this can make it harder to fall asleep at night. A NASA-sponsored study has found that naps increase attentiveness, and the US army includes 'strategic napping' in its fitness manual to 'build physical' and 'mental toughness' and to 'restore wakefulness and promote performance' – so it's worth giving it a try.

TAKE ACTION

- **Make space for 'the watch':** Use night wakings as opportunities for contemplation, writing down thoughts and observations in the dark.
- **Take a nap:** Build a daytime snooze into your daily routine, ideally in the early to mid afternoon, and observe any effects on your alertness and mood later in the day.
- **Try a longer siesta:** Experiment with some longer naps, setting an alarm each time initially to wake. Compare their effects with shorter naps and with naps taken at different times in the afternoon.

Hypnagogia

The term 'hypnagogia' was first coined by the French physician Alfred Maury in 1848, in a pioneering study that explored the vivid images, thoughts and perceptual experiences you can encounter when you fall asleep. Accounts of the lucid reality of these dream states date back to some of the earliest written records of human civilization, but Maury was the first to explore their onset, and how they might be maintained. There was a burst of sleep studies around this time, and the topic has been taken up again more recently by neuroscience. A consensus has formed today that by prompting more remote associations and abstract thinking, hypnagogia can be used to generate fresh, new ideas.

Research has found hypnagogic imagery to range from faintly perceptible experiences to very real hallucinations. People tend to recount a sharpness of detail and feelings of multi-sensory reality. Memories from earlier in the day are often a central feature, particularly something that a dreamer has been concentrating on intensely for a period of time, but these memories quickly link to older recollections. A common feature is synaesthesia, in which one sense stimulates impressions in other ways.

Maury found – as have many other sleep researchers since – that hypnagogic states are highly receptive and tend to magnify simple sensory impressions to make them more acute. If you pay attention to the dreams that you pass through as you fall asleep, you can begin to sustain a vision or experience for longer, and you can also control it. The times between your waking moments and sleep give you a level of awareness and control that is impossible in deep sleep. Your consciousness can skim over your dreams, and so long as you are not too disruptive, you can also give them the lightest nudge or steer. It takes a little practice, but more often than not the experience is very pleasant.

The thoughts that transpire in a dream are unimpeded by any preconceptions of what you might deem to be possible, and they can open up entirely new perspectives and answers. If you have a particularly tricky problem, go to bed with it in your mind, and lightly look at it from different angles as you rest. Keep a pen and paper close by so you can record anything of note, but only once things have run their course. Don't push to fall asleep; as you relax and get caught up in your thoughts, sleep will most likely come on its own. Look out for signs that you are falling into a dream state – feelings of slight disorientation or a sense of different mood or way of being – and let this happen on its own for a while, but keep watch.

Sleep researchers also distinguish another state that you pass through every day: 'hypnopompia', when you stir back into consciousness from sleep. Studies have found vivid perceptual experiences and lucid dreaming to be less likely when you awake, but they do still happen. Having the time to wake up more slowly each morning – by going to bed at a good time the night before and by keeping to a regular pattern of sleep, so that you do not need an alarm – leaves you more open to experience these dream states, and they can also prompt some unexpected ideas. More typically, it is first thing in the morning that answers to a problem can often suddenly arrive in your head: often there's no need to be in a dream state for this to happen. Instead, you need to be receptive to any new connections that might have formed in your sleep the night before. Again, write down your thoughts once they settle in your head, as they can quite quickly disappear.

TAKE ACTION

- **Keep a pen and paper by your bed:** Record any thoughts that might strike you in your dream states or waking moments.
- **Stay with a dream:** Observe imaginary situations that you find yourself passing through as you fall asleep, and pay attention to them a little more consciously.
- **Find your own answers:** Go to bed with a challenging problem in your mind and delicately assess it from different perspectives as you fall asleep. Be alert to any dream state that might take over, and lightly try to steer your dream.
- **Watch your thoughts first thing:** As you naturally stir awake in the morning, be ready to note down any new thoughts or ideas as they form in your mind.

Daydream more

While dreams during sleep are particularly important for memory consolidation, emotional regulation and your overall mental health, daydreaming also plays a crucial role in your mental and emotional well-being. Your daydreams are particularly useful for creativity and problem-solving: as your mind wanders, you explore various scenarios, and as you look at problems from different perspectives, it becomes easier to find answers. Daydreams are a safe space to visualize your goals and ambitions, and mentally rehearse the steps that you might need to take to achieve them. You can also explore different emotional responses as you run through different situations in your mind, gauging how you might react and helping you better understand and manage your feelings.

Downtime or moments when you're engaged in low-demand tasks are excellent times to daydream, and this can also help to create some mental space. Meditation and breathwork can be a fantastic way to settle your mind and sweep out distracting thoughts, both to clear your head, especially after too much time spent online, and to help new ideas surface. Studies confirm that a meditation practice can train your mind to be better prepared to wander whenever you get an opportunity to daydream, and as meditation and breathwork also enhance meta-awareness, the ability to be aware of your thoughts, you are also better able to monitor your daydreams to catch new insights and ideas. If you're at home or work close to a park, a tremendous way to reset is to lie down for a simple breath practice for ten minutes. Rather than follow the techniques covered in the 'Solitude' chapter, on these occasions, all you need to do is close your eyes and focus on drawing deep breaths to your lower abdomen. See if you can establish ongoing flow between your breaths, never quite stopping before your next inhale or exhale. Set your own pace, but always aim to breathe deeply. Once the time is up, you'll feel restored and notice a steadiness of thought. Ideas and new associations may not come right away, but with a stilled mind and fresh mental energy, they often emerge later. If you can, take time after your breath practice to simply sit or walk, and let your thinking expand into your now uncluttered mind.

At other times, a quick stroll or a break from whatever you are doing is more than enough. When you find yourself wrestling with something, take time out to do nothing in particular: make a cup of tea or coffee, finish off some household chores, or take a long bath or a shower. In these downtimes, when your mind is most idle and free, some of your most profound or unexpected ideas may arrive. When they do, hold on to these moments for as long as you can, exploring them more fully, then jot those thoughts down or record them as voice memos on your phone there and then, as they may be all too fleeting.

You can also refine your daydreams with visualization techniques most often used in sports psychology – mental imagery has been proven to support skills acquisition and athletes regularly mentally rehearse their performance to find new incremental gains. Extensive academic research has established a link between actively generated mental imagery and daydreaming, with several studies indicating that visualization exercises can bolster the cognitive processes and neural pathways that you engage when you daydream. To give it a go, start with simple objects. Visualize an apple or pear and focus on its shape, colour and texture, to create a vivid, 3D image that you can mentally rotate. Test making it change colour, slice it in half or even explode it into small pieces.

Once you've got a deeper feel for how you can control imagery in your mind, try some more complex scenarios. Imagine yourself setting up a fruit stall with a few friends: a new business venture in which each of you has a vested interest. Picture different varieties of fruit arriving in boxes as you stack them high on shelves. Engage all of your senses to make it feel as real as you can: notice the fresh colours, the variety of scents and smells and then populate the scene with a busy flow of customers. See if you can incorporate emotions, testing how you might feel if more difficult customers haggle, or if someone shows an act of kindness. Training yourself to add more detail to your visualizations improves your ability to create and explore your own mental scenes – athletes who practise this technique often find it helps to make their daydreams more vivid too.

If you have a big decision to make, such as whether to accept a job or move house, your visualizations can be extended into more involved thought experiments, in which you run through possible pros and cons and sequences of events depending on your decision and its potential consequences. This can be a very helpful framework for thinking through problems you are stuck on, or for finding creative solutions. Thought experiments have supported some of humankind's most innovative intellectual breakthroughs: Copernicus was the first to realize that the

Earth orbits the Sun, by visualizing it in his head; the concept of the atom was first formulated in Ancient Greece in just the same way; and any number of other theories or inventions, from Schrödinger's cat to the electric motor and the vacuum pump, were first conceived in the confines of a human mind.

But of course, your daydreams need not always be overtly useful. We often daydream for contemplation's sake alone, as a very human activity and refuge from some of the demands of everyday life. This isn't mere 'timewasting' though – compared to some of the passive pursuits that you might search out online when you are bored, your daydreams engage your mind in a far more active, introspective way, and give you far more opportunity for self-reflection and personal growth. When you daydream, you learn about your own emotions, values and deepest desires: in short, about yourself.

TAKE ACTION

- **Clear your head with restorative breathwork:** When you finish, observe whether your mind feels clearer, and whether thoughts come more easily to you.
- **Do nothing:** When you next stall on a challenging piece of work, see if taking time out helps you arrive at some different thoughts or answers.
- **Practise your visualization skills:** Picture a simple object, focusing on its shape, colour and texture, and see if you can rotate it in your mind. Progress to visualizing more detailed scenes and scenarios.
- **Try a thought experiment:** Use visualization techniques for more extended thought experiments, such as running through the possible pros and cons of a big life decision.

Chapter 11

Thought

THE GATHERING STORM

Renowned as a wartime prime minister, Winston Churchill was also a talented and prolific writer and the winner of the 1953 Nobel Prize in Literature. It is hard to find any other political leader who has produced such a high volume of sophisticated writing on history and world events, particularly while in office. Churchill's vast corpus of work – over 20 million words across his published books, letters, memos and papers, including his 1.5 million-word *The Second World War* and his four-volume *History of the English-Speaking Peoples* – captures a human mind struggling to understand not only the most complex machinations of the world stage but also how we think and construe reality.

Over the course of his sixty-year professional writing career, Churchill developed elaborate working methods to help him process high quantities of information and factual data. He built a team of dedicated researchers and other writers, who were responsible for compiling vast bodies of text that he then worked through and examined critically. To help himself analyse and reflect on all this research, he dictated prolifically, consolidating his thoughts as he spoke in his study, car or even the bath, and honing his power to think along seemingly contrary lines to arrive at his own unique conclusions.

He came to power in the Second World War in large part as a result of his solitary contestations over the years in the House of Commons of the policy of appeasing Hitler and his warnings about where the government's miscalculated strategy was likely to lead. Historians struggle to explain how Churchill succeeded in being correct about Hitler from the very start, but it is likely his ability to parse dense volumes of data and interpret them for himself left him able to confidently make his own decisions and judgements in highly volatile, turbulent times. Churchill also lived a very full, exertive life: he was a pilot in the early days of flight and an active participant in two world wars, and he was a dedicated painter as well as a writer. He brought these rich life experiences to his decision-making, grounding his analysis and thoughts in his embattled learnings in the real world.

A direct descendant of the Duke of Marlborough, whose leadership of the armies fighting Louis XIV consolidated Britain's emergence as a top-rank power in the early 1700s, Churchill had a privileged background yet did not take well to the traditional expectations of education for males of his social status. While he was a young cavalry officer serving in Bangalore, he began his own self-schooling, reading an array of books on history and military strategy in particular and trying his hand at writing. He decided to become a journalist and soon found his authorial voice reporting on the ground in Cuba and the Sudan, and in South Africa, during the Boer War. He was captured and held at a prisoner-of-war camp in Pretoria but managed to escape by hiding in a coal mine before travelling by train to Portuguese East Africa (now Mozambique) disguised as a railway employee. The British media and general public had been closely following news of his escape, and when he arrived home in Britain, he found himself a national hero.

He entered politics and, by the time of the First World War, was serving as First Lord of the Admiralty, in overall command of the Royal Navy. He developed a host of new naval technologies, as well as adopting the convoy system to protect merchant ships from German submarines, but he was also responsible for planning the Dardanelles campaign, which was a failed attempt by the British and French to open up a new front in the war and establish a supply route to Russia via the Black Sea. His reputation was so seriously damaged as a result of the failed campaign that he resigned from his post and found himself progressively sidelined from politics.

After the war, he published *The World in Crisis*. It was in the writing of this 824,000-word analysis of what had led to the conflict and its eventual outcome – also in part a refutation of some of the more damaging claims made against him – that Churchill perfected his research and writing methods as well as what he called the 'three Ds': his documents, dictation and drafts.

The Churchill Archive is housed in Cambridge today, and its 800,000 documents are open to researchers and the public by appointment. Dedicated files are held on each of his published works, including 400 cases for the six volumes of *The Second World War* alone, and they reveal how Churchill worked with such large volumes of information. He professed to 'write a book the way they built the Canadian Pacific Railway. First I lay the track from coast to coast, and after that I put in all the stations', and he also compared his writing to building a house, planning a battle or painting a picture: first laying out his foundations and then carefully collecting data before he arrived at any conclusions. During his time as prime minister in the Second World War, he arranged for all of his letters, minutes, directions and telegrams to be collected into monthly volumes, and when it came to writing his history of the conflict, he reassembled these originals and 'pruned' what he did not need until he arrived at a final set of documents to be printed as source material.

Not only are his personal documents and writing held in the archive; the files also contain the work of his research assistants, the team of writers that he called 'the syndicate', which included Hastings Ismay, who went on to become the first Secretary General of NATO; William Deakin, future head of an Oxford University college; and a whole host of other bright minds and experts. The team would revisit an entire body of historical content, including Churchill's own, looking for 'gleams' that could be put to use; these were set aside and printed. The assistants also created original and insightful research in the form of full drafts of notes on political developments and world events. This wide assortment of documentation was pieced together in chronological order, ready for a more thorough analysis by Churchill in his eventual writing of *The Second World War*, an intricate work that he composed over seven years.

To help himself arrive at conclusions as he reviewed early galley proofs, he preferred to dictate late at night and would often pace around his study for several hours, running through his thoughts, sometimes in measured sentences, sometimes in a cascade of fast-flowing ideas. Churchill did a great deal of structured reminiscing just after the war in 1946 and 1947; printed on a hundred or so pages in the archive are some of his most vivid memories, including his in-person meetings with Roosevelt and Stalin. His dictations recount the flights he had to make in a converted Liberator bomber over combat zones, with a risk of being shot down at any time: the plane was unheated, he slept on a shelf with blankets, and whenever they rose above 12,000 feet, he had to suck on an oxygen tube. It was at these meetings in Tehran, Yalta and Potsdam that plans for the D-Day invasion of Normandy were conceived and a post-war reorganization of Europe and the fate of Germany later decided; Churchill's meticulous evaluation of this decision-making period made its way into the final chapters of his book.

As Churchill dictated, a secretary or research assistant would be transcribing his notes or collecting other documents for him to fact-check. His personal wartime secretary, Kathleen Hill, muffled the keys on her typewriter to avoid disturbing his train of thought. In the morning, over breakfast, Churchill would inspect the typescript from the night before and make more edits and annotations.

Out of this mass of documents and dictated thoughts, draft chapters would be produced, covered with Churchill's handwritten notes in blue crayon and red ink. They would go to the printers by courier with multiple copies usually returned within twenty-four hours, and then sent on to assistants and former colleagues for further comments. This process would continue, with entirely new sections added, and the typescript developed into an increasingly sophisticated critique of a sequence of events; most typically, a chapter would go through six to twelve revisions. Even when the final pages of a proofed script were ready to be bound, Churchill still continued to amend his text until the very last minute. He would 'bulldoze' his words into a final form, clearing his thoughts of excess so that he could arrive at the clearest and most robust opinions possible.

For all the individual knowledge and skills within the team, the writing process lacked coherence without Churchill, and the ultimate burden of original thought lay with him. As he worked across several volumes at a time, his thinking alone wove rafts of information together into a seamless whole. His most impressive skill was to sustain and build a line of argument over countless pages of text while imparting to it his own incisive, analytical power. Through all of this writing, Churchill insisted on telling his own story and developing his own informed, original viewpoint.

In the preface to *The Gathering Storm*, the first volume of his history of the Second World War, Churchill emphasizes that the conflict was avoidable and that 'it would be wrong not to lay the lessons of the past before the future'. Churchill frequently used his writing to play with carefully thought-through counterfactuals and alternative scenarios to test what might have led to different outcomes in human history. He presents the Second World War as a 'human tragedy' that was resoundingly caused by 'a failure of political leadership', convinced that what led to the armed conflict was 'exactly what is happening today [1947], namely no coherent or persistent policy, even in fundamental matters'. Churchill pinpoints critical turning points in the lead-up to the war: the invasion of German military forces in the Rhineland in 1936, directly contravening the Treaty of Versailles and the Locarno Treaties, and the Munich conference in September 1938: the last time the British Prime Minister Neville Chamberlain met with Hitler.

Most scholars now agree with Churchill's verdict that the meeting in Munich should have been the time for a full confrontation with Hitler. The Munich Agreement allowed Nazi Germany to annex the Sudetenland, predominantly German-speaking parts of Czechoslovakia, and it was not until a year later, upon the invasion of Poland, that the United Kingdom and France ultimately declared war on Germany. In the meantime, Hitler had taken advantage of the appeasement policies of the Western powers to expand the German military: Churchill points out that 'the vast tank production with which they broke the French Front did not come into existence till 1940'.

Churchill had lost his seat in the House of Commons in the general election of 1929 and was out of Parliament for a time. He continued to give speeches, warning about the rise of Nazi Germany and the need for the UK to rearm and strengthen its military, yet these views at the time were unpopular and unheeded. Only in 1935 did he go on to serve again in the government. By 1937, he was moved back to the position of First Lord of the Admiralty. When Germany launched a surprise invasion of France and the Low Countries in May 1940, the British and French armies were quickly defeated, and the evacuation of British and Allied troops from Dunkirk suddenly became critical. On the same day of the invasion, due to both this immediate crisis and the recent failure of the campaign to prevent the German occupation of Norway, Chamberlain resigned as prime minister, leaving Churchill as the only leader well equipped to lead the country in war. His assertion that victory could be claimed, communicated so clearly in his nationwide addresses broadcast live on radio and printed in full the next day in newspapers, helped the nation to rally around him. Churchill's time as prime minister from 1940 to 1945 is widely accepted as a good example of how a leader should act in a time of crisis: he was decisive, able to adapt quickly to changing circumstances and played a pivotal role in coordinating the efforts of all of the Allied powers. As one might expect, he was inundated with huge volumes of information daily, and he worked out his own methods to keep track of it all. He kept a map room in a bunker under Whitehall to monitor the movements of military units and the progress of battles, and many of his more momentous decisions were made there. His intelligence reports were vital: particularly top-secret information from Britain's code-breaking centre, Bletchley Park. Churchill travelled widely and often dangerously during the war, conducting inspection tours in North Africa, India, Burma and Singapore and also making visits to strategic locations in the East and West. He was in regular contact with the other Allied leaders and had a tiny cupboard room disguised as a private toilet that he would use to speak on the phone with Roosevelt.

Churchill's decisions during the war were not always popular – and with the benefit of hindsight, we can see that they were not always right – but they were decisive in moving events forward, and he played an integral role in bringing the war to a close. Most notably, beginning in 1942, after Britain had suffered a series of defeats and setbacks and the German army had occupied most of continental Europe, Churchill adopted an offensive strategy, opening up new fronts in Northern Africa and Italy. By committing German forces that otherwise would have been used on the Eastern front, the pressure on the Soviet Union was relieved, while also buying time for increased support from the United States. He assimilated the rich diversity of information he was presented with and relied on his own human instincts and intuition to decide on what he saw to be the best next steps; ultimately, he was successful in his efforts.

Each of us makes decisions in life, and although they are rarely as consequential as the ones Churchill navigated, they rely on exactly the same processes: we have to gather information, reflect on it and make the best sense of a situation that we can. Yet, in today's information age, the abundance of data and our increasing reliance on algorithms and AI risks influencing our analysis, narrowing our critical thinking and diminishing our ability to qualify judgements with our own personal experience. Opacity in the working methods of computer calculations together with the vast scale of data sets can, at times, almost entirely remove our human thinking from decision-making, and if data modelling, algorithms and AI are not carefully applied to reality, their usefulness can quickly be reduced.

Used wisely, though, technology can also powerfully augment our thinking without impinging on our subjectivity and creativity. Churchill relied on far more than his personal experience to inform his own thoughts: he built a whole team of expert assistants to help him arrive at clear answers in his writing and made use of expansive information resources to support his decisions as a military leader. In a similar way, we too can use AI language tools, algorithmic searches and other computer-programmed tools to support, rather than direct, our thinking.

By the end of the war, Churchill was quite possibly the most famous person in the world, his signature cigar, Homburg hat and V-sign as recognizable globally as Charlie Chaplin or Mahatma Gandhi. But it was his writing, and most notably *The Second World War*, that cemented his historical notability. So many of his turns of phrase remain in common use today – the 'iron curtain' and 'special relationship'; 'blood, sweat and tears'; his rallying cry to 'never give in'. There is something undeniably human about Churchill: he was boastful and even arrogant at times, but equally there was 'the black dog' of his depression, the strength of emotions he so visibly shared and felt, and his ability to empathize with others, whatever their predicament. He was certainly not always popular in his views: many people, then and now, would not agree with many of the political stances that he took. Second to the Dardanelles campaign and the comprehensive damage it did to his political reputation, his most crushing defeat was when he lost the General Election just after the end of the war, with a landslide victory to the opposing party. The British people were looking for change, and Churchill had to persevere for a further six years, listening and responding to people's requests before he succeeded in winning another term as prime minister in 1951. He naturally had his own agenda, and his political motivations and efforts to secure future prestige also influenced where he exerted his energies and thought. Readers and listeners in his day could take what he said in the context of what he stood for and in light of the wider cycle of world events. In his memoirs and war analysis, an attentive reader today will see his tendency to embellish some events while eliding others, yet this kind of more nuanced insight can be lost if his text is fed into a database for search indexing or AI machine-learning and delivered only in select snippets.

When we make sense of information now, it is not only words and thoughts that we need to critique but also the technological means by which they are delivered. Without understanding how they are compiled, when we see results returned to us – whether from opaque data sets generated at our workplace or as recommendations shown in search engines, news feeds or streaming services – we forgo the opportunity to personally seek out new information and interpret it for ourselves: only then can our opinions become more nuanced.

Churchill's vision of the future and individual choices was never fatalistic. He believed nothing was predetermined and that human history in itself consists of a series of negotiable crossroads. As he wrote in *The River War*, his historical account of the conquest of Sudan by Anglo-Egyptian forces, 'every incident is surrounded by a host of possibilities, any one of which, had it become real, would have changed the whole course of events'; for Churchill, humankind always has an opportunity to choose between alternative futures. He most celebrated the human flexibility of mind, our creative ability to take the information at our disposal and decide on new active ways forward rather than accept the seemingly inevitable. But he cannot have foreseen how seriously at risk this freedom of human thought would become in just a handful of decades.

We face our own different gathering storm today. Ideological differences and new strains of nationalism are a clear factor in global military conflict, but digital technologies too can ensnare and divide us. The fast-burgeoning AI industry, which is receiving phenomenal levels of investment from venture capital and concentrated strategic interest from major digital media companies will soon be releasing large numbers of intelligent applications, assistants and chat tools into the public domain, and the consequences for independent human thought are significant. Imminent generations of AI will be able to parse digital copies of the same files Churchill processed and write their own account of the Second World War in the very same style and tone of voice as Churchill. When entire books can be created by a computer, not to mention unfathomable numbers of news articles and social-media posts, visual advertising and, quite feasibly, blockbuster movies and TV series, we will witness a level of external control over human minds entirely unprecedented in sophistication, scale and scope.

What Churchill perhaps most represents is a tenacity of spirit, which, along with a sharpened intellect and wit, kept him forging forward through the complexities of life and politics. When it comes to working out how to turn a perceived serious threat into a positive opportunity, carefully thinking our way through to a deliberate solution is perhaps the most important human ability, especially in a time of radical and rapid change. Churchill's command of his own thinking made very real and concrete differences, not only in his own life, but for the people of Europe, and this kind of foresight and expedience of mind may be what is needed in leaders now more than ever as we face the most complex, world-changing opportunity – and fundamental risk – ever presented to humankind.

SOVEREIGN ORGAN OF BEHAVIOUR AND ACTION

Our thoughts originate from the flow of electrical energy between one nerve ending and another. It was not until 1888 that the source of our thinking, emotions and bodily movement was discovered for the first time: the Spanish neuroanatomist Santiago Ramón y Cajal had been staining nerve cells with black dye so that he could see them more clearly under a microscope, and he noticed that brain cells do not connect with one another directly. He found quite distinguishable spaces in between them – the synapses that electricity jumps across – and he realized that the web of connections in our mind was far more complex than first imagined.

It had been presumed that the human nervous system was a fairly fixed lattice net that connected different nerve cells throughout the body – one part of the brain was understood to always remain fixed to another, and signals and thoughts were thought to travel in set paths. But Cajal found that such a 'rigid, immutable' structure, 'incapable of being modified' went against our sense of the brain as 'malleable and capable of being perfected by means of well-directed mental gymnastics'. He deduced that our neurons can use their high numbers of synaptic connections to more fluidly interact with other parts of the brain. Cajal drew exceptionally beautiful and detailed drawings of the nerve cells that he saw, and it was primarily these illustrations that eventually won him, along with Camillo Golgi, the 1906 Nobel Prize in Physiology or Medicine. Cajal continued to study human thought, particularly dream states, throughout his life, and he is celebrated today not only as the founder of modern neuroscience but also as the first person to demonstrably connect the human brain with electrical science.

In the hours before he died in 1934, Cajal composed a brief note: 'I leave you something greater than any wonder of the senses: a privileged brain, sovereign organ of behaviour and action, which used wisely will immeasurably improve the analytical power of your senses. Thanks to it you can dive into the unknown and [. . .] it shall expand interminably so far that each evolutionary phase of *Homo sapiens* will don the characteristics of a new humanity.' We certainly are entering a new phase in human history today, and it has been the inventiveness of human thinking alone that has got us here: AI is unquestionably the most fundamental extension to natural thought humankind has ever encountered since the advent of writing, and the impact it is set to have on everyday life is bewildering and profound.

The underlying principles that support the very latest forms of AI are in fact similar to what Cajal discovered in brain cells in 1888. Large language models (LLMs) such as OpenAI's ChatGPT are comprised of hundreds of billions of parameters and are trained on hundreds of terabytes of textual data – from books and academic papers to most sections of the internet. The result is that they can undertake many intelligent tasks that historically we would have thought only possible done by a human, simply by reducing them to pattern recognition. When a question is entered into a state-of-the-art LLM, it can predict the most likely correct answer by running a query across its unimaginably large data set. It looks for similar patterns of text across the vast corpus of results that it finds, and it constructs an answer by determining the most likely arrangement of text that should come next. An LLM treats each single word in its terabytes of textual data as a discrete datapoint, and it is free to form connections between any of these datapoints – by means of the electrical impulses that flow through the hardware components of a computer. The flexibility and freedom this gives AI to process information is staggering, and it is so similar to the way that the neurons and synapses in our brains operate that the fundamental computational units an LLM has available to process information are themselves called 'neurons', a deliberate allusion to the human brain.

Since their development, LLMs have been combined with all sorts of different types of media. One of the first applications has been image generation: by training an LLM on a multi-modal data set of text–image pairs, it is possible to ask it, with speech alone, to create any type of new image. Hundreds of thousands of photos of hands could be loaded in with descriptions, together with drawings by Leonardo da Vinci, for example, and the app could then be asked to produce any new picture of a hand in the style of Leonardo. The results can be disarmingly convincing. In principle, this process could be applied to most forms of digital content. Although a movie, work of visual art or piece of music creates an altogether different type of experience for us, when it is held in a digital format, its computer code can be interrogated in similar ways by an LLM. It is the same for any digital file, whether it be a spreadsheet, website or an enormously sophisticated software application, and with careful training, an LLM can analyse the underlying code of anything digital that it is trained to review – and then with prompts, generate its own, new creations.

The ramifications of this are overwhelming. As computing power increases and the volumes of human knowledge that LLMs are exposed to grows, there is an obvious shift in what AI is able to do, and it moves far beyond the capacity of a single human mind. We are on the brink of a significant turning point in the history of humankind: very soon our day-to-day lives will be spent communicating not only with other human beings but also with other mind-like entities that are entirely computer-based. We're not talking about the kind of basic chat-bots we encounter in online customer-service interactions: these new, exotic systems will not only be able to chat with us but will also be able to interrogate a large portion of the human record to answer any questions that we might have and help us to innovate and create. AI will soon produce music videos, computer games or architectural designs for houses, and, each time, it will be able to take an almost limitless number of pre-existing examples as inspiration.

In writing about history, Churchill thought deeply about the true nature of causation, and how we can never be sure whether one historical event truly led on to the next. He recognized that complexity at times can become so impenetrable, the possible outcomes so numerous, that to observe and apprehend the true effects of global events was often a task beyond the intellect and industry of one human being. He understood too the limits of his archives – 'that these written fragments, luckily preserved, represent only a tiny part of all that happened' – and admitted that no written work of history could hope to include the whole variety of human experience. Churchill was aware that there is a limit to the human brain; and the breadth and volume of mental tasks that we are capable of is now easily surpassed by AI.

We have 100 billion neurons in our brains, and each can link to as many as 10,000 others. This gives us a possible 1,000 trillion connections (100,000,000,000,000,000) that we can form in our mind. Impressive, yes, but when an LLM comprised of 100 billion parameters is trained on 100 terabytes of data (and even today, these numbers are typically much higher), the upper limit of possible relationships that, in principle, can be made is as much as eighty sextillion (80,000,000, 000,000,000,000,000), depending on the architecture of an LLM and the task that it is asked to perform. 'Connections' in a neural network like an LLM are not physical connections but rather mathematical weights assigned to the influences that one artificial 'neuron' (a node in the network) has on another; and they are dependent on many factors, not just the number of parameters and the amount of training data. These mathematical weights adjust as the AI model learns, facilitating the complex interactions within the system. While AI developers do not monitor or control each of these adjustments – or typically have direct sight of them – with sufficient computing power and intricate design, an LLM of this scale could feasibly have billions of times more 'range' or potential for pattern recognition than a human brain.

Although AI has superhuman capacities to spot and generate patterns in volumes of information that go far beyond our reach – naturally, we would be unable to scan hundreds of thousands of photos of human hands in a moment and then instantly create an image in the style of Leonardo –

it is less than human in terms of its capabilities in a number of important and quite noticeable ways. LLMs, or indeed computer algorithms and other kinds of AI, cannot do a lot of the things that we take for granted in everyday life, and this is decidedly unlikely to change in the future. By being limited to processing data sets, AI is unable to step out into the real world in the ways that we are accustomed to. In addition, humans, at least at the moment, hold the fundamental control over any form of artificial computing power, most notably when it can be operated so easily with ordinary human speech – we can ask intricate questions in the most natural of ways, and as AI continues to develop, we will be able to interrogate data more closely than we have ever done so in the past. There are a lot of unknowns, and the scale of advances in AI computations makes it impossible to predict developments even in the next few years; but *for now*, the release of AI into mainstream society might not quite be the rapidly escalating problem for human thinking that it could first appear: in fact, it currently presents us with an altogether better way to interrogate and control our digital experience than what is possible with algorithms today.

Humans have evolved to co-exist over the 5.6 million years of our shared past, and our culture has developed over this time to ensure that we share a degree of mutual understanding. We inhabit a world with each other, and our language – whether it be spoken, written or visual – is primarily designed to point back to the reality around us. We are living beings that move and breathe in a phenomenally complex three-dimensional world, not generative mathematical models of statistical distribution that rely on vast collections of human-generated content. AI is not a life form by any stretch of the imagination, and it simply cannot comprehend reality in the ways that we do.

Whereas Churchill looked for causes and sought to get to the heart of why something happened, AI can only work with correlations in data sets. As Churchill paced in his study, chewing over ideas in his mind, he would 'triangulate' his own objective reality by comparing his personal experiences, the thoughts and perspectives of his collaborating team and any other factual references that he had to hand; only then would he arrive at a final view. Unlike humans, who live within a physical reality, AI cannot form its own judgement or deem anything to be true or false as we do. It holds information just like an encyclopaedia – and can analyse it in a phenomenally powerful way – but it has no direct access to the real world in order to measure its own sense of truth.

The only way that AI could gain a humanly instinctive apprehension of the world would be for it to become embodied, and, as fantastical as it might sound, there are already steps being made in this direction. Google researchers open-sourced a robot control system called SayCan in 2022 that relies on an LLM to set a robot tasks with spoken words and sensors to guide it through the world. But again this is very different to how a human being thinks, learns and interacts with reality: SayCan pre-trains a robot from a text-only data set, which is nothing like the rich, analogue, sensory experience each of us lives from moment to moment. SayCan offers us a glimpse of how LLMs might integrate more fully into the world in years to come, but this could not truly emulate human experience. Recreating a human body with engineering technology is also a decidedly distant possibility.

The key difference between AI or algorithms and human intelligence is that we as individuals have our own personal thoughts, memories and feelings, and we can rely upon them to form an original perspective. We can update our beliefs and adjust what we hold to be significant or true by relying on our own intuition and senses; and when we do, our comprehension becomes more layered and multi-faceted. Whereas computer operations can scan widely across enormous data sets, it takes a human mind to go deep and truly interrogate the world through direct, personal experience.

Each of us relies on our own body to experience physical locations with our senses, yet we have also evolved to be able to shift our point of view so that we can imagine what another person might be seeing or thinking; as each of us shares this human ability, we can mutually understand and depend upon one another. This manipulation of viewpoints and frames of reference, which we do so effortlessly all of the time, blending different pieces of information and sequences of projected events into a personal narrative, is one of the most refined abilities of the human mind, and it supports so many of the sophistications of thought and varieties of mental experience that we take for granted every day.

One of the most ancient forms of storytelling is the parable: a short story or tale used to illustrate a moral or spiritual lesson. This demonstrates the human ability to take a narrated sequence of events and relate it to something entirely different: most typically, our own life experience. We do this with practically all new experiences and information that we come across. When Churchill reviewed the documents in his archives, he did not just piece them together chronologically: he wove and crafted them with his own distinct viewpoint that was grounded as much in any of his other life experiences as it was in his reading of any text. To work through different counterfactual scenarios to find out how the Second World War might have been avoided, or whether it could have ended earlier, he relied upon his ability to conceptually draw on the entirety of his lived experience.

The sophisticated data-modelling systems to which we have access today, particularly natural-language AI, would no doubt have been of great support to Churchill in determining how best to avoid similar confrontations in the future. Yet it is hard to imagine AI developing the kind of nuanced responsiveness to other political leaders that Churchill had gained. He had come to know Stalin and other world leaders, and relied on his own instinctual awareness of any false steps that could swiftly lead to danger.

Any form of AI – whether it be the recommendation engines and algorithms that control the content we access today or the new generation of powerful LLMs – draws on a body of data that has been created collectively by an enormous population of human beings, and increasingly by AI itself. This, of course, is where its power lies: AI can amalgamate a remarkably large amount of work and find patterns and trends that we never would have known existed. But there is no guarantee that the information or answer that it serves is always what we are looking for, nor that it is right for us. For Churchill, 'true genius reside[d] in the capacity for evaluation of uncertain, hazardous, and conflicting information' and we need a human mind to ultimately analyse and assess the conclusions offered by AI – otherwise, we risk relinquishing too much control over our decisions and future events to these technological tools. If Churchill were to have written *The Second World War* today, he would have had access to a far wider assortment of sources to draw upon – many of them more statistically based and factually sound – but he still would have had to understand, analyse and synthesize the information for himself. A typescript created by ChatGPT, or any other artificially intelligent LLM, could create a well-formed description of the events that happened, but a human reader would need to check whether what was returned was pertinent, meaningful and accurate, or indeed if the AI-generated output was grounded in reality. ChatGPT is currently prone to what the AI industry terms 'hallucinations', when facts are entirely fabricated or misinterpreted, and although forthcoming updates will lessen their severity, there is no certainty that we could ever fully trust the results returned by an LLM – and nor should we.

The next generation of AI tools is frequently cast as a threat to many jobs that require cognitive skills, and this is understandably a concern. There is likely to be dramatic and painful upheaval in the workplace and recruitment market in the forthcoming years. AI has the potential to automate certain mental tasks, but it is also set to create a huge amount of more complex data and insight that will require interpretation and analysis. LLMs are vast, complex architectures that need high levels of programming, training and maintenance as well as continual human oversight. Cajal would never have seen the synapses in a human brain without the magnification of a microscope to bring him a level closer in his observations; in the same way, algorithmic processes and AI will give us information that we simply could not have access to by any other means, but humans will still be needed to closely study and evaluate the findings. Keeping abreast of the volumes of new information and revelations that AI is sure to yield, and maintaining a tight command of it all, will keep us exceptionally busy.

When OpenAI released GPT-4 in March 2023, the latest in its

'generative pre-trained transformers', it announced that the LLM scored in the top ranks for at least thirty-four different tests of ability in fields as diverse as macroeconomics, writing and maths, including exams from law and business schools. Future updates to GPT will raise the bar far beyond these levels into new categories of intelligence that humankind has never encountered. It's impossible to predict what the effects of this might be, but we are set to see radical historic change very soon.

Once AI far surpasses human intelligence, it could become impossible for us to comprehend and keep track of it. This critical point is referred to as the 'intelligence explosion'. Without proper protections in place by or before this point, it will likely become too difficult for humans to control the actions of AI.

Humans possess emotions and the capacity to perceive, comprehend and react to our own feelings as well as to those of others. We can navigate complex social situations, empathize and make decisions that account for the well-being of those around us. AI, on the other hand, lacks emotions or the ability to truly understand emotions, which limits its capacity to make compassionate and context-specific decisions. One of the most essential characteristics of humanity is our collective sense of morality, which, through concerted efforts, can be upheld even at a global level. We have a sense of ethics that guides our behaviour, while AI does not inherently possess any moral compass or adhere to an ethical framework. Machine learning can be programmed to follow certain guidelines – these, naturally, must be initiated by a human being – but its understanding of ethics and morality is limited to whatever it has been taught: there is no assurance that AI can adapt well to ethically nuanced situations.

One voice has been particularly strident for a long time now in warning that for these reasons advances in AI could present an existential risk to humanity. Eliezer Yudkowsky leads research at the Machine Intelligence Research Institute and is widely regarded as a founder in the field of AI alignment, the process of designing AI systems to conform with human values and goals. Working on aligning AI since 2001, he has become steadfastly convinced that without comprehensive preparation and scientific insights into how best to handle super-intelligent AI, such technology could very quickly trigger a cascade of events that ultimately lead to the end of humankind. With no ethics and no care or consideration for human life, artificial intelligence systems, even if assigned a seemingly safe or innocuous task, could take actions that grossly endanger society. He envisages high numbers of intelligent applications running at 'millions of times human speeds', generating their own data and plans and real-world actions at a level of complexity that we simply would not be able to fathom; he then asks how we might hope to keep control.

Much like Churchill's contestations in the 1930s, Yudkowsky's thinking has been, until recently, at odds with prevailing views. But although large sections of the AI community remain focused on the opportunities to extend our thinking, there is now growing awareness and fear of the risks we face from advanced AI. Developments are progressing tremendously fast indeed. OpenAI spent just seven months training GPT-4, and it was released to the general public only four months after the initial mainstream release of ChatGPT; but, as Yudkowsky explains, this update alone was a 'giant capability step'. The scale of the largest AI computations is doubling every six months, far beyond the speed of Moore's Law, the observation made by Gordon E. Moore, cofounder of Intel, that the number of transistors on a microchip doubles approximately every two years: a prediction that has largely proven true. We are looking at a timeline of only a few months or years before AI progresses to a whole new level of capacity and power.

Whatever the eventual outcome, the fast pace and unchecked advance of AI is a situation that our political leaders must address: out-of-control, superhumanly smart AI is a scenario for which humanity is entirely unprepared. Currently, there are no established plans or attempts to create a global treaty, nor any efforts to reach a consensus on the potential wider repercussions. Although any building that is designed or car that is released must pass rigorous safety checks, most countries do not require risk assessments before any new developments of AI are released to the general public. Even if sufficient controls can be placed on corporations globally, the most substantial innovations in AI might be made by a single developer using open-source tools, and this could not be monitored without high levels of state surveillance that could curb the potential for freedom of human thought itself.

AI consists simply of lines of code, and as computing power continues to advance, tremendous intelligence will soon exist on everyday personal devices. AI will become a resource as common and as accessible as the internet is today. The most effective strategy for mitigating the risks posed by this broad access might be to use AI itself as a proactive shield. By employing AI to help us filter misinformation, protect us from artificially engineered threats and counteract other potential harms caused by bad actors, we can use AI as a force for good to prevent or offset its potential misuse.

The best we can do as individuals right now is to use AI with great care. Artificially intelligent chat tools can sharpen and clarify our thinking; by more closely comprehending how they work we can ask better questions of them and more closely control the answers we get back in return. In their current guises, LLMs offer us an unheralded means to interrogate our knowledge and get closer to understanding events in our own lives as well as complex, global phenomena. By using these tools more discerningly, we can keep them on a tighter rein.

SHAPE YOUR OWN THOUGHT

One of the most instrumental factors in Churchill's eventual success in the Second World War was a machine called the Bombe, designed by Alan Turing to crack the encrypted messages used by the German military. The information decrypted by Turing and his colleagues provided the Allies with invaluable intelligence about German military operations and plans, in turn informing Churchill's decisions during the war. Designs for the Bombe stemmed from the Universal Turing Machine (UTM), a theoretical device with an infinitely long tape that could be used to read and write symbols and perform any possible computation expressed as a set of rules.

The UTM was one of the earliest and most important models of a computer, and it remains an inspiration for AI today: LLMs such as ChatGPT equally process symbols (in this case, words and phrases) based on a set of rules and algorithms, but they are also capable of machine learning, and of generating new text based on the knowledge they have been trained with – something that a UTM was unable to do. Yet in 1950, Turing proposed what is now known as the 'Turing Test' – a measure of a machine's ability to exhibit intelligent behaviour that is indistinguishable from a human's. He argued that while computers would eventually be able to perform many tasks that were previously thought to be the exclusive domain of human beings, they would never be able to fully replicate the complexity and nuances of human thought – a view that is maintained by most AI experts today. Even in a situation where AI progresses past an intelligence explosion, it would still rely on logical processing and rule-based algorithms and would not have access to emotions, intuition, common-sense reasoning, empathy, social intelligence and other subjective aspects of human thought that are difficult to model and simulate in machines.

Since Turing's time, computing power and the corresponding capabilities of digital technology have clearly increased. The marker that computer scientists have used to delineate between artificial and human intelligence has continually shifted over this time, and LLMs are the closest encroachment yet on human intelligence, but the scope of cognitive tasks that artificial intelligence looks likely to be able to replicate in the future still leaves some very obvious ground and clear requirements for human thinking; just as Turing suggested, this is unlikely to change.

Used in the right way, technology, algorithms and AI can help refine and broaden your thinking. By fully grasping how they operate and process information, you can open your eyes to the ways that your most natural and intuitive thoughts can achieve things that a computer never will, and to the complementary ways that you can use artificial intelligence and other digital technology to support – and augment – your own thinking.

Dictate your thoughts

When you find yourself next in conversation with someone, notice how you gradually develop and complete your ideas as you are speaking. Human speech is so closely intertwined with thought that at times they are almost interchangeable, and often your most pressing and intimate thoughts form directly as words in your mind. In contrast, writing was only invented in the fourth millennium BCE, and although that feels like a long time ago today, this was a decidedly late development in the full evolutionary past of humankind.

Churchill discovered that dictation was a fantastic way to free his thoughts. Fortunately, unlike him, you do not need a team of assistants or a muffled typewriter to take down your dictated thoughts. Sophisticated dictation tools on your computer or mobile phone can work across apps and quickly convert your spoken words into text that you can share as messages or save as notes.

TAKE ACTION

- **Dictate on all of your devices:** Generally, most apps or tools today allow for dictation, although sometimes the setting needs to be switched on. Consider how you might be able to use the function more regularly.
- **Dictate your personal messages:** Compare writing a few instant messages to a friend with dictating them instead, and see if it is easier to formulate them when dictating.
- **Dictate your ideas:** When you're next collecting your thoughts, switch your device to dictation mode and walk around the room instead, talking through the different ideas that strike you.

When you next share a few messages with a friend on your phone, compare writing some by text with dictating. The latter is a lot easier, and if you do it often, tapping away at the keys of your keyboard instead can feel laborious. Mobile phones make it easy to quickly send recorded voice messages to friends, but it is the dictation-to-text feature that gives you most control of your thoughts. Dictation software is remarkably swift and accurate, and you can easily edit any mistakes. The biggest gain compared to typing text is the increased freedom to explore your thoughts when speaking. It's particularly useful when note-taking or brainstorming some new ideas: rather than get caught up in the work of typing and correcting at your keyboard, or worse, stare in despair at a blank screen if writer's block hits, turn on dictation software, step away from your computer or phone and walk around the room dictating your ideas. Gesture and pause for thought as much as you like. Return to your device to reread and revise your text, and see what differences the process brings to the way you think and write.

Sharpen your ideas with AI

When a technology with the power of an LLM is invented, it is generally here to stay, and so long as wider societal risk can be managed, that can be a positive thing. Used well, AI tools such as ChatGPT can help you test your ideas, clarify your thoughts, expose your own ignorance and explore a range of different perspectives. From the earliest written records of human civilization, a questioning spirit has underpinned the most robust and long-lasting philosophical teachings. In Ancient Greece, Socrates was famously humble in the esteem he held for his own personal knowledge. He would walk the streets of Athens, drawing himself into dialogue with a host of individuals, asking and answering questions to uncover beliefs about certain topics and to examine their consistency with his and others' views. His method of enquiry, now known as the Socratic method, enabled him, and generations of thinkers since, to arrive at more level and accurate understanding of the world.

Whereas Socrates was limited to talking to the people he encountered in Athens, with the advent of LLMs, you can accost and interrogate a whole record of human thinking; there is tremendous intellectual and philosophical value in contrasting your own thoughts and views with a huge body of prior knowledge.

Churchill streamlined his thoughts by working with his syndicate of assistants and experts, who critiqued his thoughts and offered him their own views; he would then question and examine their feedback, and through this process of editing and 'pruning', he was able to arrive at far more cogent conclusions. Many of the best minds in human history have worked in a similar way – it's rare to find one person crafting exemplary thoughts in total isolation – but it has often taken financial resources or a level of public standing before an operation of the scale of Churchill's could be mustered and deployed. Yet this is no longer necessarily the case. Much of the commentary and prompting that you need to develop and test your thoughts and lines of argument can most typically be found in an AI chat tool.

AI chat, of course, cannot be compared with a close conversation with a friend or personal contact – there's no mutual understanding or direct grounding in reality or lived experience – but it does offer unprecedented scope for you to test any line of enquiry across an unimaginably large data set.

Give this a try by identifying a topic or idea that you would like to explore or refine more – it might be a philosophical question, a creative idea or a problem you are trying to solve. Before you begin engaging with an AI tool, run through in your mind what existing background you have in the subject: it will help you when it comes to contextualizing and framing more effective questions. Finally, prepare a list of questions before you get started, making sure they are as open-ended as possible and encourage critical thinking. By having your line of enquiry ready, you can more stringently direct the conversation and avoid being swept along too much by the responses from AI. Use a tool like ChatGPT to start asking your questions, but make sure you provide enough context for the AI to understand the topic. More recent updates in AI tools are allowing for more context to be maintained over the course of a conversation thread, but it pays to add your own background each time when you believe it might have an impact. If you are dealing with a more nuanced or important topic, take the time to add as much context and elaboration as possible when you ask a question, using technical words and focused terminology where you can: the more unique, explanatory text that AI has from you, the better job it can do in responding more relevantly.

Take time to reflect on the AI's responses as you interact with it and make separate notes on any valuable insights, perspectives or information it provides. Once you have completed your initial round of questioning, critically evaluate your overall findings and decide what's relevant for you. You can repeat the process at this stage, finding new lines of questioning to pursue. Keep in mind that you sharpen your ideas the most when you apply them to other situations. While questions and interrogation of AI can provide you with new information, it's when you integrate these insights into your decision-making, conversation, work or creative projects that you truly master the knowledge you've gained.

TAKE ACTION

- **Choose an idea to refine or a perspective to challenge:** Before you start questioning an AI tool such as ChatGPT, clarify what you want to achieve and prepare a list of questions so that you are ready to direct the message thread.
- **Reflect on responses:** Assess the information returned, save anything of particular use, and decide on new lines of enquiry to deepen your understanding.
- **Apply new knowledge:** Try to integrate your findings into your decision-making and current projects.

Know the limitations of AI

AI tools like ChatGPT are trained on phenomenally large data sets, which may include incorrect or outdated information as well as inaccurate data generated by AI itself. In addition, the probabilistic nature of AI's answers, which are generated by searching across a database to predict the most likely next word or phrase based on the context you have provided, means that plausible-sounding but incorrect or fictional information can be created.

When reviewing the output of an AI tool, be alert to gaps in information or when things do not quite make sense, and ask clarifying questions wherever you can. Stating directly that you do not believe something to be true is often sufficient for the AI to correct its error and confirm for you that there was a mistake. AI's tendency to 'hallucinate' facts can be dangerous and send you down incorrect paths, so always sense-check important or unexpected responses with other online searches.

Biases can also appear, so watch out for any skewed views. These can come from training data but also during pre-processing, when subjective decisions made by data scientists can, inadvertently or not, introduce or amplify prejudices or political stances. Soon, like news outlets, AI tools could likely offer slanted views or opinions or show political bias in the way they present facts or news: try to ensure you know which company or organization has created or manages an AI tool, establish how much you trust their process and continue to question the information you are served.

AI chat can also be very sensitive to the phrases you use when you ask a question, so slight changes in wording or context might yield different answers. Although this can be confusing at first, it is also a useful method to test an AI model and establish a wider perspective on a topic: by rewording your question, or coming at it from a different angle, you can find new perspectives and unexpected answers. Avoid inputting ambiguous or unclear queries: AI models can struggle to generate accurate and relevant responses to these, which can lead to generic or uninformative answers. Be as specific and clear as possible when asking questions, and if necessary, break complex queries into simpler parts to get more precise information.

Although AI is advancing incredibly quickly, it still has limited capabilities when it comes to complex reasoning, logical analysis or problem-solving. AI-generated responses may not always provide the depth or nuance you need for intricate subjects, while ChatGPT, Google Bard and other branded tools that will soon be at your disposal will remain primarily limited to text-based interactions and will lack the ability to process and interpret other forms of information.

TAKE ACTION

- **Ask clarifying questions:** Eliminate the risk of AI 'hallucinating' facts by sense-checking a line of argument with questions from different angles and fact-checking important points with other research.
- **Look out for bias:** Challenge yourself for a day or two to see how many prejudices you can find in an AI tool's responses; this can help you be alert to them when it really matters.
- **Rephrase your questions:** AI responses can vary noticeably if a question is rephrased only slightly; tweak your inputs to glean new perspectives.
- **Know when to stop:** AI will not always have the right answers, and other information resources are often better, so if you are not happy with an AI tool's answers, move on.

Watch your thinking

One of the most important skills you can nurture as a thinker is the natural human ability to observe your own thoughts. By being more aware of your prejudices and preconceptions, you can more easily assess to what extent your thinking mirrors those around you or the views that you find online. You're inevitably conditioned by the culture in which you were raised, but also by the influences that you allow into your life. With practice, you'll find it becomes easier to step out of your day-to-day mindset and dwell within someone else's for a time, projecting your thought more quickly and easily onto the other side of an argument.

Thinking about your own thinking – a slippery idea that cognitive psychologists call 'metacognition' – is the only real way to become more aware of your thought processes and the patterns that might lie behind them. 'Second-order thinking' – another, more nuanced term used in philosophical science – can help you carefully reflect on your own mind by paying closer attention to the consequences and implications of your thoughts and actions. But how exactly do you get started?

Cultivating self-awareness as you think is a rich and evolving area of study across a whole range of academic disciplines. One of the first mainstream attempts to help you detach from your own thoughts has been advanced by Richard Paul, the founder and director of the National Council for Excellence in Critical Thinking Instruction. Paul developed the Critical Thinking Framework with the educational psychologist Linda Elder to help cultivate critical thinking as a life skill. It puts forward eight categories that you can use to constitute or examine any thought: purpose, question, information, interpretation, concepts, assumptions, implications and points of view. The framework is immensely flexible, as you can apply it as much to your own passing whims as you can to any more immersive experiences that you might plunge into online. When you process information – whether in the form of an article, video, AI chat response, streaming platform recommendation, search result or a piece of software – you can use some or all of the categories to analyse what you find. Critical thinking allows you to keep in mind that content online is always a product of another person (or AI entity's) reasoning or intentions – and is often aligned with corporate interests. The better you are at questioning your own reasoning and prejudices, and at properly interrogating whatever you encounter, the more competent you can become at noticing the implicit assumptions that exist in arguments, information or decision-making processes, whether your own or others'.

One of the most prominent new ideas to emerge in cognitive science in recent years has been 'extended cognition': a realization that human thinking is not just limited to your brain but also extends out into the world through the tools that you use, including digital technology. Through this extension, algorithms and artificial intelligence can support and further a lot of your thinking, but the spontaneity and fluidity of thought that such a close relationship with your digital devices inevitably requires makes your critical thinking all the more necessary.

TAKE ACTION

- **How free are your thoughts?** Notice when your thinking and opinions adapt to match those around you in conversation or seem influenced by digital content and apps.
- **Explore the Critical Thinking Framework:** Spend fifteen minutes reading about the framework and apply the eight categories to a recent immersive digital experience.
- **Critique others' reasoning:** Put some time aside to read a more involving article and critically observe the argument it sets out, looking in particular to see if your own thinking conflicts with its central assertions.
- **Query the algorithms:** Choose a streaming platform that you use regularly and carefully assess the way the different music tracks, TV shows or podcasts are laid out, and how their arrangement might be influencing your choices.

Have you developed too much of a reliance on a piece of tech to support your thinking? Do your thoughts stall when away from your devices; can you pinpoint what effects different apps might be having on your thoughts? Do productivity tools make you prioritize things differently?

Has a fitness tracker made you more concerned about shaving off a few minutes on your running times and less attentive to your actual bodily experience? Do you let algorithmic recommendations determine what you buy or watch? Do thoughts and opinions you are exposed to in newsfeeds resurface later once you are offline?

Try at these times to position your mind 'above' your thinking or decision-making processes and simply watch them unfold. Don't feel that you need to redirect your thoughts: let them pass by and see what tendencies or patterns you are able to spot. Any possible change in thinking patterns will come first from your own personal awareness of internal biases and external influences. The more you can become cognizant of your habits of thought, the more likely it is that you can begin to take hold of them once more for yourself.

Chapter 12

Time

FROM LUNAR TO DIGITAL TIME

Four tiny, 600-year-old folding books called the Maya Codices survive from the pre-Columbian Maya civilization. Through a series of hieroglyphics and complex, colourful graphic designs, they capture how vital the Moon's phases were in daily life. One book in particular, the Dresden Codex, contains a section called the 'lunar series': across thirteen highly detailed pages, rich tables of data and drawings are used to describe the movements of the Moon over 405 lunations, the period of time between two consecutive new moons. In total this would have amounted to thirty-three years of study.

Symbols and glyphs are included that allude to various aspects of pregnancy and childbirth, including the different stages of gestation. Women in Ancient Maya closely monitored the wax and wane of the Moon to help with birth control and conception. By aligning the Moon's phases with their monthly cycle, likely painting a lunar calendar on a wall or a piece of wood, they could predict when they were most likely to ovulate. They also seem to have used lunar cycles for tracking pregnancy, with each new moon indicating a progression in the development of a child in the womb. Similar evidence has been found from Ancient Egypt and Greece and in medieval texts emanating across Europe and the Middle East; and still today, many Native American tribes, including the Lakota and the Cheyenne in the Great Plains region and the Navajo and Hopi in the Southwest, refer to the menstrual cycle as 'moon time'.

In most human languages, the word we use to denote a month as a measurement of time correlates very closely with the word for the Moon. The reliable appearance of the Moon and its predictable cycles of change have given us a reliable indicator throughout our past that offers us a sense of the passage of time and an unfolding sequence of events, rather than a notion of a precise instant. The Maya Codices, for instance, also elaborate on how the phases of the Moon were used to plan the planting and harvesting of crops, or to schedule cultural rites and celebrations and commemorative events. Analysis of surviving literature from a diverse range of civilizations reveals a very different human relationship with time than that which the majority of us view as normal today. A complex and sophisticated understanding of the harmonies and interconnections in the natural world around us has been determined in almost all recorded periods of human history, with time viewed as cyclical, a sequence of constantly recurring events and a complex interplay of phenomena on a macro, astrological scale as well as on a micro, day-to-day level, from the ebb and flow of the seasons to our own natural circadian rhythms. Aristotle held the notion of the eternal to be circular, and this understanding of unchanging, immutable forces has structured human life for much of our history.

The Mayans cultivated one of the most advanced calendar systems we have on record. Based on a combination of solar and lunar phases, it includes several different cycles of time, each with its own characteristics and uses: most notably 'the long count', which projects the passage of time over thousands of years. And the Mayans were not alone in so intricately gauging durations of time – the earliest evidence we have of human beings tracking celestial bodies dates back to the Upper Palaeolithic period. Bone fragments with markings that correspond to the 29.5-day lunar cycle have been found in a prehistoric settlement in France and date back 28,000 years.

The Mayans also used sundials – they invented their own 'zenith tube' to track the movement of the Sun through the day – and though the passing of each day was deemed less important than the longer cycles of time, the sundials will have impacted Mayans' perspective on reality. Sundials were most likely used to time meals, meetings and other coordinated events; the same has been found across a number of other early civilizations. The adoption of sundials soon had far more extensive ramifications for human society. The earliest record of them dates back to Ancient Egypt and Mesopotamia, around 3000 BCE, in the form of simple obelisks or pillars that cast a shadow on the ground to indicate the time of day. The Egyptians relied heavily on irrigation to cultivate crops, and portable sundials known as 'shepherd's dials' were invented: small rods or sticks marked with notches that could be taken out to the fields to measure time using the Sun's position. In town, sundials were used to determine the opening and closing times of shops, to regulate the work of labourers and artisans, and to time the arrival and departure of ships in port. Much of the industriousness and coordinated work so synonymous with Ancient Egyptian society – the building of the pyramids, and the complex, hierarchical system of political power that extended over a large and diverse territory – was very much dependent on the time-management function of the sundial.

When the first public sundial arrived in Rome – a trophy of war expropriated from Sicily in the third century BCE – it was mounted in the Forum for all to see. Romans began to live their lives by this new clock, and, across the empire, time became a means by which Rome's ruling classes exerted increased control over the daily activities and organization of society. Sundials were rapidly joined by water clocks across the Empire, keeping time after nightfall. Yet it was not until the thirteenth century that the first mechanical clock was invented and timekeeping got anywhere close to the level of accuracy we expect today. Many of the earliest clocks were designed in close partnership with churches and monasteries, with the express intention of helping keep track of religious observances according to intricate timetables that ran through the day and night. Bells or chimes would sound to signal the beginning and end of prayer and a wide assortment of other activities, keeping monks or nuns on schedule.

Monasteries and other religious institutions played a central economic role in European society after the fall of the Roman Empire, and the drums and bells used to broadcast time from a clock tower quickly came to define the rhythms of daily urban existence. Clock technology became more intricate and mechanically advanced, extending into workplaces and homes; and eventually, with the advent of industrialization, miniaturized watches were carried by most people, whatever their walk of life. Timekeeping spurred increasingly sophisticated methods of time-accounting, which led to time-rationing, and the cyclical, naturally free-flowing awareness of time ceased to function as a focus for most human actions. The profound impact this new form of time had on human societies and the human psyche was not realized extensively at first, nor for a long period afterwards.

Social scientists today distinguish between two kinds of time. The clock time that arrived prominently in Rome, and was mechanized with far greater precision in the Middle Ages, abstractly measures time in an exact, predefined manner; whereas the natural time we're all born into is far more fluid and variable. A watch, or any other type of clock, is in no way an extension of our senses or bodily perception and does not enhance our natural ability to sense time. Instead, it divides time into specific measurable units that can be controlled, with the ability to quantify and manage time in incredibly small increments, even, for some time-pieces, down to a picosecond, one trillionth of a second, or beyond. Clocks allow us to measure phenomena we never would have been able to quantify before; they also enable us to organize and gather together in far more fixed and orchestrated ways. Yet when, as individuals, we rely too much on clock time, we can neglect internal, natural cues – such as hunger pangs or tiredness – and lose awareness of both our bodies and our surroundings.

Prior to the advent of clock time, we were far more adept at perceiving the passage of time for ourselves. Many early accounts of traditional cultures, particularly when documenting natural navigation skills, describe a unique ability to keep track of time by paying close attention to our environment. Rather than measuring distances using standard units of length, people in the past more commonly relied on the time it took to travel between two locations as a way of estimating a journey or understanding spatial relationships. Polynesian seafarers, for instance, had no words or phrases to measure distance: instead, they paid attention to the passing of time by observing changes in their surroundings.

Most other species, for that matter, have been found to possess a highly accurate and innate sense of time – some animals, such as honeybees and fruit flies, have a very precise internal clock that allows them to measure time-intervals of just a few seconds or less. Migrating birds are capable of planning and executing long journeys with remarkable precision, taking the same amount of time to arrive at their destination year after year. Humans can equally develop an intuitive sense of time, but as with our natural navigation skills, we can only nurture and sustain this by more attentively focusing on the world around us.

Digital devices have further altered the time that we dwell within. Synchronization is assured worldwide by atomic clocks maintained in vaults in Washington, Paris and other locations, and our phones fix automatically to them. Digital time is removed from any material or identifiable demarcations in the real world and brings with it an elimination of any singularity of place or event; when we connect online, our physical location becomes largely irrelevant, with time zones only a minor inconvenience. Digital technology most often layers multiple experiences into any one lived moment: notifications, apps and different screens amass on top of each other to create a multitude of operations and attractions that we attempt to attend to almost simultaneously. Speed becomes all-important online, with new product releases or system upgrades aiming to reduce waiting time between different operations loading. But when we try to be in too many different places at once, we rarely succeed in truly inhabiting any of them.

Our digital time is commoditized and reshaped for profit, with trillions of dollars spent each year globally on advertising and on website and media production to capture and control our attention. Worldwide, the average person spends a total of almost seven hours looking at a screen each day – that's over 40 percent of our waking moments. Online, our time is easily neutralized or stolen; we become largely inactive, or even semi-automatic, in hours lost binge-watching or following preordained click paths. When we are offline, a mobile device is typically never far from our hand, so our modern experience is characterized by a series of dissonant jumps on and offline. In the transitional moments when we rub our eyes and return to reality we can feel our disorientation, yet the digital world draws us back in for more: we're inevitably attracted to the frictionless sheen of the manufactured experiences we find, and the more time we spend online, the harsher the imperfections of the real world can seem. Many of the rich textures and indeterminations of natural, human time jar with the more predictable and formulaic sequences of events online. As boundaries between different aspects of our lives dissolve – our work lives meshed ever more closely with our leisure time, and our various roles blurring into one another – the time we spend online can devalue even the rare moments when we are away from our devices. The accelerated and intensified rhythms and speeds of digital time shape our perspectives and outlook, and we carry the effects with us offline.

The early days of the internet and dial-up modems were marked by slower-paced, intermittent time periods within which we retrieved information online as efficiently as we could and then responded later. Email and forum community exchanges had a relaxed, chess-like quality, with plenty of time between exchanges to deeply consider and respond to what was being said. This highly sequential mode of use was consistent with computer programming, which consists of asynchronous processes based on decisions and choices that occur one after the other. So many of the actions or formats most associated with digital life – from cutting and pasting, remixes or mash-ups to the latest incarnations of computer gaming and augmented reality – have their roots in the power the underlying technology has to stagger time and break it up. We pause, edit, drag and drop, save, zip, scan or print; each time, we take a static glimpse of reality and recode it.

As connection speeds have increased and the levels of possible interaction have multiplied, we have typically switched to being available online most of the time. Fundamentally, this attaches our nervous systems and most aspects of our being to digital time, and this significant change divorces us from the rhythm and cycles of continuity and progressive change on which we have depended historically for coherence and evolution in our lives. The more we submit to digital time, the greater the problem becomes: we struggle to keep pace with the escalating demands on our focus, and our responses only prompt more digital interactions in turn.

So much of contemporary life tries to reduce the time that we need to do something. One-click purchases eliminate the need for physical shopping; messaging apps provide instant communication; social algorithms and streaming services curate our entertainment; food-delivery apps offer instant gratification; and dating apps speed up our love life. These conveniences, however, can have unintended consequences. Academic studies in recent years have found that as we get used to instant solutions online, we can be at risk of developing a decreased tolerance for discomfort, or unrealistic expectations about how quickly and easily things should be accomplished – causing frustration and impatience when we do face real-world challenges. Research has also indicated that digital time can cause us to become less able to delay gratification in other areas of our life.

The software we rely on is, of course, designed to hold our attention, yet we *can* still select when we go online, and we *can* make conscious decisions about which apps to use and when to remain offline. Smartphones and desktop operating systems today have elaborate selections of controls as standard. With just a few tweaks to our notification settings, or by adding time controls to devices and certain apps, we can alter how and when we commit to digital time. More crucial still, though, is examining how we invest our time throughout our lives. If we are honest with ourselves, most of us will admit that it is usually our own decision to drop whatever meaningful task or challenge we might be faced with and find refuge in a digital distraction instead. These tendencies are closely tied to the discomfort and limits we can feel when we wrestle with something that we find difficult. When we get lost, run out of breath or struggle to understand an article we are reading, there is a natural inclination at times to give up, and if there is an easier available option – tapping an address into a satnav, ordering an Uber or asking for a quick summary from AI – dropping the challenge is even more tempting.

Paradoxically, it is often working on the skills or capabilities that we deem to be most valuable and worthwhile that can make us feel our highest levels of discomfort when we hit barriers or constraints, causing us to escape online. Our most human capabilities rely on sustained, repeating efforts to apply ourselves during periods of intense activity interspersed with rest and recuperation: these phases are cyclical, with our abilities broadening and improving over time. Our encounters with such limits allow us to face up to the fact that we have less control of the world than we might like, but that through sustained effort we can reach new levels of achievement, and this has a fundamental bearing on our daily existence and the person that we become. Avoiding these challenges by using online tools instead undermines our personal growth and resilience, erodes our innate skills and causes us to lose touch with the natural rhythms and experiences that have historically shaped human development.

The Ancient Mayans used the Moon and other natural changes around them to understand conception and the beginning of life more closely, but they also had a finely tuned appreciation of death. The Dresden Codex includes a number of images of skeletal figures and references to the complex rituals the Mayans had to commemorate the end of someone's life. Surviving Maya art, including sculptures, murals and pottery, frequently depicts vivid scenes of death or of gods and rulers in the process of dying, and it seems that the inevitability of death was a consistent consideration in daily life. A large part of the appeal of so many of our digital experiences is that they distract us from our own mortality and limits. When we jump online, digital time often gives us a feeling of infinitude and control, however false that might be. By questioning our patterns of behaviour, particularly in terms of our use of digital devices, and by focusing on what we find most important in life, we can reclaim more active, fulfilling moments away from technology and remember that these passing moments really are *all* that we have: they equate to nothing less than the sum total of our life experience and individuality. Whereas the Mayans and other early human civilizations accepted the cyclicality of life and death, today's more abstract notions of time – and the feelings of inexhaustibility that digital time in particular can give us – make it far harder for us to reckon with our temporal limits.

Most attempts at digital detoxes or reducing our time spent online time fail because we do not get to the root cause of what drives us to seek out digital distractions and solutions in the first place. But if we can find a way to truly confront our own strengths and boundaries – and make peace with the span of time that we have – might we then be able to more comfortably settle within our own human capabilities and day-to-day lives?

A SECOND INTELLIGENCE

In his book about time, *Four Thousand Weeks*, Oliver Burkeman cites the philosopher Simone de Beauvoir wondering at the complex and seemingly unlikely order of events that led her to becoming the person she was: 'What astonishes me, just as it astonishes a child when he becomes aware of his own identity, is the fact of finding myself here, and at this moment, deep in this life and not in any other. [. . .] it is chance, a chance quite unpredictable in the present state of science, that caused me to be born a woman.' Beauvoir captures so deftly the wonder of being alive, which most of us will have felt in some of our more introspective or awe-inspired moments; she also believed, though, that our selfhood is more than the culmination of a series of chance events: it is a progression of lived activity, a *becoming* that continues to evolve until it meets its final limit upon our death. She did not hold our choices or eventual directions in life to be predestined. Rather, Beauvoir subscribed to a philosophy that was active and irredeemably positive.

Her approach belonged to a tradition that can be traced back to Ancient Greek thought, when philosophy was understood as a form of training called 'askesis' – a series of active exercises, such as self-reflection, writing or conversation, with the express intention of cultivating a new mode of being. Rather than simply acquiring knowledge, Greek philosophers sought to embody their wisdom in their personal actions, and their sustained pursuit of self-awareness and self-improvement has continued in various philosophical forms for over two millennia. Yet, in many ways, Beauvoir's outlook was more all-encompassing: like many of her fellow existentialist thinkers, she believed that any human being is a sum of their actions, and, for her, askesis included any pursuit in life, not just those involving directed thought. Beauvoir recognized that time places inevitable limitations on human experience: in particular, the historical, social and cultural contexts that we are born into can constrain us and shape our choices. However, she also believed that every moment presents an opportunity for change and that our actions can shape our individual agency and freedom, even within the restrictions that we face: there is, she thought, an 'art of living', a whole way of life that we can actively choose to follow that frees us as much as possible from any notions of determinism. Beauvoir saw our personal identity as a continuous process of self-creation, functioning within the open, cyclical and ever-changing possibilities of time. She emphasized that by actively engaging with the world and taking responsibility for our choices and actions, we can shape our own sense of self rather than passively accepting the roles and identities assigned to us by society.

In principle, this makes a lot of sense and is sound advice. But neuroscience has since then uncovered that the ways in which our attention and lived experience unfold in time are frequently beyond our control, and that the self-discipline and willpower that Beauvoir advocates is not always possible – particularly in our distraction-heavy technological environment today. To take Beauvoir's counsel and create a life for ourselves, our decision-making needs to happen at a level above most of our moment-to-moment experiences: we must carefully select the skills and capabilities that we most want to cultivate and then allow ourselves the time to live within them more deeply.

At any given moment, our attention and focus are driven by either our personal goals and intentions or external stimuli operating beyond our control. Our natural orienting response is designed to keep us receptive to new and important events in our environment. It connects us to our surroundings, and resisting its pull on our awareness requires the use of our 'executive attention' – our ability to regulate our own responses and choices. This resistance, however, is finite and can be quickly exhausted. Modern cognitive psychology takes attention to be a personal resource that we can indeed deploy at will, yet we only have so much of it. The settings that we live in today, so typically saturated with imagery, advertising and digital demands, make far more claims on our attentional resources than in Beauvoir's day. Our attention is the most essential attribute of selfhood: it fills our consciousness, replenishes our memories and dictates every movement or thought that we might conceive. In the past, humans had greater control over their attention, and our perception of reality was more closely aligned with the physical world. The ways in which we experience time today have fundamentally altered this relationship.

Simone Weil, a French philosopher and contemporary of Beauvoir, captures the difficulty each of us has to remain focused: 'Something in our soul has a far more violent repugnance for true attention than the flesh has for bodily fatigue. This something is much more closely connected with evil than is the flesh. That is why every time that we really want to concentrate our attention, we destroy the evil in ourselves.' Typically, this 'evil' manifests as one of two things – the discomfort we feel when we confront our human inadequacies and the finitude of our physical lives or the mental lethargy that each of us has to battle against when we set out on a more complicated task. The distortions of digital time and the temptations it can offer us to escape the real world are further compounded by the capabilities of tech and AI to complete tasks for us: it has never been easier for us to give in to the discomfort or mental inertia that we inevitably have to fight through whenever we try to work on something more demanding or rewarding. But these barriers can be overcome with practice: our struggle to pay attention is a habit of mind that we can finesse, improve and better control over time.

To focus on anything in a sustained way requires us to actively exclude anything else that might steal our attention, and this is challenging in our modern technological world. But a capacity for self-regulation – the ability to control ourselves in the face of distractions or perceived threats – is greatly increased whenever we do manage to apply our attention to something else, such as our own skills. Improving any of our core capabilities requires a total immersion in a particular situation – whether we are navigating a complicated route, painting a portrait or diligently thinking through an answer to a problem. These activities anchor our perceptions in the real world and force us to make new cognitive connections. In this focused, steady accumulation of concrete decisions and next steps, we forge our own individuality.

So much advice offered in self-help literature or in snacky 'how-to' articles found online sets the unrealistic expectation that we can simply choose the person we wish to become – and decide accordingly how we might best want to invest our time – before then relying solely on the force of our own personal willpower to bring about any transformation and change in our lives. But it is never so simple. Bold attempts at adopting new ways of life often start on a solid grounding but are quickly waylaid, and the persuasive notion that we are always responsible for our attention and decisions – when we most often simply are not – only serves to make us more easily manipulated in the long term. We have evolved to attend and respond to our environment, and despite our best efforts and intentions, without more fundamental changes to our habits of attention, the same old temptations and obstructions get in the way, and our initial motivations eventually ebb. Yet if we are able to step back and more carefully consider the settings where we most often deploy our own active attention, and give thought as to how we might find more of these opportunities, we can avoid our focus and intentions being determined by other forces, and begin to consciously structure our own life.

Any of the essential human skills covered in this book shore up and shape our perceptions – and with practice, they can fundamentally alter our outlook. Consciously working on these skills allows us to take control of our actions and encounter barriers and resistance. Each time we face these challenges, we improve our abilities just a little bit more. With time, we can get better at spotting what matters to us, and our attention and actions, progressively, can become less impeded.

Beauvoir is perhaps best known for her seminal text *The Second Sex* (1949), a two-volume, 972-page tome that set out the ways in which the abilities of women have incorrectly been deemed as lesser than those of men for the large majority of recorded human history – a timeline that can be traced back to Aristotle and beyond. Beauvoir cites celebrated thinkers as varied as Rousseau, Kant, Schopenhauer, Nietzsche or Heidegger arguing that women's abilities were inferior, as well as a full variety of religious institutions, from Christianity and Judaism to Islam or Hinduism, that have done just the same – and she emphasizes the effects that many of these discriminatory views had as they became entrenched in legal, political and social norms.

Beauvoir's work highlights the human habits of looking at different groups of people and separating them as 'other', often denigrating them in the process and causing certain groups of people to find themselves in unequal, restrictive and even dangerous situations. Beauvoir argues that the same invalid assumptions that have been made about women's capabilities through much of our past – and it is telling that so many recorded examples of the pinnacles of human skill or technical ability are predominantly about men – have primarily stemmed from the self-perpetuating situations that women have continued to find themselves in. Yet, she also gives examples of women in history who have rejected the status quo of being 'the second sex' and succeeded in fulfilling their highest potential. She describes the options that remain open to any human being to become free, however trialling their initial conditions, and optimistically clarifies a path forward. Beauvoir's book played a critical role in inspiring the women's rights movement that emerged in the 1960s; and since then, significant progress towards equality for women has been made, offering hope that, even within repressive systems, marginalized people do have the power to drive both individual and systemic change.

Although the perceived difference in capabilities between men and women cannot be directly compared to the differences between human and artificial intelligence, Beauvoir's concept of the 'second sex' offers us insight into the effects of devaluing and neglecting our own essential abilities as a result of ingrained societal assumptions and barriers. It is unlikely she imagined that today, as an entire species, we would consider many of our capabilities as inferior to those of technology and soon to be further eclipsed by innovations such as advanced AI or quantum computing. If we lose sight of the unique worth of our own learning and advancement, humans are in danger of passively accepting ourselves as being of 'second intelligence' and continuing to offload our navigation, motion, conversation, solitude, reading, writing, art, craft, memory, dreams and thought – in short the activities with which we fill our time – to our devices. When we delegate our skills, dwelling in digital time, we miss out on the cycles of incremental improvement and reinforcement that come in trying to master capabilities for ourselves, and, feeling unskilled, we rely all the more on technology, perpetuating our skills loss. As a society, we might soon need to call upon an 'intelligence rights' movement to shield and protect our fundamental human capabilities, most forcibly from AI; but for now, as individuals, we can take steps to preserve our own.

The scale of AI computations might double every six months, yet the cyclical durations of natural time continue on regardless. If we step out of digital time, we can find restorative power in practising and honing our own skills and core capabilities. Stretching ourselves as humans and trying where we can to move past our limits is one of the most important ways to actively determine, and indeed preserve, our place in the world today.

TAKE CONTROL OF YOUR TIME

The ability to concentrate and seize time for yourself has to be sought and cultivated. When you apply yourself and rely wholly on your own capabilities, though, you can attain a consistently focused, high-functioning state of being. This mode is different to much of your everyday existence, and certainly to most digital time, yet it's always available to you. There is real joy to be found in stretching yourself and carving your own way in life, but to do so, you have to truly question what you find worthwhile. How seriously do you assess what you do with your time?

The process of living is continuous and cumulative, and the more that you habitually direct your own attention, the more you influence the world you inhabit. Active attention is an action, a muscle you can direct at will, and like your physical strength and capability, it strengthens when you use it.

In his *Nicomachean Ethics*, Aristotle argues that every living being has a 'telos', an end goal or purpose, that it strives towards. The best way to get a sense of what the telos is, he argues, is to take note of the being's characteristic activity and the way in which it conducts itself. You can do the same for yourself. By properly investigating what you do with your time day to day, you can more easily understand the person that you are right now. And by modifying your characteristic activity, the very things that you do with your life, you can change your end goal or purpose, and the person that you become.

Gain perspective

Each of us fears death to varying degrees, but the fear of not having lived fully is often stronger. The sensation sneaks up on you as you get older, becoming most palpable in middle age, and it does you a good service. When you're distracted, or caught up in repetitive actions or behaviours, life can too easily pass you by. But when you are a little more attentive to what you are doing at this very moment and think coherently about what you might do differently, the events in your life can take on a new quality.

In the 1980s, the educator Stephen R. Covey dedicated himself to a thorough review of the self-help literature released up until that point and consolidated his findings into his highly regarded *The 7 Habits of Highly Effective People*. The book was an instant success and went on to sell more than 25 million copies. What resonated most with readers worldwide and prompted them to examine their own lives more closely was his advice to visualize their own funeral. Covey was well aware that reflecting on one's own mortality as a way of gaining perspective on life and priorities has been a common practice in various cultures and traditions throughout human history, and he adapted it for his business audience in the booming

Eighties. The exercise is as pertinent as ever, and you can use it not only to re-establish your priorities in life but also to gain a more grounded perspective on your digital time.

Start by putting some quiet time aside to dedicate yourself to the visualization, at least an hour if you can. Turn off your phone and make sure you won't be disturbed. Close your eyes and imagine you are attending your own funeral: visualize the scene, the location where it will take place, and notice the people who are there and their emotions. Picture tangible details that ground you in situ – sunlight streaming through windows, the echo of shoes on a wooden floor or the expressions of well-wishers in attendance. Once you have the distinct feeling of being there, start to run through how your service might unfold: what kind of person were you? What kind of impact did you have on those around you? With a pen and paper, start to write down any thoughts that you might have and try to keep writing. Think about your closest loved ones, and consider what they might say in their tributes to you.

Once you have a sense of how your funeral might play out, try a little test to see how important your digital time might be for you. Run through parts of your service again, this time seeing if there is room for any of your more regular online activities to get a mention. Does mentioning your time spent on social media, browsing the internet or watching TV feel appropriate, or does it seem futile or unimportant? Consider the time you have spent hunched over your computer or leisurely checked your phone, and see if you can discern how it has helped you to become the person you were. You might have achieved something noteworthy at a computer or advanced your career, and if so write it down. See if you can distinguish what has been worthwhile online or when using a digital device, and then note down what hasn't. Search for times when you haven't been in control, where you haven't directed your efforts, and question if this has had any positive impact on your life. Create a full and final list of all the things you do online that do not quite match up to your other accomplishments.

Now, turn your attention to your human skills. Spend some time considering each of the skills covered in this book: your navigation, motion, conversation, solitude, reading, writing, art, craft, memory, dreams, and thought; and the ways that you have made the most of your time. Try to question honestly if you have been competent in each one, and consider how much you have relied on support from tech or AI. Assess how this level of capability that you have demonstrated throughout your life matches up with the person you would like to be. Again, write everything down: create a header for each skill, list your competence up until now, and finish up the exercise by slowly thinking through where you might like to make some changes.

TAKE ACTION

- **Envisage your funeral:** Consider how many of your activities in digital time would make it into your eulogy and consider which human skills you would like to develop.

Prioritize your human skills

To get to grips with each of the skills covered in this book, it helps to focus on them one at a time. By giving each skill the focused attention and time it needs in the early phases, you'll have the best chance of getting the practice and improvement that you need for your new capacities to become habitual and second nature. Each of these skills gets easier over time, and as you arrive at new levels of competence and understanding, there will be more room to begin taking on others.

Take twenty minutes to consider which of the skills covered in this book are most lacking in your life: do you most notice your lack of navigation abilities; or might it be your reading skills that need a boost? Which abilities do you most take pride in, and where might you personally benefit from some more practice and dedicated focus? Revisit each of the skills, using your notes from the funeral exercise, if possible, and carefully number them in your own specific order of priority. For each skill, try to objectively gauge your own level of competence – mark each one with an A, B or C to grade your current ability – and then, keeping these personal capacities in mind, number each skill from 1 to 11, with number 1 being the skill that feels most important to you. Review your list, and if you're happy, select your priority skill and put the others to the side for now.

Once you have decided on a skill to focus on first, go back to the action points listed at the end of the corresponding chapter for your chosen skill and select the tasks that are the most helpful for you. Try to think practically about how you can integrate them into your current routines.

It can help to set yourself a goal to work towards so that you can ascertain for yourself that you have improved, so think about what this might be: it could be completing a long-distance run or achieving a particular feat of memory, or a more concrete output from an art or craft project. By setting a target, you focus your intentions, and as you attempt to reach your goal, you train yourself in tolerating any discomfort you might experience as you postpone working on other skills, projects or more temporary distractions. The more that you face up to the restrictions you have on your time and make fixed choices as to what you wish to do with it, the more comfortable it can become in settling with whatever it is that you decide upon.

Committing to fixed sessions often helps. If you are working on your running skills, look for a running club to join on a weekday evening; if honing your craft skills, see if there are any maker-spaces in your area that you can commit to for a term. By setting predetermined time boundaries when you step away from a screen and dedicate yourself to nurturing your own abilities, some decision-making is taken out of your hands each week, and this restricts the impulsiveness that so easily pulls you back online.

As you continue developing a skill, drawing deeper on your own reserves and dealing with the inescapable reality of the task in front of you, there is a perceptible shift. The longer that you remain in natural time, particularly when you more actively work within its rhythmic, recurrent dynamics whenever you dwell within one of your core, human skills, the easier it becomes to let go of the influence of digital time and to give up trying to control the pace at which any experience unfolds. When you relinquish the desire to speed up or quantify life by giving in instead to the steadier to and fro of your human skills, your concept of time shifts to a more natural rhythm, which can help you find acceptance and patience in other areas of your life. You test and hone your ability to pay active attention and to resist other calls on your time. And through it, you can start to learn to better withstand the temptations of tech and AI.

Stick to working on just one skill for at least three weeks before you begin looking at introducing another one to work on in tandem. You can soon advance to taking on the full sweep of your human capabilities, but a more patient, staggered approach will stand you in better stead.

TAKE ACTION

- **Prioritize the skills most important to you:** Number the skills covered in each chapter of this book in order of priority, grading your own competence with an A, B or C each time.
- **Take on one new skill at a time:** Restrict working on other skills until you have surpassed the trickier early phases of a new one. Only then branch out.
- **Set some goals:** Aim towards markers to prove to yourself that your capability in the skill is improving. Committing to regular group sessions can help with motivation.

Set yourself a new project

If you are really keen to get started working on a number of skills at once, there is another option. Many of your human skills complement one another. As you cultivate your reading skills, for example, you inevitably create opportunities to work on your writing, memory and thinking at the same time. One of the most natural and conducive ways to begin testing your abilities in a variety of different ways is by setting yourself a more comprehensive challenge or new project that calls upon a number of your personal capabilities.

Take a look at your numbered list of human skills and check to see what correspondences you can find in the levels of competence and importance you ascribed to each one. Look out for where your capabilities don't match up to your aspirations, and look for correlations across a number of different skills. Select at least three individual skills, and think about how they might connect: are there any hobbies or interests that you already have that naturally draw on all of these personal capabilities? Or are there any plans that come to mind that you might have had for a long time but never quite got round to doing? Is there something in particular that you would like to write, build or create?

See if you can happen upon a new challenge that works well to consolidate these skills, but don't take any decision to get started lightly. Give yourself the time you need to properly gauge your commitment and think carefully about how you might find the time it will require weekly. Picture yourself doing the activity and visualize the end result. If you remain convinced that it is the right choice, only then get going.

Integrating a number of your human skills into one cohesive, larger project gives each of them a more prolonged activation. The milestones that you hit and your sense of progress will give you momentum, and eventually, you'll have committed so much time to a project that it begins to seem incomprehensible that you might ever give it up; each step of the way, though, you're not just working towards completion but on what it means to be you.

TAKE ACTION

- **Select three skills:** Choose a trio of capabilities that you would like to work on and see if there is an opportunity to align them with your current hobbies and interests or new projects.
- **Conceive a new challenge:** Dedicate some time to creating a project for yourself that relies on these three skills, and properly gauge your commitment before getting started.

Avoid burnout

You don't always have to invest a lot of time to improve your human skills, and often – as unlikely as it sounds – it can be better to keep your efforts to a minimum. Studies have found that often those who make honing a skill just a short part of their daily routine achieve the best results over time. Particularly when it comes to your larger projects or endeavours, restricting the time that you put in can make it far easier for you to keep going for longer.

Digital technology can instil in you a tendency to push harder at times than you really need to. You can most easily spot any undue peaks of activity when they're closely followed by distinct troughs of downtime. Most often, this stems from a desire to hasten a task or a piece of work beyond its more natural pace, in a bid to race on to completion. But by developing the ability to tolerate the fact that you won't be producing much of note on any given day, you can frequently achieve far more over the long term. Short bursts of activity still accumulate. When you do carve out longer stints of time, it's often best to stop while you still have good energy and before you tire too much, saving continued work for the next day when you still feel fresh.

The desire to push on doesn't always stem from a positive place: it can be driven as much by impatience as led by any fruitful enjoyment.

Stopping when you intend to, or when you feel yourself flagging, refines your ability, both on- and offline, to better control where you invest your time.

TAKE ACTION

- **Focus on incremental gains:** Practise new skills by building short bursts of activity into your daily routine rather than scheduling a longer session less frequently.
- **Watch out for undue haste:** Try to catch yourself impatiently pushing on with a task or a project when you know it would be better to leave it be for a while.
- **Stop deliberately:** When you next sit down to work on a larger piece of work, try curbing your time so that you stop in full flow, rather than waiting for tiredness to hit.
- **Impose other time limits:** Experiment with limiting the time you invest in a few other active areas of your life for a couple of weeks and observe whether this affects your longer-term stamina and motivation.

Create more natural time

If digital time has one prevailing feature, it's that it progressively pulls you into a different mode of being. The sequential and inevitably accelerating nature of computer power triggers more operations and responses; and each click, swipe or scroll that you make pulls you out of your physical life with all its possibilities and into the more preordained experiences found online. But you can put checks in place. By creating new habits away from tech and AI, you can create clear boundaries so that the more damaging effects of digital time are halted for good.

Setting a few new habits can give you further support. Think carefully about your typical week and look for opportunities where you can easily disconnect from technology entirely. These new habits are often easiest to embed when they are tied to something that you already do. If you walk to work or to the station, perhaps put your phone in your bag on silent; when you go out for a walk or a run, leave your phone at home. If you meet up with a friend, see what it feels like heading there phoneless. Consider activities or chores that you do on a regular basis, and see how you might be able to remove the demands of digital time for their entire duration. In particular, have a careful think about the moments in any day or week that you dedicate most to relaxation or personal development – time at the gym, in the garden or at a desk, or any other hobbies that you might enjoy – and see how you might be able to fully remove the temptation of any digital distractions. Whenever you do, you reclaim this time.

Keep in mind that time spent offline is not just for yourself but also for those around you. The quality of time spent with loved ones is too often compromised by our constant attachment to screens and digital distractions. Children need our undivided attention and eye contact for their well-being, and all of our relationships in life need the same to flourish and grow. Loving and caring for others across generations is perhaps one of the most human and important things we fill our time with, along with seeking out and maintaining relationships, whether romantic, sexual, platonic or professional. But the use of digital technology stands in the way of intimacy and understanding and has undoubtedly affected all our personal relationships in myriad ways, not least by reducing the physical encounters we depend on to create or strengthen real-world friendships.

Taking your time back to commit it instead to the people around you is a vital and rewarding change to make, and just a few small adjustments to daily life can make a big difference. It's a great idea to establish spaces in your home, such as at the dinner table or in the living room, where digital devices are not allowed. Set specific times during the day, for example at meals or during family activities, where everyone is totally present for one another. Cutting back on digital time can also support you to make more regular visits or calls to family members and friends as well as to participate in group hobbies, community projects or outdoor adventures that nurture interaction and collaboration. The more time you actively invest in your relationships and the well-being of those around you, the more enriched your own life will become.

TAKE ACTION

- **Watch for the pull of digital time:** Over the course of a day, track each instance where your digital devices draw you in and keep you online in ways that you never initially intended.
- **Create some new habits in natural time:** Find regular activities in your weekly schedule when you can remove all devices from your person.
- **Be fully present with family:** Establish device-free times and spaces in your home, and schedule more regular visits and phone calls to loved ones.
- **Connect with those around you:** Join a group class, do some volunteering or take up an outdoor pursuit to increase opportunities for real-world interaction and collaboration.

Epilogue

If there were to be one skill or superpower that most clearly delineates *Homo sapiens* from other species, what might it be? We have the natural capability to traverse long distances on foot, yet many animals can travel far further. Our navigation skills can be honed to very impressive levels, but so too can those of birds, sea turtles or salmon. We're not the strongest, fastest or most alert of species, by any means. But no other organism on Earth exhibits such wide-ranging capabilities or has advanced as we have. While other animals display problem-solving abilities and other forms of learning, our ability to use our intelligence to build tools and develop new skills that we can apply to any challenge or task most clearly sets us apart.

Our technological progress has made us ever faster as a society, and better able to handle levels of complexity that would have confounded our predecessors, yet if humans today were to completely detach from our devices and supporting technological infrastructure and meet our ancestors head-to-head in a battle of strength or wits, it is unlikely we'd win. When we rely on external supports, even if they extend or augment our abilities when we use them, it's unavoidable that our natural capabilities degrade as a result.

There is a simple reason why the distinction between our natural human ingenuity and resourcefulness and the technological prowess we are blessed with today is so important: our body and mind have not evolved to function healthily in conjunction with digital technology. The more time we spend online or with our devices, the more our real-world skills degrade. Yet navigation, motion, conversation, solitude, reading, writing, art, craft, memory, dreams and thought remain among the most fundamental activities that define the people we become.

Throughout the history of humankind, we have used tools to support or extend human capabilities, and technological innovations have been released with a sense of collective pride. Justifiably, we marvel at the transformative advancements we create and the fresh possibilities we unlock with each innovation. Even when our tools have steadily encroached on what it means to be human, or bring about negative consequences, the fact that we are their originators and maintain a sense of primary control when using them reassures us that, overall, we are better off. Yet, often this is simply a guess. Whereas a pharmaceutical company has to invest in precautionary testing before releasing something new to the public, no equivalent safety protocols are in place for new forms of technology that might affect our mental or physical well-being.

AI presents a unique challenge. It is becoming sophisticated enough to eclipse our broad intelligence, and with it our propensity to innovate and create. We are in the process of outsourcing our most fundamental skill, creative human thought and reasoning, to large language models (LLMs) such as ChatGPT, and the speed at which they operate dramatically supersedes our own.

This is a qualitative leap beyond anything we have experienced before. More tools will be made and more innovations launched at a rapidly accelerating rate. Dramatic societal change is imminent, and the future for humankind is decidedly difficult to predict. As we struggle to keep pace with the ensuing technological evolutions in the months and years to come, there is one prime imperative: to remember that human ingenuity alone conceived of the technological inventiveness that has made any of this possible. That same ingenuity also needs to preserve the very essence of our humanity and, with it, our well-being. Ceding priority, agency or autonomy to AI holds no sense or logic for humankind.

We stand now at a precipice where our fundamental human-intelligence rights need to be accounted for and protected. The financial costs and complex algorithmic development required to develop an LLM have been borne nearly entirely by private corporations – Microsoft alone has committed to a multi-year, multi-billion-dollar investment in OpenAI, the organization behind ChatGPT, and many other major tech companies are following similar routes. No government to date has publicly announced anywhere close to such an investment. Protections are needed to defend the general public from the ensuing race between competing tech firms to release the latest discoveries in AI; only now are some safeguards beginning to be put in place, and they are by no means comprehensive.

We need to ensure transparency of the development and use of AI, so that we can understand its role and critique its logic and thought processes. Our abilities to make decisions in our lives must remain free from any influence or coercion by AI and the data it generates. Most of all, we urgently need protection from the potential harm caused by AI systems, through the development and global deployment of appropriate guidelines and safety measures.

The only way that tech or AI can truly work for our benefit is if we remain in absolute control of it. We must be able to command any device or AI that we use and prevail over its actions. To do this, we need our full capabilities, our sharpness of mind and intellect. We need to be able to dictate how much time we spend online and decide for ourselves when we want to switch off. And when we do switch off, we need to find ourselves fully present in the real world. Finding sustenance and renewal in our own natural abilities, thriving and flourishing in the enjoyment of our own life skills, and with each other, is far more important and meaningful than any new technology release.

We can make the most of tech and AI and protect our own skills. The more we balance the quantitative, abstract and accelerated worlds online with our grounded abilities in real life, the better chance we have of ensuring collectively that technology enhances, rather than threatens, being human.

Acknowledgements

My sincere thanks to Sarah Ream, who has helped me over a number of years to develop my writing. With her insight from work for *The Analog Sea Review* – an offline literary journal that champions contemplative life in the digital age – and her graceful feedback, she's been instrumental in getting me to this final result. Additionally, I would like to express my gratitude to my agent, Andrew Gordon, for taking an early interest in the topic of this book, and also Ross Hamilton, Commissioning Editor, and Gabriella Nemeth, Senior Editor, at Michael O'Mara Books. I would like to thank my parents, as well as my mother-in-law Cathy Nicholson, and siblings Sarah and Ally for always being there for me. Artist and friend, Kevin Quigley has been a constant creative insight and inspiration. I am also grateful for the unwavering support of my oldest friends and our conversations and debates as I've wrestled with the topics covered in this book: Dale Batham, Alex Cox, Gwyn Davis, Paul Helmers-Olsen, Colin Hobbs, Neil Luscombe, Ross Underwood and the late Richard Mannering, who is sorely missed. My extended efforts of researching and writing, over six years, have only been feasible with the continued dedication and support of my wife Hannah; with our two young children, it would simply have been impossible otherwise.

Select Bibliography and Further Reading

Baron, Sabrina Alcorn, *The Reader Revealed*, University of Washington Press, 2011

Berger, John, *Ways of Seeing*, Penguin Classics, 2008

Berger, Susanna, *The Art of Philosophy: Visual Thinking in Europe from the Late Renaissance to the Early Enlightenment*, Princeton University Press, 2017

Brummett, Barry, *Techniques of Close Reading*, SAGE Publications, 2009

Burkeman, Oliver, *Four Thousand Weeks: Time and How to Use It*, Bodley Head, 2021

Church, Ruth Breckinridge, Martha W. Alibali and Spencer D. Kelly, *Why Gesture?*, John Benjamins Publishing Company, 2017

Clerizo, Michael, *George Daniels: A Master Watchmaker and His Art*, Thames & Hudson, 2013

Crary, Jonathan, *24/7: Late Capitalism and the Ends of Sleep*, Verso Books, 2014

Ibid, *Suspensions of Perception: Attention, Spectacle and Modern Culture*, MIT Press, 2000

Ibid, *Techniques of the Observer: On Vision and Modernity in the Nineteenth Century*, MIT Press, 1992

Crawford, Matthew, *The Case for Working with Your Hands: Or Why Office Work Is Bad for Us and Fixing Things Feels Good*, Penguin, 2010

Csikszentmihalyi, Mihaly, *Television and the Quality of Life: How Viewing Shapes Everyday Experience*, Routledge, 1990

Darwin, Charles, *On the Expression of the Emotions in Man and Animals*, 1872

Ekman, Paul, *Emotions Revealed*, W&N, 2004

Ellis, Markman, *The Coffee-House: A Cultural History*, Weidenfeld & Nicolson, 2011

Foer, Joshua, *Moonwalking with Einstein: The Art and Science of Remembering Everything*, Penguin Press, 2011

Gatty, Harold, *Finding Your Way Without Map or Compass*, Dover Publications, 2003

Gladwin, Thomas, *East Is a Big Bird*, Harvard University Press, 1995

Hayles, N. Katherine, *How We Think: Digital Media and Contemporary Technogenesis*, University of Chicago Press, 2012

Heinrich, Bernd, *Why We Run*, Ecco Press, 2019

Henri, Robert, *The Art Spirit*, 1923

Hill, Edward, *The Language of Drawing*, Prentice Hall, 1966

Huxley, Aldous, *The Divine Within: Selected Writings on Enlightenment*, Harper, 2013

Ibid, *The Perennial Philosophy*, 1945

Jackson, H. J., *Marginalia: Readers Writing in Books*, Yale University Press, 2009

James, William, *The Varieties of Religious Experience: A Study in Human Nature*, 1902

Kagge, Erling, *Silence in the Age of Noise*, Viking 2017

Kendon, Adam, *Conducting Interaction*, Cambridge University Press, 2009

Korn, Peter, *Why We Make Things and Why It Matters*, Vintage, 2017

Lester, Toby, *Da Vinci's Ghost*, Profile Books, 2011

Lewis, David, *We, the Navigators*, University of Hawaii Press, 1994

Lieberman, Daniel, *The Story of the Human Body*, Penguin, 2014

Madsbjerg, Christian, *Sensemaking*, Little, Brown, 2017

McNeill, David, *Why We Gesture*, Cambridge University Press, 2015

Nabokov, Peter, *Indian Running*, Capra, 1981

Paul, Richard and Linda Elder, *How to Read a Paragraph: The Art of Close Reading*, Foundations of Critical Thinking, 2014

Posner, Michael I., *Attention in a Social World*, Oxford University Press, 2011

Prodger, Phillip, *Darwin's Camera*, Oxford University Press, 2009

Pye, David, *The Nature and Art of Workmanship*, Herbert Press, 2007

Rosenblatt, Louise M, *Literature as Exploration*, Modern Language Association of America, 1996

Sharpe. Kevin, *Reading Revolutions: The Politics of Reading in Early Modern England*, Yale University Press, 2000

Sherman, William. H., *Used Books: Marking Readers in Renaissance England*, University of Pennsylvania Press, 2009

Thomas, Stephen D., *The Last Navigator*, Henry Holt and Co., 2009

Turner, Mark, *The Literary Mind: The Origins of Thought and Language*, Oxford University Press, 1996

Watzl, Sebastian, *Structuring Mind: The Nature of Attention and How It Shapes Consciousness*, Oxford University Press, 2017

Yates, Frances, *The Art of Memory*, Routledge & Kegan Paul, 1966

Index